A History of English Spelling

Edinburgh Textbooks on the English Language – Advanced

General Editor
Heinz Giegerich, Professor Emeritus of English Linguistics, University of Edinburgh

Editorial Board
Heinz Giegerich, University of Edinburgh – General Editor
Laurie Bauer (University of Wellington)
Olga Fischer (University of Amsterdam)
Willem Hollmann (Lancaster University)
Marianne Hundt (University of Zurich)
Rochelle Lieber (University of New Hampshire)
Bettelou Los (University of Edinburgh)
Robert McColl Millar (University of Aberdeen)
Donka Minkova (UCLA)
Edgar Schneider (University of Regensburg)
Graeme Trousdale (University of Edinburgh)

Titles in the series include:

The Pragmatics of Fiction: Literature, Stage and Screen Discourse
Miriam A. Locher and Andreas H. Jucker

English Syntax: A Minimalist Account of Structure and Variation
Elspeth Edelstein

Construction Grammar and its Application to English 2nd edition
Martin Hilpert

Pragmatics
Chris Cummins

Corpus Linguistics and the Description of English, 2ⁿᵈ edition
Hans Lindquist and Magnus Levin

Modern Scots: An Analytical Survey
Robert McColl Millar

Contemporary Stylistics: Language, Cognition, Interpretation
Alison Gibbons and Sara Whiteley

A Critical Account of English Syntax: Grammar, Meaning, Text
Keith Brown and Jim Miller

English Historical Semantics
Christian Kay and Kathryn Allan

A Historical Syntax of English
Bettelou Los

Morphological Theory and the Morphology of English
Jan Don

A Historical Phonology of English
Donka Minkova

English Historical Pragmatics
Andreas Jucker and Irma Taavitsainen

English Historical Sociolinguistics
Robert McColl Millar

A Historical Morphology of English
Don Ringe

World Englishes: The Local Lives of a Global Language
Bertus Van Rooy

A History of English Spelling
Simon Horobin

Visit the Edinburgh Textbooks in the English Language website at
https://edinburghuniversitypress.com/series-edinburgh-textbooks-on-the-english-language-advanced.html

A History of English Spelling

Simon Horobin

EDINBURGH
University Press

Edinburgh University Press is one of the leading university presses in the UK. We publish academic books and journals in our selected subject areas across the humanities and social sciences, combining cutting-edge scholarship with high editorial and production values to produce academic works of lasting importance. For more information visit our website: edinburghuniversitypress.com

Edinburgh University Press Ltd
13 Infirmary Street
Edinburgh EH1 1LT

Typeset in Janson MT
by Cheshire Typesetting Ltd, Cuddington, Cheshire, and
Printed and bound in the UK

A CIP record for this book is available from the British Library

ISBN 978 1 3995 0022 7 (hardback)
ISBN 978 1 3995 0023 4 (paperback)
ISBN 978 1 3995 0025 8 (webready PDF)
ISBN 978 1 3995 0024 1 (epub)

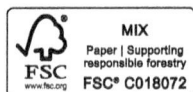

FSC
www.fsc.org

MIX
Paper | Supporting
responsible forestry
FSC® C018072

This book is printed using paper from well-managed forests, recycling and other controlled sources

Contents

Preface   vi

Introduction: Writing Systems   1

Part I: History

1. Old English   13
2. Middle English   23
3. Standardisation   36
4. Early Modern English   49
5. Late Modern English   61
6. US English   73
7. Present-day English   85
8. Spelling Scots   96

Part II: Perspectives

9. Prescriptivist attitudes to correct spelling   111
10. Female spelling   123
11. Reforming spelling   135
12. Creating your own research project   150

References   162
Index   171

Preface

Popularly viewed as eccentric and illogical, dismissed by linguists as fixed and therefore uninteresting, English spelling is the Cinderella of modern linguistics. However, recent scholarly developments, such as the contributions to Cook and Ryan (eds), *The Routledge Handbook of the English Writing System* (2016), have revealed the English writing system to be a complex and fascinating subject. With a rich history of variation, English spelling has much to offer diachronic sociolinguists, while study of its history helps to explain many of today's apparent irregularities and anomalies. The story of its standardisation, beginning with the introduction of the printing press, and the de-standardisation currently being witnessed on social media sites like Twitter and Facebook, offers new perspectives on how technology drives linguistic change, and reveals fascinating insights into the ways in which variable spelling is being repurposed today.

This book is divided into two main sections. This first section is intended to offer an updated history of English spelling, going beyond classic introductions like Scragg 1974 and Cook 2004 by drawing on the latest scholarship, as well as considering more recent changes and a wider selection of varieties. The second section takes a thematic approach, considering how changes in the functions, media and attitudes towards the written word have affected the way English is spelled. A final chapter introduces a number of key corpora, describes some sample analyses and suggests avenues for future research.

I am grateful to Professor Heinz Giegerich, the series General Editor, for many helpful suggestions during the writing of this book, and to Laura Quinn and Sam Johnson of Edinburgh University Press for their support and patience during the writing process. I also wish to thank Professor Jeremy Smith and Dr Annika Ester Maresia for reading the entire draft and for making numerous important suggestions for its improvement.

Introduction: writing systems

'A language and its written form constitute two separate systems of signs. The sole reason for the existence of the latter is to represent the former' (De Saussure in Harris 2013: 27). While De Saussure is evidently correct in distinguishing speech and writing in this way, his subsequent statement that writing is entirely dependent upon speech helps to explain why written language has been overlooked in much linguistic research. As a secondary mode of linguistic representation, written language has typically been ignored by linguists in favour of the primary mode of speech. This is regrettable, not least because all analysis of historical states of English that predate the invention of speech recording must necessarily be based on written forms of the language. Because of this, any study of the pronunciation of the historical stages of English must necessarily involve consideration of its written forms. One of the problems that stems from this chronic neglect of the written language as a subject of study in its own right is a relative lack of linguistic theorisation of the written mode and the ways in which it relates to speech. In order to understand the written language better, we need to develop a stronger understanding of its difference from speech than that offered by Saussure. For instance, where speech is generally ephemeral, writing can remain available long after it has been written down. While writing is clearly related to the spoken mode, the nature of that relationship is more complex than is usually understood.

There are two major ways in which a writing system relates to the spoken system that it represents. An individual written symbol may either directly represent a concept, or it may represent the word by which the concept is conventionally known. This first kind of written symbol is known as an ideograph; examples of ideographs used in the English writing system include the Arabic numerals (1, 2, 3), the ampersand <&>, mathematical symbols, the pound sign (a stylised form of <L> for Latin libra 'pound') and the @sign now widely used in email and social media: < +, −, £, @ >. A number of these are employed in English as they

1

are convenient shorthands; this is especially apparent when attempting to render complex numbers, such as five million, four hundred thousand, six hundred and twenty-two and a half. This is a much lengthier way of rendering this number than simply using the equivalent numerals: 5,400,622.5. Another clear advantage of the numeric system is that it is comprehensible by speakers of any language, whereas the longer version can only be understood by speakers of English.

The second type is the phonographic system, in which written symbols map on to speech segments; these could be syllables, phonemes (both vowels and consonants) or consonantal phonemes only. The English writing system is phonological, with written symbols representing phonemes: the sound unit that distinguishes one meaningful sound from another, e.g. the contrast between /b/ and /p/ in **big** and **pig**. The contrasting alphabetical unit is known as the grapheme. So, in a phonological system like English, individual phonemes like /b/ and /p/ map on to graphemes like <b> and <p>. In some cases, a single phoneme maps onto two graphemes, as in /Θ/, a single sound that is represented by the consonant cluster <th>; this is known as a digraph. In linguistic discussions, phonemes are conventionally marked using slash brackets, //, while graphemes are signalled by the use of angle brackets, <>.

We have seen that, in phonographic systems like that of English, letters map on to phonemes. This is because phonemes mark meaningful contrasts, such as that between /b/ and /p/ in the example of **big** and **pig** cited above. If the same letter were used for both the voiced and voiceless bilabial plosives, the two words would be spelled identically. During the Old English period, the distinction between voiced and voiceless fricatives was not phonemic, and consequently the single letter <f> was used to represent both voiced and voiceless sounds. If the letter appeared at the beginning of a word, it was pronounced without voicing, e.g. **finger** FINGER; where it appeared between vowels it was pronounced with voicing, e.g. **ofer** OVER. This example shows that in a phonological system it is not necessary to signal distinctions that are allophonic: ones that do not carry meaningful distinctions.

It would, of course, be possible for a writing system to represent allophonic distinctions, but since these are not meaningful, it would serve little purpose. A system that represented, say, the two different /l/ sounds in **laurel**, [l] and [ɫ], would be inefficient in communicative terms, since the distinction is not phonemic. The result would be an uneconomical writing system, which required a learner to acquire spelling distinctions that were of no meaningful value. Similarly, different accents of English have alternative realisations of phonemes, such as the Northumbrian burr, a voiced uvular fricative [ʁ], or the alveolar tap, [ɾ], found in Leeds and Liverpool. It would be possible to mark such distinctions in the writing system; indeed, such a system does exist in the International Phonetic Alphabet, but this is designed to represent precise distinctions for use by experts in phonetics and not as an everyday writing system. For general readers it is not important how the /r/ is realised, but whether it is /r/ or /l/, as this distinction is meaningful, cf. **rot** and **lot**.

While the basic principle of a phonographic system is that a single sound maps onto a single letter, there is in practice considerable variation. In English the letter <c> may signal /s/ or /k/ or /tʃ/, as in **city, cake** and **cello**. The relatively small number of vowel letters in English compared to the much greater number of vowel sounds means that these letters have an especially wide range of functions. Individual sounds can also be rendered in a variety of ways; for instance, /uː/ can be spelled <o>, <oe>, <oo>, <ew>, <ou>, while <a> can map on to /æ/ in **hat**, /ɑː/ in **grass** (in Received Pronunciation), /ə/ in **China**, /ɛ/ in **any**.

There is a limit to the permitted combinations of graphemes in an orthographic system; it is unusual, for instance, to find English words where <q> is not followed by <u>, or words that include the consonant combination <kk>. Certain constraints operate so that particular combinations of graphemes can only be found in certain positions, e.g. <tch> cannot appear in initial position even though it is a representation of /tʃ/ in **catch**; similarly, <ck> is never used for initial /k/ though it does appear frequently for this sound in words like **brick** and **stick**. By contrast, the graphemes <wh> for /w/ and <j> for /dʒ/ cannot appear at the ends of words. The study of these constraints was termed 'graphotactics' by Venezky (1967: 77). The significance of graphotactics for a full appreciation of English spelling is apparent from a closer consideration of George Bernard Shaw's famous claim that English spelling is so irregular that it would be possible to spell the word **fish** as **ghoti**, by analogy with spellings such as enou**gh**, w**o**men, mo**ti**on. The <gh> spelling is very rare at the beginning of words (exceptions are **ghost** and **gherkin**) and never represents [f] in this position. Similarly <ti> only signals the [ʃ] when it appears within a word and never at the end. Despite this, attempts to highlight the unpredictability of English spelling have sought to find ever more eccentric examples; perhaps the best is the following: **ghoughphtheight-teau**. If the <gh> is pronounced [p] (as it is in **hiccough**), the <ough> sounded as in **dough**, the <phth> pronounced [t] (as in **phthisis**), the <eigh> as in **weigh**, the <tte> as [t] (as in **gazette**), and the <eau> as in **gateau**), the word becomes a possible alternative spelling of **potato**.

Since the phonemic make-up of a language can change over time, the number and nature of such contrasts are not fixed. Earlier we saw that there was no phonemic contrast between voiced and voiceless fricatives in

Old English, and thus no written distinction was made. But this distinction became phonemic in the Middle English period, as we will see in Chapter 2, resulting in a need for a written distinction. As a consequence the letter <f> continued to be used for the voiceless labiodental fricative, while <v> was employed to signal its voiced partner.

To recap, the English writing system is phonological, in that individual graphemes map on to phonemes, meaningful units of sound, but not allophones, variant manifestations of particular phonemes. Just as a phoneme can be seen as constituted of a class of sounds that represent that single sound, so is a grapheme made up of a series of letterforms, known as allographs, that represent different ways of realising that letter. There is no agreed convention for marking allographs, although double angle brackets are often found and will be adopted in this book: <<>>. Historical examples of allographs used in English include the various forms of the grapheme <s> used by medieval scribes: the long-s, an 8-shaped form, or the Greek letter sigma. A more modern example can be seen in the way different computer fonts represent the grapheme <g>, <<g, g, ɡ>>. The relationship between grapheme and allograph may change over time. An example of this is the letters 'u' and 'v'; in modern English these are separate graphemes, but in Middle English they were allographs, <<v>> and <<u>> of the grapheme <v>. Another instance concerns the letters 'i' and 'j', which in modern English are separate graphemes, but which were allographs in Middle English. Yet this is not true of all words, since there are examples in English of discontinuous or split digraphs in which a silent letter can indicate a different pronunciation of another. This is clearest in the function of final <e>, which signals the difference in pronunciation between **bit** and **bite**.

Classical grammarians employed a different set of terminology in order to distinguish between the *littera* (the overall superordinate term for a letter), its written (*figura*) and spoken manifestations (*potestas*), and the name of the letter (*nomen*). This is drawn from the writings of the Latin grammarians Donatus and Priscian, who developed the doctrine of the *littera*. Aelius Donatus was a mid-fifth-century teacher, whose grammatical works, *Ars minor* and *Ars maior*, were standard reading in the Middle Ages, to the extent that any grammatical textbook came to be known as a *donet*. Priscianus Caesariensis, or 'Priscian', flourished in the early sixth century AD and was the author of the *Institutiones grammaticae*, 'Grammatical foundations', a key grammatical textbook. Priscian's work was the basis for Ælfric's *Excerptiones de arte grammatica anglice*, 'Extracts on grammar in English', a Latin grammar for novice monks, written in Old English. Priscian began by describing 'voice' (Latin *vox*), which he divided into four different categories: articulate, inarticulate, literate and illiterate. He defined the *littera* as a sound that can be written separately, deriving its name from *legitura*, a 'reading-road', and thus the pathway by which people read. In his section on the *littera*, Donatus listed those letters employed to write Latin and their various functions, ending with a definition of their three properties: name (*nomen*), form (*figura*), and force (*potestas*). When rendering this doctrine into English, Ælfric translated these concepts as *nama*, *hīw* and *miht*, and explains them as follows: 'Nama: hū hē gehāten byð (a, b, c); hīw: hū hē gesceapen byð; miht: hwæt hē mæge betwux ōðrum stafum'. This may be translated in the following way: 'Name: how it is called; form: how it is shaped; power: what it has the power to do among other letters'. This is a useful formulation since it enables us to distinguish the uses of a letter, that is the *potestas* 'power', or *potestates* 'powers', with which it is associated, from the form of the letter itself.

The arbitrary relationship between sound and symbol in any alphabet is an important concept in the study of written language. There is no particular reason why the letter 'b' should be connected with the phoneme /b/; these connections are simply conventions agreed by particular communities. As such the conventions themselves frequently differ across different languages and their users. This can be seen from examining how the Roman alphabet used for writing English is employed in the writing of a variety of other European languages, with certain key differences. For example, <j> represents /j/ in German, Dutch, Danish, Swedish and Norwegian, but /ʒ/ in French and Portuguese, /x/ in Spanish and /dʒ/ in English. In German the grapheme <w> maps on to the phoneme /v/ rather than /w/, while <v> maps on to the phoneme /f/.

Priscian made a distinction between *litterae* and *elementae*, so as to separate the written symbol and its spoken counterpart. This terminology was still being employed in the seventeenth century, although spoken and written elements were often confused. The schoolteacher Simon Daines wrote in his spelling book *Orthoepia Anglicana* (1640) that:

According to the Etymologie, or strict sense of the term, Letters are but certain Characters, or notes, whereby any word is expressed in writing: and for this cause were they by the antient Latinists distinguished into Letters, as they be Charactericall notes, and Elements, as the first grounds or Principles of speech. But this nicety is confounded in the generall accep-tion, which promiscuously terms them Letters; and this we shall follow.

In 1633, Charles Butler used the term 'uncharactered letters', evidently a reference to spoken sounds rather than written symbols. Dr Johnson's definition of *letter* in his *Dictionary of the English Language* (1755) is 'one of the elements of syllables; a character in the alphabet', which conflates both spoken and written aspects. Other ways of distinguishing the speech sound and the written symbol included John Hart's employment of *letter* to refer to writing and *voice* for speech. Using this classical nomenclature we could say that the *littera* 's' maps on to the *potestates* /s/ and /z/ in modern English, while the following are alternative *figurae* that have been associated with this *littera* throughout the history of English: the Greek sigma <<σ>>, an 8-shaped form found in medieval scripts, and the long-s, <<ʃ>>, used in printed books up to the eighteenth century.

English, therefore, employs a phonographic writing system, which encodes the phonemic structure of the language. Given this function, it is evidently true that the written system is dependent upon speech to a significant degree. However, a writing system cannot reflect all the relevant features of a spoken system: suprasegmental features such as intonation, stress and pauses are generally not signalled. Even at the segmental level, English spelling offers a broad phonemic transcription, revealing underlying phonemic contrasts and telling us nothing about the exact pronunciation of the phonemes themselves.

So far, I have focused on the way in which a phonological writing system represents phonemic units. But there are instances in English where the writing system encodes morphological information. A good example of this concerns the spelling of inflectional morphemes, such as the past tense inflexion <ed> and the plural marker <s>. In English there are two major classes of verbs, strong and weak, which differ in the way they form the past tense. Strong verbs form their past tenses by changing the vowel in the stem, e.g. **run/ran**, **swim/swum**, while weak verbs add a dental suffix. This dental suffix is pronounced slightly differently depending on the sound to which it is added: /d, ɪd, t/. Compare the pronunciation of the final unstressed syllable in the following words: **parted**, **talked**, **called**. In the first of these the <–ed> ending is pronounced /ɪd/, in the second it is sounded with a /t/ and in the final instance it is pronounced with /d/. This distinction is predictable from the phonetic context. Where it follows a stem which ends in /t/ or /d/, the ending is pronounced /ɪd/. The distinction between /d/ and /t/ depends on whether the preceding consonant is voiced or voiceless. If the dental suffix follows a voiced consonant (apart from /d/), it is pronounced /d/, e.g. **amused**, **raved**. Where it follows a voiceless consonant, it is pronounced /t/, e.g. **missed**, **laughed**. Because of this predictability, and the fact that its function does not change with the different pronunciation, English has evolved a system whereby a single <ed> spelling is used to mark the past tense morpheme, irrespective of pronunciation: **talked**, **parted**, **raised**. A similar example concerns the way in which the plural inflexion <s> represents [s] in **hats**, **lips**, **rocks** but [z] in **dogs**, **mounds**, **rhymes**. The distinction here again relates to the nature of the consonant which it follows. If the plural marker is added to a voiceless consonant, it is voiceless, [s]. Where it follows a voiced consonant, it is voiced, [z]. In both cases it would be possible to signal these distinctions in the spelling system so that we write **partid, talkt, calld** and **dogz, moundz, rhymez**. These spellings would have the effect of making the words more phonetically transparent, but they would disrupt the morphological principle whereby the weak preterite ending is spelled <ed> and the plural ending is spelled <s>.

In some instances, a spelling convention may encode etymological rather than phonological or morphological information. For example, the /f/ sound in English is represented by the grapheme <f>, a convention that can be traced back to Old English. However, a number of words have been subsequently borrowed into English from Greek, where they were spelled with the Greek letter 'phi': <Φ>. In Old English the Greek letter phi in such words was spelled with the grapheme <f>, as if they were of native origin, e.g. **fenix** PHOENIX. But in later borrowings the digraph <ph> was adopted to render the Greek letter phi. As a consequence, the <ph> digraph is now found in a number of Greek loanwords, such as **philosophy** and **philology**, where it renders the Greek letter <Φ>. In addition to signalling the sound /f/, therefore, the <ph> digraph also indicates that such words are of Greek origin and may be distinguished from native words where the /f/ is spelled <f>, e.g. **food, free**. As we shall see in Chapter 6, the <ph> diagraph has recently taken on an expressive function in the digital realm, where it appears in words that have no etymological connection with Greek. In the case of **phreak**, the <ph> may be due to an association with **phone**, since the term is a 1970s coinage used to refer to people who manipulate phones in order to place long-distance calls without paying the charges. A more recent example is **phish**, an alteration of **fish**, used of a fraudster who sends out emails intended to trick recipients into parting with confidential financial details.

As will be apparent from some of the examples we have discussed above, the relationship between spelling and pronunciation in a phonological system is subject to change over time. An important reason for this is that pronunciation is constantly subject to variation and change, while writing systems tend to remain stable over longer periods of time. When it was first used to write down Old English, there was a much closer relationship between spelling and pronunciation than there is in Present-day English (PDE). One obvious way in which the gap between spelling and pronunciation widens over time as a result of sound change concerns the simplification of consonant clusters. For instance, Present-day English has a group of words containing a <gh> digraph that is not sounded: **night, bought, taught**. Given that English is a phonological system in which graphemes encode phonemes, this seems a strange situation. What is the point in such a system in having silent letters? Would it not make more sense for these words to be spelled **nite**, **bawt**, **tawt**? But these spellings are a legacy of a time when the <gh> digraph mapped on to the fricative sound /x/. This sound was recorded in Old English, when it was spelled with the grapheme <h>. In Middle English this fricative sound came to be spelled with <gh>. However, during the fifteenth century the fricative sound ceased to be pronounced in some dialects, but not that of the London dialect which was the basis of the standard spelling system. It was only after the standard spelling system had become established, with spellings like **night**, **bought**, **taught**, that all dialects of English came to drop the /x/ sound. The result of this is a group of spellings like **night** (including **right**, **might**, **sight**, **fight**) which contain a digraph that has no spoken equivalent. But, while this may seem an unhelpful development in a phonographic system, such spellings do serve to reduce the number of homonyms in English. In a strictly phonographic system, homophones – words pronounced identically – would also be homonyms – words with identical pronunciation and spelling. But the preservation of the now redundant <gh> in **sight** and **might** means that their written forms are easily distinguished from **site** and **mite**.

The example of the <gh> digraph shows how the development of a standard form leads to a spelling system that is no longer able to reflect changes in pronunciation as they emerge. In pre-standard varieties, changes in spelling offer key evidence of changes in pronunciation. However, a standard written variety tends to fossilise distinctions that are no longer active in the language. A good example of this is the distinction between <ee> and <ea> in modern English pairs like **meat** and **meet**. This represented a genuine distinction in pronunciation in Late Modern English, but today the two are pronounced identically, although in a small number of exceptions, such as **greet** and **great**, a distinction in pronunciation is maintained.

The principle of 'orthographic depth' refers to the relationship between symbols and sounds in a writing system. In shallow systems there is a one-to-one relationship, so that words can be read aloud or written down in a predictable way. By contrast, a deep orthography has a less direct relationship between spelling and sound. English has a comparatively deep orthography, in that there are individual symbols that map on to more than one sound, e.g. <x> which represents the sounds /ks/, while individual sounds can map on to multiple symbols, as <gh> can represent /g/ in **gherkin**, /f/ in **enough** or nothing at all in **thought**. The extent to which English spelling is not predictable from a sounding out of the individual symbols is apparent in specific words such as **through** and

thorough, and even more so in proper nouns such as the place name **Bicester** 'Bister') and the personal names **Cholmondley** ('Chumley') and Featherstonehaugh ('Fanshaw').

While most changes serve to drive spelling and pronunciation further apart, it is also possible for pronunciation to change to reflect spelling, bringing the two modes into closer alignment. An example of this concerns the word **herb**, which was borrowed into English from French **herbe**, in which the initial <h> was silent. The word was usually spelled **erbe** in Middle English, but the initial <h> was sporadically included under the influence of the Latin form **herba**. By around 1475, the spelling with initial <h> became regular. In the nineteenth century, the spelling with initial <h> triggered a pronunciation of the word with initial /h/, a change that was encouraged by the stigmatisation of so-called 'h-dropping' – the failure to sound initial /h/ – in native words like **horse** and **how**. This change only affected British English; US English continues to pronounce this word without the initial /h/, reminding us of the importance of both regional and global variation in both spelling and pronunciation systems. These changes in spelling and pronunciation to **herb** were paralleled by a number of related changes in words like **adventure** and **host** (Middle English **aventure** and **ost**). However, not all words whose spellings were changed to reflect etymology had their pronunciations shifted to reflect the altered written form. In the case of **hotel**, the initial /h/ was only restored in the twentieth century, while the h-less pronunciation can still be heard in some accents. Uncertainty over whether a word beginning with a vowel should have initial <h> or not has resulted in its introduction in words where it is not found in the Latin etymon, e.g. the common ME spelling **habundant** (from Latin **abundans**) and **hermit** (from Latin **eremita**). Other examples of spellings that have triggered changes in pronunciation are ones involving compounds such as **waistcoat** (previously [wɛskət]) and **forehead** (previously [fɒrɪd]).

These examples remind of us of the complexity of studying the history of pronunciation, given that it has to be carried out through analysis of the written records. Spelling, therefore, is of primary importance for the historical study of spoken language. Despite this, or perhaps as a consequence of this, spelling has been comparatively neglected as a linguistic discipline in its own right. The view that writing exists purely as a means of encoding speech has a long pedigree; the seventeenth-century spelling reformer Thomas Smith claimed that 'writing exists to express what is uttered'. But it is oversimplistic to consider a spelling system as nothing more than a system for mapping sounds onto written characters. Such a view was strongly refuted by Venezky (1967: 77): 'For centuries philologists have approached the study of English orthography with the purblind attitude that writing serves only to mirror speech, and that deviations from a perfect letter-sound relationship are irregularities'. The purpose of this book is to demonstrate the importance of studying English spelling in its own right, to showcase some of the increasingly wide range of research that has been conducted into spelling and the insights this has made possible, as well as to make suggestions as to how this research agenda could be taken forward in the future.

Part I

History

1 Old English

1.1 Origins of Old English

Old English is the name given to the earliest written records of the English language, found in manuscripts copied between 650 and 1100. It was spoken by the Angles and Saxons who came to the British Isles in the fifth century following the departure of the Roman armies and who settled throughout England and southern Scotland. These tribes set out from their homelands in southern Denmark and northern Germany, where they spoke a language belonging to the Germanic language family. This language family is derived from a single common ancestor known today as Proto-Germanic, for which no written records survive. Proto-Germanic subsequently split into three major language groups: West, North and East Germanic. The language varieties spoken by the Angles and Saxons belonged to the West Germanic group; as they came into contact with each other in Britain, a new variety emerged, which they termed *Englisc* and which is now known as Old English.

The Anglo-Saxons were introduced to Latin literacy by the Romans and Irish missionaries at the end of the sixth century. However, the Anglo-Saxons were literate before their conversion to Christianity, since they used an alphabetic system known as runes, although runic literacy appears to have been limited to the Anglians.

1.2 Runes

The runic alphabet originated in Scandinavia and was used on the continent before it was transported to England. It consists of a series of letters formed using straight lines, and was created specifically for inscribing on hard materials such as wood, metal and stone. There are some important differences between the system used by the Anglo-Saxons, and its Scandinavian ancestor, known as the 'futhark', from the opening six letters. Some of these differences are purely visual, such as the

13

addition of a second crossbar to the *h* rune: ᚻ. Others, however, reflect changes in pronunciation between Old English and the wider Germanic language family. For instance, in Old English and the closely related Old Frisian (collectively known as Ingvaeonic), the sound represented by the *a* rune, ᚠ, came to be rounded; in recognition of this change, the shape of the rune was altered to ᚪ. The placement of this modified rune in fourth position led to the Anglo-Saxon runic system becoming known as the 'futhorc' rather than the Scandinavian 'futhark'. The Old English fronting of *a* in some positions created the need for further modifications. As a consequence, the ᚫ rune came to be used for the fronted vowel (known as *æsc* 'ash-tree'), while a variant version, ᚪ, was devised for the back vowel (termed *ac* 'oak'). Anglo-Saxon runemasters also introduced two new runic characters, ᚷ and ᚳ, to represent the sounds /g/ and /k/, required as a result of the palatalisation of these sounds before front vowels.

Although runes are popularly thought to have been employed for magical purposes, their principal use was considerably more mundane. Many surviving examples of runic writing are simple ownership inscriptions, or records of the name of the object's maker. An example of the latter is the Gallehus horn, a drinking vessel from the fifth century, which bears an inscription recording that it was made by one Hlewagast, son of Holt. A more puzzling example is a fifth-century inscription on the bone of a roe deer which reads **raihan**, an archaic and inflected form of Old English **ra**, ROE DEER. Although recording the material on which the inscription was made may seem an unusual practice, another example is found in the better-known Franks Casket. This casket preserves a riddle inscribed in runes, the answer to which is **hronæsban**, or whalebone, the material from which the small box was crafted.

It is often assumed that runes were particularly associated with Germanic paganism. But, if this were the case, we would expect to see them fall out of use following the conversion of the Anglo-Saxons. But the runic and Roman alphabets continued to be used alongside each other. The tolerance of runic writing following Christianisation is particularly apparent from the appearance of a runic inscription on the Ruthwell Cross, a ninth-century monument produced in the kingdom of Northumbria. This cross, which now stands in Ruthwell Church, in the Scottish county of Dumfries and Galloway, contains a series of inscriptions in Roman and runic script. The main inscription corresponds to passages voiced by the cross in the Old English poem *The Dream of the Rood*.

The modified form of the runic alphabet used by the Anglo-Saxons is also found in inscriptions found in Friesland, reflecting the similarities between Old English and Frisian. The Anglo-Saxon invaders probably brought this modified version of the futhark with them. By the end of the tenth century, we find records of the complete futhorc, as can be seen in the Thames scramasax, a one-sided sword found at the bottom of the Thames in 1857 and now preserved in the British Museum. In this inscription we see the use of the modified ᚠ in fourth position, the double-barred ᚻ in ninth place, and the ᚠ and ᚠ runes, which were added at the end of the sequence.

1.3 Roman alphabet: script

Old English was written using a form of writing known as the 'insular' script, developed in Ireland and then exported to Anglo-Saxon Northumbria as part of its conversion under King Edwin in 627. Edwin's successor, Oswald, was baptised into the Celtic church on Iona, whose monastery dates back to its foundation by Columba in circa 563. The insular script employed by Anglo-Saxon scribes comprises a number of letter forms which look quite different to the equivalent forms found in the Caroline minuscule script, developed at the court of Charlemagne and adopted by the Anglo-Saxons in the tenth century for writing Latin. Distinctive features of insular minuscule include the long forms of **f**, **s**, and **r**, which all extend below the baseline, a form of **t** that does not project above the crossbar, and a flat-topped form of the letter **g**.

1.4 Roman alphabet: spellings and sounds

In many ways, the adoption of the Roman alphabet by the Anglo-Saxons was simply a case of applying the conventions for representing Latin to Old English. So, for instance, the phonemes /b, p, t, d/ were spelled using the letters <b, p, t, d> from the Latin alphabet. But the process of adoption was not always quite this straightforward. This is because Latin employed a sound system that differed from Old English in several important ways. We noted above that Old English belongs to the Germanic language family; Latin formed part of a different language group, known as Italic. While both Germanic and Italic are members of a much larger family, known as Indo-European, they had undergone a number of changes that set them apart from each other. For instance, Latin did not make use of the dental fricatives, /ð, θ/; consequently, there was no established Latin convention for scribes to follow. In order to fill this gap, Anglo-Saxon scribes turned to the runic alphabet and borrowed the letter 'thorn': <þ>. A similar problem concerned the representation of the /w/ phoneme, which in Latin was spelled using the letter <v>, which in turn came to be used to represent the /v/ sound in Vulgar Latin. To avoid confusion, Anglo-Saxon scribes employed the runic equivalent <ρ>, known as wynn, meaning 'joy'. Since the letters <j, w> were not part of the Roman alphabet as used for writing Latin, they are also not found in Old English.

In the Northumbrian dialect, influence from Irish practices meant that the earliest texts used <th> for /θ/ and <u> for /w/. In the version of Cædmon's Hymn in CUL Kk.5.16, a copy of the Latin version of Bede's *Historia Ecclesiastica Gentis Anglorum*, 'An Ecclesiastical History of the English People', we find the spellings **uard** and **tha** for the West-Saxon dialect equivalents **weard** and **þa**. Another dialectal variant is the use of <vv> for /w/. The inscription that is found on the Alfred Jewel reads 'Ælfred mec heht gevvyrcan', with <vv> representing the /w/ sound in **gewyrcan** MADE. Old English made little use of the letters <q> and <z>, mostly reserving them for foreign names or technical terms.

Other differences concern the conventions with which Anglo-Saxon scribes employed the letters shared by both orthographies. Instead of following the Latin practice of using <qu> for the /kw/ sound, Old English used <cw>, e.g. **cwēn** QUEEN. The adoption of <qu> in such words is a Middle English development triggered by the influence of French practice (see further Chapter 2).

The phonemic inventory of Old English differs in important ways from Present-day English. For instance, although Old English included both voiced and voiceless sets of fricatives, only the voiceless sounds were phonemic. There were voiced fricative sounds, but they were in complementary distribution with the voiceless fricatives, so that the choice between the two was governed by the position in the word. When a fricative appeared at the beginning or end of the word it was voiceless, as in **hūs** HOUSE; where it appeared in the middle of a word it was voiced, as in **dysig** DIZZY, i.e. 'foolish'. In the word **hlāf**, the ancestor of modern English LOAF, the final <f> is voiceless; but in the word **hlāford**, the origin of PDE LORD, it is voiced. This is also true of the voiced and voiceless dental fricatives, which could be spelled with the letter <þ> or using an alternative letter, <ð>, known today as 'edh'. Because the distinction between [θ] and [ð] was not phonemic in Old English, no attempt was made to employ these two letters to mark this distinction. Instead, the letters <ð, þ> were used interchangeably; hence **ðicce** THICK and **tið** 'grant' (PDE TITHE).

The voiceless velar fricative /x/, no longer a feature of PDE although still found in some accents of Scots and Scottish English, was spelled <h> in Old English; it appears in words like **niht** and **miht**, where its legacy can be seen in the use of <ght> in Present-day English equivalents like **night** and **might**. This sound also appeared at the ends of words, as in **heah** HIGH and **seah** SAW.

Unlike PDE, Old English did not make use of the /ŋ/ phoneme; this sound was only ever found before /g/, as in **hringan** 'to ring', and so remained allophonic, as in some Midlands and Northern accents today. The letter <c> mapped on to two allophones: [k] and [tʃ], depending on whether it was followed by a front vowel or a back vowel: compare **cild** CHILD and **cuman** COME. But note that <k> was sometimes used before front vowels where the [k] sound might otherwise be erroneously rendered [tʃ]: **kyning**, alongside **cyning** KING. Such examples arose where a front vowel followed [k] as a result of 'i-mutation', a prehistoric sound change by which a back vowel was fronted where an /i/ or /j/ appeared in the following syllable. Similar use was made of the grapheme <g>, which reflects [j] before and after any front vowel, <i, æ, e>, as in **gear** YEAR and **dæg** DAY. Elsewhere it renders the [g] sound, as in **gan** GO, **gold** GOLD, **gylt** GUILT. Between and following back vowels, and between <l> and <r>, <g> signals [ɣ], as in **dagas** DAYS; in final position it can alternate with <h>: **burh, burg**. After <n>, <g> can signal [dʒ], e.g. **engel** ANGEL, although this sound is more usually spelled <cg> as in **brycg** BRIDGE. The [ʃ] sound was spelled with <sc>, as in **scip** SHIP and **biscop** BISHOP. In order to signal where the consonant was palatalised, some Old English scribes employed <e> as a diacritic, as in **sceolde** SHOULD, alongside **sculde**. Because the spelling <eu> was generally avoided in Old English, **sceolde** is spelled with an <o>. This is also found in words like **geoguð** YOUTH and **Geōl** YULE, where the <o> represents the [u] sound. An alternative way of spelling these words with <iu> can also be found in Old English: **iuguð** and **Giūl**.

Old English also made use of a number of consonant groups that have not survived into PDE. These include the clusters [hn, hl, hr, hw] found in words like **hnutu** NUT, **hlāf** LOAF, **hring** RING, **hwæt** WHAT, **gnagan** GNAW, **wrīðan** WRITHE; in each of these cases both initial consonants were sounded. Comparison with their PDE equivalents reveals that in each instance the initial sound has since been dropped, a development that took place in the Middle English period. Old English was also rhotic, meaning that the <r> was pronounced after vowels and at the ends of words, as in **hord** HOARD and **bār** BOAR.

Old English also made use of geminate, or long, consonants in medial position. Contrast **hoppian** HOP with **hopian** HOPE, **sunne** SUN and **sunu** SON. Although gemination is no longer a phonemic feature of Present-day English, it is found across morpheme and word boundaries, as in BOOK KEEPER and BAD DOG.

1.5 Vowels

The following letters were used to represent the monophthongs in Old English: <y, i, e æ, a, o, u>. There was no written distinction between long and short vowels in OE, hence **god** could signal either GOD or GOOD. Despite this lack of written marking, length is an important distinction in OE, as can be seen in additional pairs of words like **mētan** MEET and **metan** MEASURE, **wendon** TURNED and **wēndon** BELIEVED. It is for this reason that modern editors typically add a macron to indicate where a vowel is long.

OE also differed from PDE in having a three-height instead of a four-height vowel system. At the front of the mouth, there were the following three sets of vowels: /i, i:/ (accompanied by the equivalent rounded vowels /y, y:/), /e, e:/, /æ, æ:/ and three sets of back vowels: /ɑ, ɑ:/, /o, o:/ and /u, u:/. Another difference between OE and PDE is that there appears to have been no qualitative distinction between long and short vowels in OE, whereas such a distinction can be seen in the PDE pronunciation of e.g. *fit* (/fɪt/) and *feet* (fi:t). The front rounded vowel /y(:)/, no longer found in PDE, was spelled using the <y> grapheme, a convention which was established for the transliteration of Greek words in Latin. Although [y] was accommodated to [i] in Latin, its association with [y] in Greek was preserved and appears to lie behind the usage in Old English (as is suggested by Ælfric referring to the letter as 'se grecisca y' [the Greek y]). In order to distinguish between /æ, æ:/ and /ɑ, ɑ:/, the letter <a> was used for the back vowel, while a modified form, <æ>, was employed for the front vowel. In origin, this letter is a ligature formed using the letters <a> and <e>. It was given the name **æsc** ASH, from that of the ᚠ rune that was used for the same sound in the futhorc.

Scholars have traditionally distinguished three sets of diphthongs which were spelled <ea, eo, ie>; early West-Saxon also includes examples of <io> which was later replaced by <eo>. These are generally thought to have reflected both short and long diphthongs; thus the <ea> in **bearn** CHILD is considered to have been short, while the equivalent digraph in **bēam** BEAM is thought to have been long. However, the exact status of the short diphthongs remains a matter of scholarly debate. One reason for this, as stated by Richard Hogg (1992: 18), is that it is very unusual for a language to show a phonemic contrast between short and long diphthongs. Furthermore, no such contrast is found in PDE, nor is it thought to have been attested in Proto-Germanic. An alternative hypothesis suggests that the digraphs were not intended to indicate a short diphthong, but instead meant to convey information concerning the quality of the following consonant. We have already seen how such spellings were used to indicate the palatal nature of the preceding consonant in words like **sceolde** and **geoguð**. Thus, Marjorie Daunt (1939) suggested that the <ea> and <eo> spellings of words such as **eald** OLD and **eolh** ELK could be intended to signal the monophthongs /æ/ or /e/ followed by a back consonant, a practice which Anglo-Saxon scribes may have learned from Old Irish.

1.6 Dialects

The Angles and Saxon tribes who invaded Britain from the continent originally settled in the south and east. But they subsequently spread out, extending their area of settlement into southern Scotland and all of England, apart from Cornwall, which, along with Wales and north-ern Scotland, remained Celtic speaking. As a result of this migration throughout the British Isles, seven smaller kingdoms emerged, known as the Heptarchy: Kent, Sussex, Wessex, Essex, East Anglia, Mercia and Northumbria. These last two are collectively known by the term Anglian. The names of the kingdoms are also used to designate the major varie-ties of Old English, whose distribution roughly corresponds to these same geographical distributions. Traditionally, four distinct Old English dialects are identified by scholars; these are termed West-Saxon, Kentish, Mercian and Northumbrian.

West-Saxon corresponds to the kingdom of Wessex, an area of the south-west of England, which had its administrative centre at Winchester. The strength of this kingdom and the success of Alfred the Great (871–99) in attempting to unite the country led to the wider adoption of the West-Saxon dialect. As a consequence, texts written in other regional dialects are only found for the earlier part of the Old English period; from 900 onwards, texts written beyond Wessex typically adopt West-Saxon dialect wholesale, or show a mixture of local and West-Saxon forms.

Although the kingdom of Northumbria stretched from Edinburgh in the north as far south as the river Mersey, the texts that survive are mostly connected with the ecclesiastical centre located at Durham. Here a monk called Aldred, Provost of the monastic house at Chester-le-Street, wrote a vernacular gloss between the elegantly written lines of Latin in the Lindisfarne Gospels, a highly deluxe manuscript originally produced at the monastery at Lindisfarne by a monk called Eadfrith. Similar problems of coverage affect our reconstruction of the Mercian dialect, for which we have very little evidence of the Eastern, and especially the East Anglian, area. Two of our major sources of evidence, the glosses on the Rushworth Gospels and the Vespasian Psalter, are both likely to have been produced at Lichfield, a major ecclesiastical focal point. The linguistic continuities that are apparent between these two texts and the Middle English AB language (see further Chapter 2) hint at a longer tradition of copying in the Mercian dialect, although, apart from an eleventh-century life of St Chad, bishop of Lichfield, much of the evidence for this has not survived.

1.6.1 Late West-Saxon

We have already noted that the evidence for Old English dialects is complicated by the wider adoption of late West-Saxon outside its local geographical area in the tenth century. Some scholars consider this to be indicative of its adoption as a standard written form of Old English, a kind of *Schriftsprache*, with an internally stable orthographic system (See Hogg 1992: 3). N. F. Blake (1996: 90) is explicit in his identification of the late West-Saxon dialect as a form of Standard English, characterised by internal consistency of forms and words. Gneuss (1972) was also content to identify the late West-Saxon dialect as 'Standard Old English', arguing that its success was due to the political prominence of the kingdom of Wessex and its large concentration of reformed Benedictine monastic houses. But while Gneuss could refer to the conclusive evidence of the teaching of a standard vocabulary, there is little to support his claim that this was also true of regularised forms of spelling, morphology and syntax.

Other scholars have noted that, despite late West-Saxon becoming established as a literary dialect, and being used beyond its Wessex origins, many manuscripts contain a variety of non-West-Saxon features in their orthography and inflexions (Campbell 1959: 9). This internal variability is especially apparent in the four major poetic codices that survive, all of which date from the end of the tenth century. While they all attest a number of features of late West-Saxon, these forms are found alongside a mixture of features drawn from other dialects. While the late West-Saxon forms are explicable as the influence of this dialect at the time of copying, the source of the non-West-Saxon forms is more debatable. These may preserve the original dialect of composition, or descend from various stages of textual transmission. A more controversial theory is that their language reflects a poetic koiné: a mixed dialect, comprising forms that would be of limited currency in prose or speech, and which poets and their audience associated with verse composition (Sisam 1953). A related view considers this dialect to have been developed for the transmission of such works, into which scribes translated exemplars composed in other dialects (Raw 1978). This may take the evidence too far and accord more meta-linguistic consciousness to scribes than is appropriate. However, there is clear evidence that scribes who copied poetic codices were prepared to tolerate forms that were not part of their own spontaneous usage, such as the spelling **aldor**, alongside the customary West-Saxon form **ealdormann** (Stanley 1969b). Stanley analysed the spelling variation between <ea> and <a> before <l> followed by another consonant. He noticed that, as West-Saxon became more widely adopted, Anglian scribes adopted <ea> instead of their usual <a>. However, not all such words were spelled <ea> in West-Saxon. An exception is the word **waldend**, which a scribe of the Junius manuscript corrected to **wealdend**. From such evidence Stanley concluded that this corrector was attempting to impose the West-Saxon standard, but was unaware that the usual <eald> sequence is not found in the word **waldend** in West-Saxon. While such examples do indicate a tendency towards the preservation of non-West-Saxon spellings in poetry, it is probably stretching the evidence too far to consider this a poetic dialect.

Other scholars have viewed late West-Saxon as a kind of standard that functioned in a similar way to the various house styles adopted by modern printing presses. In a later stage this local standard was gradually adopted outside its Wessex heartland by scribes writing in Kent, Mercia and Northumbria (Scragg 1974: 9). Since the wider adoption of late West-Saxon is closely linked with bishoprics, such as those located at Canterbury, Worcester and York, Hogg suggested that it would be more accurate to consider it an ecclesiastical rather than a literary standard (1992: 13).

Jeremy Smith has sought to explain the mixture of late West-Saxon with other dialects by viewing it as a focused rather than a fixed stand-ard: one that permits internal variation alongside a degree of stability rather than insisting on a single correct spelling form for all words (see further Chapter 3). As well as noting that certain distinctive lexical habits were restricted to specific monastic scriptoria, Smith observed persistent orthographic distinctions across manuscripts copied in late West-Saxon (Smith 1996: 67). The work of these scholars indicates that, while there is considerable support for a late West-Saxon variety, it remains difficult to determine its limits and the degree of internal variability that it toler-ated. Perhaps the clearest evidence of a concern with implementing a consistent and standardised spelling system is found in the manuscripts of Ælfric, some of which were corrected by Ælfric himself, in order to ensure accuracy in their orthography (Godden 1979). An important interven-tion by Faulkner (2020) examined two large datasets, one of over 19,000 morphemes from 100 texts and a second comprising 91,000 spellings from 941 texts across 198 manuscripts, in order to approach the debate from a more empirical perspective. Faulkner's quantitative study found that, across this extensive body of texts, the infinitive morpheme was written <–an> 96.1% of the time and the diphthong /æa, æːa/ was spelled

<ea> 96.5% of the time. This leads Faulkner to conclude that scholars have been too cautious in their willingness to accept the existence of a homogeneous variety of West-Saxon.

The widespread adoption of this variety was facilitated by a period of political stability under King Edgar (959–75) and the Benedictine reform that brought with it improvements in literacy. But, where some scholars have drawn attention to the remarkable fixity attested by the spelling system of late West-Saxon, others have stressed its internal variability. The upshot of the spread of this standardised variety is that in the first half of the eleventh century, manuscripts produced in regional centres such as Canterbury, Worcester and York show little evidence of regional dialect.

2 Middle English

Middle English refers to the period in the history of English from roughly 1100–1500. The major extralinguistic factor that precipitated the shift from Old English to Middle English was the Norman Conquest of 1066, since this led to the replacement of English with French as the principal vernacular used for literary, administrative, legal and other written functions. This created a distinct break with the late West-Saxon standard that had developed before the conquest, and triggered numerous subsequent changes in the spelling of English. The existence of a late West-Saxon standard meant that there was a relatively large gap between the spellings used in this period and the way these words were pronounced. This is because, as pronunciation changed over time, the spelling system was not modified to accommodate these changes. Furthermore, the use of the late West-Saxon standard throughout the country meant that it was being used by scribes whose native dialects included different pronunciations not represented by the late West-Saxon spelling conventions. As late West-Saxon ceased to be used, we witness a process by which scribes remodelled their spelling systems to reflect their contemporary, local systems of pronunciation.

One obvious way in which Middle English spelling looks very different to that of the pre-Conquest period is the dropping of the special characters employed for writing Old English. The loss of these letters, however, happened at different times in different dialects. The letter ash <æ> was used until the thirteenth century; in the West Midlands it was exploited by the poet Layamon to create a faux-archaistic appearance to his text. The letter <ð> fell out of use at a similar time, being replaced by the digraph <th> or the runic <þ>, which survived up to the end of the fifteenth century, although it became increasingly restricted to use in abbreviations like þᵗ THAT and in determiners such as þe THE and þis THIS. The most decisive factor in the loss of <þ> from the English writing system was the advent of the printing press. Since printing types were initially produced on the continent, William Caxton, England's first printer, tended to use <th> rather than <þ>. Where he did use <þ>, particularly in abbreviations, he employed the similar-looking letter <y>, following a practice that had already been established in northern and eastern dialects, in which spellings like **yai** THEY, **yan** THEN and **yre** THREE were common. In northern dialect use of the fifteenth century, thorn was reintroduced in the legal and administrative register, but often used mistakenly in contexts where <y> is required, e.g. **wþll** WILL and **þong** YOUNG. At first, <th> began to replace both <þ> and <y> in initial positions where it represents [Θ], **thin**, **think**, then medially where it signals [ð], **other**, **mother**, and then finally in words where [ð] appears initially, e.g. **they**, **them**. The convention of using <th> to signal [Θ] goes back to the Romans, who employed this digraph when transliterating this sound in words borrowed from Greek, and later in the names of the Germanic peoples with whom they came into contact. That this convention was already known in Anglo-Saxon England is apparent from the early Northumbrian spellings considered in the previous chapter.

As we saw in Section 1.4, [w] was represented by the runic letter wynn in OE, although modern editors routinely replace it with the modern equivalent <w>. Wynn continued to be employed in England after the Conquest; however, its similarity to both the letters <y> and <þ> created the potential for confusion. The dot over the <y> was not sufficient to create a clear distinction and was no help in avoiding confusion between <þ> and <wynn>. Up until the thirteenth century, wynn continued to appear in ME texts, often alongside the alternatives <u> or <uu>, the 'double u' from which the letter gets its name, which ultimately replaced it. This convention was also found in the spelling of Old English names when they appeared in Anglo-Latin texts, as in Ætheluuald and Ætheluulf, where wynn, along with either thorn or eth, would be used if the surrounding text were in Old English. It is also possible that the popularity of certain French names with <w>, e.g. Walter and William, contributed to this process of replacement.

We saw in Section 1.3 that Old English scripts employed an insular form of <g> <<ʒ>>, although this is usually represented by <g> in modern editions of Old English texts. During this period, a Carolingian script was introduced from the continent, which included the letter <g>, but this was used for copying Latin rather than Old English. In the Middle English period, this letter was borrowed into English to represent the sound /g/, while a modified version of the insular g, <ʒ>, which was termed 'yogh', was employed for the sounds /j/ and /x/ – hence its name, which is a representation of these two sounds. Yogh continued to be used throughout the Middle English period, although it was gradually replaced by the letter <y> for /j/ and <gh> for /x/. The <cg> combination that was used for [ʤ] was replaced by <gg> in ME, as found in words like **brigge** (OE **brycg**).

The shape of the letter yogh resembled that of the letter <ȝ>, as that was rendered in French scripts. The letter <z> was not widely employed in OE, mostly being reserved as an alternative means of marking [ts] in words like **bezt** BEST. However, its use increased in ME, leading to potential confusion in words where it appeared alongside the letter yogh, e.g. **boȝez** BOUGHS. Since both <ȝ> and <y> could be used to represent /j/, scribes for whom <y> and <þ> were identical would also use <ȝ> for [Θ] or [ð], e.g. **ȝat** THAT, **ȝem** THEM.

The /x/ sound that appeared in words like KNIGHT and BRIGHT was lost during the fifteenth century, although the <gh> has been preserved due to the standardisation of spelling. Because the standard was based upon a southern dialect, where the /x/ was preserved longest, this spelling has become part of the modern standard variety. In northern dialects, a pronunciation with [f] developed, producing spellings like **dafter** DAUGHTER; this northern variant is the origin of the standard pronunciations of ENOUGH and ROUGH (Old English **genoh** and **ruh**).

The <gh> digraph represents a development in which <h> developed a role as a diacritic, also employed in a number of similar instances: <ch, wh, sh, th>. Alongside <sh> there were a number of dialectal variants used for representing the /ʃ/ sound, e.g. <ss, sch, x>. The last of these was only attested in the Norfolk dialect, where it was mostly restricted to the modal verb SHALL: **xal**.

The replacement of <sc> with <sh> was also helpful in avoiding confusion with words borrowed from Old Norse, which contained the consonant combination /sk/. This combination was found in Proto-Germanic, but in the West Germanic dialects it had shifted to /ʃ/: compare Old English **scip** and Old Norse **skip**. Words borrowed from Old Norse during this period were spelled <sk>, e.g. **sky** and **skyrte** (compare the cognate Old English form **scyrte** (PDE SHIRT). The /sk/ cluster also appeared in some French borrowings, where it was spelled <sc>, sometimes alongside alternatives with <sch>, as in **escap** and **eschap**, often reflecting dialect variation in Old French. In some instances, such as **catel** and **chatel**, the variant forms became attributed to different words.

The distinction between /w/ and /ʍ/ was maintained throughout much of the ME period. However, some dialects began to use spellings with initial <w>, e.g. **wan** WHAN, **wich** WHICH, while others employed back spellings such as **whas** WAS, suggesting the loss of the [ʍ] sound. In the northern dialects, this sound was preserved longer and spelled <quh>, as in **quhilk** and **quhan**. In the more conservative south-west midland dialects the <hw> found in Old English was preserved longer than in other parts of the country. The loss of initial /x/ also affected the consonant clusters <hl, hn, hr>: ME **lofe** (OE **hlāf**), **nut** (OE **hnutu**), **roof** (OE **hrōf**). This process occurred early in the ME period and was complete by around 1200; transitional forms such as **lhord** (OE **hlāford**) are recorded in the Kentish dialect of circa 1300.

In other consonant clusters, such as <wr>, <kn>, <wl> and <gn>, both consonants appear to have been pronounced throughout the ME period in words like **wrong, knight, gnawe**.

2.1 Vowels

Where OE had no written distinction between short and long vowels, ME employed vowel doubling to indicate vowel length, e.g. **stoon** STONE and **taak** TAKE. In ME the following letters were used to represent the short vowels [ɪ, ɛ, a, ɔ, ʊ]: <i/y, e, a, o, u>. The long vowels [iː, eː, ɛː, aː, ɔː, oː, uː] were written using the following combinations: <i/y, e/ee, a/aa, o/ oo, ou/ow>. An important feature of this inventory is that there was no written distinction between the mid close and mid open vowels. The front vowels [eː] and [ɛː] were both spelled <ee>, while the back vowels [oː] and [ɔː] were both spelled <oo>. Another notable feature of this inventory is the disappearance of <æ>, which took place in the Early ME period, being replaced by <a, e, ea>. A further difference from OE concerns the use of <ou, ow> to represent [uː], a usage that was introduced from French and replaced the OE practice of using <u>. Dialect variation means that this inventory differs depending on the area in which a text was written. For instance, in the southern dialects of ME the <ā> vowel of OE was rounded and raised and written with <oo>, as in **stoon**. However, in the northern dialects the ā was preserved and continued to be spelled <a, aa>. Different dialects came up with alternative methods of marking vowel length; for instance, northern varieties of ME used <i> as a diacritic following the vowel to indicate its length, as in **guid** GOOD. The levelling and loss of inflexional endings during the ME period meant that final <e> became redundant and so began to be repurposed as a length marker. Since inflexional levelling affected the northern dialects earlier than those of the south, because of contact with Scandinavian speakers, this device is found first in the dialects of the north and Scots, e.g. **gude** GOOD.

A significant difference between OE and ME concerns the diphthongs. OE diphthongs monophthongised and merged with other sounds, so that OE **beo** became ME **bee** and OE **heorta** became ME **herte**. A series of vocalisations of certain consonants created a new set of diphthongs in ME:

[aɪ]   <ai, ay, ei, ey>
[ɔɪ]   <oi, oy>
[aʊ]   <au>
[ɔʊ]   <ow>
[ɪʊ]   <ew>

These are the result of the vocalisation of the consonants <w, g, h>, as in **pley** (OE **plega**) PLAY, **throw** (OE **þrawan**). French loanwords with [ɔɪ] were spelled using the <oi, oy> digraph.

In unstressed syllables, a process whereby qualitative distinctions that had begun to be lost in late OE continued into ME. This resulted in the widespread use of schwa, which was spelled <e>. Thus in ME the strong noun plural inflexion was <–es> rather than the <–as> found in OE. There was some variation in this according to dialect, with western dialects using <–us> and northern dialects having <is/–ys>.

2.2 Consonants

The consonant system of ME shows a number of key changes from that inherited from Old English. Some of these are the consequence of internal changes reflecting shifts in pronunciation, while others are the result of influence from French and Latin.

As we saw in the previous chapter, in Old English <c> was used for both [k] and [tʃ], with the choice of sound being guided by whether it was followed by a front or back vowel, e.g. **cū** COW but **cild** CHILD. Subsequent changes in pronunciation, however, increased the number of words in which the [k] sound was followed by a front vowel, e.g. **cēne** KEEN. To avoid confusion the letter <k>, a feature of the Latin alphabet that was more widely used in French, was introduced in such environments, while <ch> was adopted as a marker of [tʃ]. The letter <c> was also used in French loanwords like **centre** and **citee** to signal [s]; this practice was extended to words of Old English origin too, as in the plural form **mice** (OE **mys**). Another French convention that was adopted in the ME period was the use of <qu> for [kw], a usage that was originally found in Latin; this was also spread to native words, as in **queen** (OE **cwēn**), replacing entirely the Old English practice of using <cw>.

The letters <z> and <v> began to be used in order to introduce a written distinction between the voiced and voiceless fricatives. This was unnecessary in OE because they were in complementary distribution, but in ME the distinction became phonemic as a result of contact with French. Borrowings of words like **fine** and **vine**, **seel** and **zeel** created a need for a written distinction. In southern dialects of ME, initial fricatives were voiced, and so <v> often appears for <f>; this is the origin of the word for the female fox, **vixen** (OE **fyxen**). The levelling and loss of inflexional endings also contributed to this process of phonemicisation. For instance, the OE verb **husian** became ME **hous**; but, while the two words, HOUSE (n.) and HOUSE (v.) are distinguished in speech, no written distinction has been introduced in PDE.

The use of the letter <v> differs from that found in PDE, since it could be used interchangeably with <u>. In general, the letter <v> appeared at the beginnings of words, as in **vntil**, and <u> within the word, as in **haue** HAVE, whether they represented a vowel or a consonant. Also interchangeable in this period were the letters <y> and <i>. This was due to the unrounding of the close rounded front vowel /y/ in most dialects; in the West Midlands where the rounded vowel was preserved it was spelled <u>. The selection of <y> rather than <i> was often due to situations where a sequence of single strokes, known as minims, was liable to cause confusion. Since the letters <n> and <m> were written as two consecutive minims, a word like **winne** WIN could be open to misunderstanding. In order to minimise this potential for confusion, scribes would often use a <y> instead of an <i>: **wynne**. For the same reason, an <o> was used instead of <u> in similar environments, as in ME **loue** (compare Old English **lufu**). However, <o> also appeared in environments where minim confusion was not a factor, such as **borough** and **thorough**, while a number of words are spelled with <u> despite the potential for such confusion, e.g. **hunt**, **thumb**. Another factor that may have influenced the decision to use <o> rather than <u> was to avoid creating homonyms, as in pairs of words like **sun** and **son**; **tun** and **ton**.

2.3 Early Middle English dialects

The dialects of ME derive from those identified for the OE period: a northern dialect based on the Northumbrian dialect of OE, a south-western variety (corresponding to West-Saxon), south-eastern (from the OE Kentish dialect); the Mercian dialect of OE is divided into West and East Midlands dialects in ME, while a further East Anglian dialect can also be identified with forms distinct from those of the East Midlands. Scholars have identified one variety of Middle English which has been considered to show early efforts towards standardisation of spelling, albeit at a purely local level. This is the South-West Midlands variety known as the 'AB' language, a term that was first coined by the philologist J. R. R. Tolkien (1929). This variety is attested in two manuscripts, Bodleian Library MS Bodley 34 [B], containing five religious prose works, the lives of St Katherine, St Margaret and St Juliana, *Hali Meiðhad* [Holy

Maidenhood] and *Sawles Warde* [Soul's Guardian], and Corpus Christi College Cambridge MS 402 [A], containing *Ancrene Wisse* [Guide for Anchoresses]. These two manuscripts were copied by two different scribes in the early thirteenth century; their early provenance suggests connections with Herefordshire. In his study of these two manuscripts, Tolkien was struck by the similarity of their spelling practices, which he considered to have been devised by 'some school or authority' and then taught to individuals like the two scribes who copied the A and B manuscripts (Tolkien 1929: 108–9).

2.3.1 AB language

The AB language was quite conservative and shared many features with its OE ancestor. For instance, it preserves rounded vowels that had unrounded in other ME dialects, e.g. **heorte** HEART and **dude** DID; it also shows the rounding of OE <a> before nasals that is characteristic of the Mercian dialect of OE, e.g. **nome** NAME and **mon** MAN. Also found in this western dialect are spellings like **feole** MANY and **eoten** EAT, the result of a sound change known as 'back mutation'. Another specifically western feature is the appearance of <e> rather than <a> in words like **efter** AFTER, and **dei** DAY, the result of sound change known as 'second fronting' that only affected the Mercian dialect of OE. Related to these forms are those showing <ea> for the short [æ] sound, e.g. **fearen** FARE and **wealle** WELL, a development that is particular to the AB language itself. It has been suggested that such conventions indicate a continuous written tradition in the West Midlands, across which spelling conventions were passed down from West Mercian scribes to their Early Middle English ancestors. But these distinctive rounded vowels, diphthongs and raisings reflect features of pronunciation rather than spelling, and thus could as easily be explained as the result of scribes independently attempting to devise written conventions to reflect a local spoken form. Rather than inheriting specific spelling forms that have been passed down in an unbroken Mercian tradition, the AB scribes could simply be reflecting their current pronunciation using similar conventions.

Where there are direct continuities with specifically written features of OE, these are with late West-Saxon rather than the Mercian dialect. For example, the AB language includes spellings that show the late West-Saxon convention of employing <e> as a diacritic to indicate the palatal nature of the preceding consonant. To demonstrate this we can compare AB **cheafle** JAW and **scheome** SHAME with late West-Saxon forms **ceafl** and **sceomu** (Black 1999: 160). From such examples, Merja Black concludes that there is no reason to assume a specific line of descent from

OE to AB; rather, the correspondences simply reflect the continued presence of late West-Saxon as part of the cultural and linguistic contexts of both the AB texts and others from the South-West Midlands milieu in which they were copied. But, while the AB dialect does show continuities with its Old English ancestor, it also adopts a number of developments that are common to other dialects of this period. The digraph <ch> is found instead of <c> to mark the /tʃ/ sound; <c> appears for /k/ before back vowels, while <k> is used before front vowels. The /ʃ/ sound is indicated by <sch>, a convention widely adopted as an alternative to <sh> in this period.

AB scribes employed the Carolingian <g> for the plosive sound, /g/, while the insular letter yogh was used for /j/. But there were also conventions that stand apart from developments elsewhere in the country, which did not work towards disambiguation and greater transparency. For instance, the AB dialect chose the letter <u> to represent the high back rounded vowels /u(:)/, found in **hus** HOUSE and **ure** OUR. This same symbol was also used for the front rounded vowels /y(:)/, as in **lutel** LITTLE and **dude** DID, which had been unrounded in other Midlands dialects and were typically spelled <y> or <i>. In OE this sound had been spelled with a <y>, so that the use of this same symbol for both front and back sounds resulted in the loss of a distinction found in OE.

The AB dialect's concern with clarity and precision in the mapping of sounds on to spellings is apparent in the introduction of several conventions that are peculiar to its system. For instance, in Section 1.5 we noted that OE did not distinguish between pairs of words like **god** GOD and **god** GOOD. In order to introduce such a distinction, the AB dialect consistently spells the former **godd**. Another example is the systematic disambiguation of **oþer** OTHER and **oðer** OR, which disrupts another consistently applied system in which <þ> only otherwise appears at the beginnings of words, leaving <ð> for use medially and finally.

Another striking feature of AB dialect is the use of <h> to represent the voiced velar fricative [ɣ], a sound that was more typically spelled with <ʒ> in early ME. Although the letter <h> was also used for [x], there was no difficulty in using the same letter for both sounds as the distinction was allophonic. The reason for this decision may have been to avoid any potential confusion in the use of <ʒ>, which was employed for both [j] and [ɣ], although the AB dialect uses <i> for [j], e.g. **deien**. As Dance (2003) has noted, the distinction being observed here was no longer a living feature of the dialect; it is an indication that the devising of this writing system probably took place in the late twelfth century. Its maintenance into the early thirteenth century is further evidence of the extent to which the AB dialect was concerned with its role as a written language, resolving potential ambiguities in the visual medium.

The AB dialect, therefore, appears to reflect an attempt to remodel the spelling system to reflect a local, western pronunciation, drawing upon new innovations as well as conventions established for the copying of late West-Saxon. These continuities with the past are also evident in another manuscript copied in the West Midlands dialect, Cotton Caligula MS A.ix, containing a lengthy verse account of the history of Britain known as the *Brut*, by a priest called Layamon. This manuscript was copied in the second half of the thirteenth century, but some of its spellings appear to be deliberately archaistic. One example of this concerns the representation of OE ā, which, in the early part of the manuscript, is spelled <o, oa, ao>. As the copying progresses, however, the scribe switches to the use of <a>. This runs contrary to the expected development, since this sound was undergoing a shift to [ɔː]. Alternative spellings, with <æ> or <eo>, cannot be understood according to this phonetic development, suggesting that they were intended to evoke the flavour of an archaic language rather than to represent actual pronunciations. Similar examples can be found in the representation of vowels in unstressed syllables, such as **blissæ** and **oðeræ**, where the vowels had already been levelled to [ə], and so must also reflect deliberate archaism rather than an attempt to reflect pronunciation. It is possible that the retention and ahistorical use of these OE features reflect attempts by scribes to imitate the written conventions of late West-Saxon. It is not clear whether the archaic and archaistic spellings are the contribution of the author or his scribes. Eric Stanley (1969a) suggested that the archaisms reflect a deliberate attempt to connect the text with the glorious pre-Conquest history represented by late West-Saxon. While it is perhaps most likely that the scribes were responsible for enhancing and extending this attempt to archaise, the stimulus was probably found in the authorial exemplar itself. A similar strategy to employ archaism to invoke an earlier period of history may lie behind the spellings employed by the scribe of the Proclamation of Henry III; despite being written in 1258, this document contains a number of forms that reflect earlier spelling practices (Machan 2005).

Our consideration of the AB dialect has suggested that this is better seen as evidence of scribes reworking spelling conventions from late West-Saxon in order to represent their local pronunciations more accurately. A particularly striking example of this can be seen in an early twelfth-century work known as *The Ormulum*. This lengthy verse work survives in a single manuscript (Bodleian Library MS Junius 1), which is the author's own working draft. In writing down his work, Orm devised an idiosyncratic spelling system which he employed with great consistency. A particularly striking feature of Orm's orthography is the use of double consonants to indicate where the vowel in a preceding closed syllable is short, hence: **mann**, **att**, **hiss**. A closed syllable is one that has the structure -VC (where V = any vowel and C = any consonant). In open syllables (ones with the structure CV-), Orm does not make such a distinction. Thus, in a disyllabic word like **faderr**, which is made up of an open syllable followed by a closed syllable, the <d> is not doubled. A consequence of this is that Orm's spelling practices provide an abundance of evidence relating to the length of vowels in this period. Spellings like **king**, **lamb**, **land** witness to the lengthening of short vowels when followed by pairs of homorganic consonants in the late twelfth century, while the spelling **lanng** indicates that this lengthening had not taken place before the <ng> cluster. The different spelling of the singular **child** and its plural form **chilldre** (OE **cildru**) exemplify how this lengthening did not occur when the pair of homorganic consonants was followed by a third consonant.

Orm's concern with accurately reflecting the pronunciation of his text can also be seen in his treatment of the <eo> digraph in words like **cneow** KNEE and **beon**. Orm spelled such words with <eo> for the first 13,000 lines of the text, but then switched to <e>: **cneww**, **ben**. This change provides useful evidence for dating the monophthongisation of this sound in Orm's spoken dialect. Being of a highly pedantic disposition, Orm returned to the earlier instances of such words and deleted all instances of the letter <o> in such environments, thereby bringing these spellings into line with his revised orthography. Another development that is particular to Orm concerns his devising a special form of the letter <g> with a horizontal line at the top, which he used to distinguish /g/ from /j/ and /dʒ/, which he spelled <ʒ> and <gg> respectively. A further innovation introduced by Orm is the use of a yogh with a superscript <h> to represent the /ʒ/ sound; the only word in which the two letters are written alongside each other is the feminine pronoun **ʒho** SHE. The consistency of this practice suggests that the two spellings are intended to reflect a phonetic distinction. It is likely that the <ʒh> in **ʒho** is intended to reflect the palatal fricative sound /ç/, which has been argued to witness to a stage in the development from OE **heo** to later ME **she** (Britton 1991).

Scholars have traditionally viewed Orm as eccentric in his orthographic habits. More recently, however, it has been acknowledged that his somewhat idiosyncratic conventions are merely similar attempts to repurpose inherited conventions to reflect his own pronunciation (Anderson and Britton 1999). It is also apparent that, while *The Ormulum* does attest to a number of distinctive and idiosyncratic spelling conventions, other of its usages are familiar from contemporary documents. For instance, it shares the practice, seen above in the AB dialect, of using <sh> for /ʃ/, e.g. **shollde, englissh**, and <ch> for /tʃ/, e.g. **child.**

2.4 Late Middle English dialects

Although we have surveyed some early ME writing, the majority of texts written down in this period were in French or Latin. English was largely a spoken vernacular and so there is comparatively little surviving evidence of its regional spelling systems. By the mid-fourteenth century, however, this situation changed, so that English began to be used more frequently and widely as a written language. Since there was at that time no standard written form of the language, the late ME period witnessed huge variation in spelling. Some of this variation reflects differences in pronunciation, as noted above in the north/south divide in the pronunciation of reflexes of OE ā, while others are purely orthographic. While we can assume that spellings like **stan** and **stoon** reflect differences in pronunciation, it is unlikely that the same is true of distinctions like **shal** and **schal**. Despite this important difference, it is evident that both types of distinction reflect different regional conventions. In setting out to map the different written conventions of late ME, the ME Dialect Project drew upon both types of linguistic data.

Another important methodological principle introduced for this project was that of dialect 'translation'. Previous dialectologists had ruled out much of the surviving ME manuscript material because of its status as '*mischsprachen*', accidental types of language composed of forms derived from the various dialects contributed by the scribes responsible for earlier copies of the text. Where earlier scholars had dismissed the possibility of scribes converting the forms of their exemplars into another dialect (Tolkien 1929), the ME Dialect Project argued that many ME scribes consistently translated their exemplars into a single consistent dialect which could be analysed like that of an autograph copy (Benskin and Laing 1981). Where *mischsprachen* were found to occur, the mixture they preserved was frequently ordered, with mixed dialect forms at the beginning of a text giving way to a more consistent dialect as copying progressed and the scribe became more confident at translating the dialect of the exemplar into his own usage.

Adopting the same techniques used in modern dialect surveys, the researchers applied a questionnaire to more than a thousand ME manuscripts. The results of this were published as a series of linguistic profiles, presenting the variant spelling forms recorded for hundreds of linguistic items. The majority of ME manuscripts were copied by anonymous scribes whose dialect and place of writing are unknown. In order to localise these profiles, a comparison was carried out with the much smaller quantity of ME material whose place of copying is known. Using this 'fit-technique', the researchers were able to locate around a thousand ME manuscripts, thereby vastly increasing our understanding of ME dialects from this period.

The linguistic profiles assembled for this project give an insight into the huge range of diversity found in ME texts from this period. For instance, *A Linguistic Atlas of Late Mediaeval English* (*LALME*) recorded hundreds of variant spellings of SUCH, include **schech**, **scwche**, **sewych**, **shiche**, **sich**, **souche**, **soyche**, **sqwyche** and **sutche**. It is important, however, not to over-exaggerate the extent to which ME was a period of rampant orthographic licence, since many of these variant spellings, e.g. **schch**, **schiche**, **schute**, **shoche**, are recorded in just one manuscript, and often are minor variants within those scribes' usage. As such, these rare items tell us little about the broader patterns of variation within ME spelling. Some of them, such as the four spellings **suuch**, **suuche**, **suuech**, **suueche**, are only found in one manuscript, and so reflect the idiosyncratic usage of a single scribe. The same is true of a number of spellings recorded just once, e.g. **sch**, **scwche**, **shych**, **suth**; since many of these are only found as minor variants in the sole manuscript in which they are recorded, they may even be little more than scribal errors. Some of the rarer forms do, however, fall into pronounced regional clusters, such as **swech**, found in eastern and south-eastern areas, or **schuch**, found only in western manuscripts. If we focus on the most widely attested forms, it is apparent that most scribes employed a small number of spellings which vary little from each other: **sech(e)**, **sich(e)**, **soch(e)**, **such(e)** and **sych(e)**. So, while there was considerable variation in the written mode in ME, accounts which suggest that this situation was communicatively dysfunctional have tended to focus too heavily on the more minor variants.

Given this vast quantity of orthographic variation, there is a wide variety of forms that can be used to distinguish the major dialect regions from each other. However, there is a smaller group of features that are particularly useful diagnostic indicators. An important marker of a northern dialect is the representation of OE *ā* as <a>, e.g. **ham** HOME; dialects south of Lincolnshire typically spell this sound with <o>: **hom**. Also typical of northern dialects is the use of <g> and <k> in **giue** GIVE and **kirk** CHURCH, where southern dialects employ <y> and <ch>, **yiue** and **chirch** – the direct result of Scandinavian influence. Northern dialects can also be identified from the spelling of OE hw as <quh>; spellings with initial <q> are also recorded in Older Scots (see Chapter 8). The West Midlands dialect is characterised by the representation of OE long and short *y* with <u>, e.g. **sunne** SIN (OE **synn**), <e> for OE *æ*, e.g. **deg**

DAY (OE **dæg**), <o> before nasal consonants, e.g. **nome** NAME, **hond** HAND (compare with the discussion of AB language above). In the West Midlands and South-West dialects digraphs like <eo> and <ea> are sometimes recorded, along with spellings reflecting the voicing of initial fricatives, e.g. **zuich** SUCH, **vox** FOX.

Such evidence points to widespread variation in the written mode throughout the late Middle English period. However, during the fifteenth century, spelling variation began to be replaced by greater regularisation and consistency and the more marked regional spellings were dropped in favour of forms of wider currency. This process, and the extent to which it witnesses to a process of standardisation, will be examined in the following chapter.

3 Standardisation

Central to accounts of the emergence of a standard spelling system is the concept of 'Chancery Standard', first identified by M. L. Samuels as one of four 'types', or 'incipient' standard varieties, in 1963. This article drew upon Samuels's ongoing work for the Middle English Dialect Project and sketched out some preliminary suggestions of the kinds of research questions that the survey would be able to answer. The essay was tentative and exploratory in its approach, as was necessitated by its appearance at a relatively early stage in the project; Samuels himself stressed that the maps he provided in this article were 'necessarily simplified, schematic representations of the evidence', and could not do justice to the extensive body of detailed, diatopic linguistic data the Dialect Project was in the process of assembling. Since the project's aim was the publication of a dialect atlas, accompanied by extensive linguistic profiles of all their sources and detailed maps of individual items, any attempt to offer a definitive account of such features at this early stage would have been premature. Samuels suggested that the most important contribution that this project would enable was the provision of a 'frame of reference for isolating and classifying those types of language that are less obviously dialectal, and can thus cast light on the probable sources of the written standard English that appears in the fifteenth century' (1963: 66). As a first step towards establishing such a framework, Samuels sketched out his fourfold model for the development of a Middle English written standard, identifying four 'types' of standardised usages.

Despite employing this numbering system, the four types identified by Samuels were not chronological. The first of these, Type I, was associated with manuscripts copied in the second half of the fourteenth century. Type II, however, was found in manuscripts produced in London from the period ca. 1340–80. The reason for this apparent discrepancy is that Type II represents the earliest of three distinct types of usage recorded in London (Types II–IV). Samuels's decision to treat Type I first was presumably prompted by a desire to set it apart from the types of London

English with which it had formerly been grouped. Previous scholarship on this dialect, such as that by Karl Brunner (1950), had located its use in London, while an earlier generation of scholars such as Skeat and Dibelius had placed it in Oxford. Using the evidence collected for the ME atlas, Samuels was able to show that this variety drew its forms from the dialects of the Central Midlands counties, particularly those of Northamptonshire, Huntingdonshire and Bedfordshire. Representative forms cited by Samuels in support of this localisation are: **sich** SUCH, **mych** MUCH, **ony** ANY, **silf** SELF, **stide** STEAD, ȝouen GIVEN, siȝ SAW.

While noting that this dialect was most closely associated with manuscripts containing the works of the religious reformer John Wycliffe, Samuels stressed that it was not limited to copies of Wycliffite texts and should not be considered to represent Wycliffe's own dialect, nor viewed as a 'religious prose koiné'. But, while the Lollards should not be seen as its originators, they did play an important role in its dissemination: 'once they had adopted it, they copied it faithfully, probably fanatically so' (Samuels 1963: 85).

As we have seen, the written forms associated with Samuels's Types II–IV are attested in manuscripts produced in London. Type II is recorded in a total of eight manuscripts, of which the main hand (Scribe 1) of the important Auchinleck manuscript (National Library of Scotland MS Advocates 19.2.1) was offered as typical. This manuscript, produced around 1340, is one of the earliest texts to witness to this type; at the other end of its period of use are three manuscripts copied by the same scribe ca. 1380: Cambridge, Magdalene College Pepys 1498, Bodleian Library MS Laud Misc 622 and British Library MS Harley 874.[1] Although the language of London, this dialect shows the influence of forms drawn from the Norfolk and Suffolk dialects – the result of immigration into the capital from those areas. Type II replaced an earlier form of London English which was essentially southern in its make-up, with some Essex influence, as may be seen in the dialect of Henry III's Proclamation issued in 1258 (Machan 2005: 21–70).

Type III is recorded in manuscripts copied in London in the final quarter of the fourteenth, or first quarter of the fifteenth centuries. The best known of these are the Hengwrt and Ellesmere manuscripts containing Chaucer's *Canterbury Tales*, probably copied in the first decade of

---

1. The other Type II manuscripts listed by Samuels are British Library MS Additional 17376, containing the English Prose Psalter, British Library MS Harley 5085, St John's College Cambridge MS 256, and Glasgow University Library MS Hunterian 250.

the fifteenth century.[2] Other manuscripts copied in Type III London English are the autograph manuscripts of Thomas Hoccleve, a copy of the B Version of *Piers Plowman*, now Trinity College Cambridge MS B.15.17, and a collection of London documents and wills.[3] Given that there is a relatively short period between the last manuscripts copied in Type II and the earliest to appear in Type III, Samuels concluded that the London dialect changed 'suddenly and radically' around 1380. But, having identified these types of language, Samuels proceeded to stress that both Types II and III showed considerable internal variation, especially by comparison with Type I: 'There is a heterogeneity of orthography that contrasts strikingly with the comparatively uniform spelling system of Type I' (1963: 71). Since the other London manuscripts produced at this time, such as the earliest copies of John Gower's *Confessio Amantis*, were not written using Type III, Samuels concluded that there was considerable tolerance of dialect variation in London ca. 1400, insisting that 'any form of written standard is conspicuous by its absence'. Type III differs dialectally from Type II in showing the influx of forms typical of the Central Midlands counties, brought into the capital through immigration from that area.

The third stage in the development of London English identified by Samuels is his Type IV, or 'Chancery Standard', which is attested in 'that flood of government documents that starts in the years following 1430' (Samuels 1963: 71). Since the earliest of these documents were copied shortly after the latest Type III witnesses, Samuels again concluded that the London dialect had witnessed rapid change, as might well be expected for a capital city at a time of considerable flux. Since Type IV was adopted by scribes employed in government offices for their regular business ('backed by the full weight of the administrative machine'), Samuels considered it natural that it should have been this variety that became accepted as the national standard, ousting the previous varieties; he concluded by identifying Type IV as the ancestor of modern standard written English: 'it is this type, not its predecessors in London English,

---

2. The Hengwrt manuscript is National Library of Wales Peniarth MS 392D and the Ellesmere manuscript is San Marino, Huntington Library MS El 26.C.9.

3. Samuels does not identify individual documents, but rather refers to 'a number of the documents printed in Chambers and Daunt, London English 1384–1425, and in Furnivall, Early English Wills' (70). See further R. W. Chambers and M. Daunt, with the assistance of M. Weale, *A Book of London English 1384–1425* (Oxford: Clarendon Press, 1931) and F. J. Furnivall (ed.), *The Fifty Earliest English Wills in the Court of Probate, London, A.D. 1387 to 1439; with a priest's of 1454*, Early English Text Society (London: Trübner, 1882).

that is the basis of modern written English'.[4] Dialectally, Type IV shows a continuity with Type III in accepting more forms derived from the Central Midlands dialects, although among these are found a larger proportion of originally northern Midlands forms.

Further research has extended, refined and also challenged some of Samuels's conclusions concerning each of these types. Irma Taavitsainen (2005) has identified Type I spellings in a group of scientific manuscripts, thereby emphasising the extent to which it would be wrong to view Type I as a purely Wycliffite phenomenon. As well as posing new questions about the relationship between scientific and Wycliffite writing of the fifteenth century, Taavitsainen's findings throw up new problems concerning the origins of the Central Midlands spelling system. Connections with the work of the translator John Trevisa, who spent time in Oxford and may have been involved in Bible translation, led Taavitsainen to propose him as the originator of the Central Midlands dialect, as part of a conscious policy to increase the intelligibility of his text over a wide geographical area. According to this scenario, the Wycliffite adoption of the Central Midlands dialect was influenced by its earlier use by Trevisa, rather than the other way around.

Further doubt has been cast on the concept of a Central Midlands dialect, at least as attested by Wycliffite manuscripts. Peikola (2003) surveyed the spelling of Samuels's diagnostic forms in sixty-eight scribal copies of Matthew's gospel in the Late Version [LV] of the Wycliffite Bible. He found no evidence in support of a Central Midland Standard, concluding that 'the alleged status of LV as the prototypical "invariable" Type I text has to be questioned' (Peikola 2003: 40). Hudson (2017) reached similar conclusions from her detailed examination of characteristic Type I forms in three major Wycliffite works – the Wycliffite Bible, the English Wycliffite sermon cycle, and the first two revisions of Rolle's English Psalter commentary.

While orthographic variation was found to be the norm across these manuscripts, Peikola did note the sustained use of a set of forms characteristic of Type I, although he considered these to be the result of textual descent rather than the adherence to an external standard. A bigger problem highlighted by Hudson concerns the number of forms under investigation: the restriction of the investigation to a set of twelve individual words is considered too small a sample upon which to base any conclusions. Hudson also objects to the attempt to locate these Wycliffite texts and the Central Midlands dialect; instead, she suggests that the Midlands forms may have been deliberately chosen because of their lack

---

4. Samuels, 'Some Applications', 71.

of regional distinctiveness – a useful strategy of concealment for scribes copying heretical texts. Most importantly, Hudson concludes that the orthography of the manuscripts she surveys lacks both the internal consistency and the adoption by other writers required to be considered a standard. The spellings of individual manuscripts are characterised by the idiolects of their copyists; where two or more manuscripts are orthographically similar, these connections are due to the co-occurrence of a single scribe, or to shared textual descent.

A similar conclusion was reached by Solopova (2017: 202–21) following an examination of the manuscripts of the Early Version of the Wycliffite Bible. Her study found little evidence of internal consistency and almost no conformance with Samuels's supposed Type I. There was little evidence of dominant forms in a single scribal output; where dominant forms did emerge, there was little agreement across the different manuscripts. Solopova concludes that there is no evidence for standardisation of spelling in the majority of manuscripts of both versions of the Bible translation, reflecting a lack of consistency in the most deluxe copies, such as the presentation volume that is now Bodleian Library MS Bodley 277, perhaps made in consultation with the translators (Solopova 2017: 217). What is apparent from these subsequent studies is that Samuels's account of this type, coming at an early stage in the dialect survey, has tended to overplay the homogeneity of the manuscripts in which it is attested, and the extent to which it should be considered a literary standard.

Reservations about Samuels's typology are not restricted to his Type I. In a wide-ranging discussion of London literature before 1380, Ralph Hanna (2005) has critiqued Samuels's concept of a Type II London English, arguing that Samuels's 'totalising approach' led him to misrepresent the linguistic complexity of these documents which witness to considerably more variation than Samuels admitted. Hanna also notes how the material evidence for Type II further undermines the claim that it represents a widely adopted standard. Three of the manuscripts identified as attesting to this variety by Samuels were written by a single scribe, while four are copies of the same text: the Middle English translation of Robert of Gretham's Anglo-Norman sermon cycle known as the *Mirur*. Hanna suggests that the apparently sudden shift from Type II to Type III postulated by Samuels is a result of the lack of material evidence from this period in fourteenth-century London book history. The lack of variation in Middle English writing of this period is thus due either to the paucity of surviving books, or to a break in book production. Hanna also takes Samuels to task for his dismissive rejection of the possibility of co-existing dialects – a possibility that would better explain the way in which Type II books continued to be copied in the late fourteenth and early fifteenth centuries, as seen in Bodleian Library MS Holkham misc. 40, a copy of the Middle English *Mirror* attesting to Type II forms, copied ca.1410. Hanna's analysis of these manuscripts leads him to question Samuels's attempts to categorise London English according to a system of chronological types:

> As one expects in any urban locale, the language of London is not easily subjected to clear typing, and the evidence would support a more robustly variant set of alternatives than Samuels allows. A more plausible reading of fourteenth-century London evidence would show that Type II already is a great deal more like Type III than Samuels is willing to credit, and that early fourteenth-century language allowed considerably greater variation than he states. (Hanna 2005: 29–30)

Similar problems have beset Samuels's formulation of a Type III form of London English. As with the other varieties, detailed analysis of its constituent texts has revealed considerably more variation than Samuels implied. The publication of full-text digital transcriptions of Type III documents has considerably facilitated the construction of linguistic profiles, revealing many more occasional forms, and allowing a much more detailed picture of relative frequencies of variant forms (Horobin 2003; Horobin and Mooney 2004). Using this methodology, it has become apparent that even the Hengwrt and Ellesmere manuscripts – copies of the same text written by the same scribe – can be shown to differ in ways that complicate the concept of a Type III standard language.

3.1 Chancery Standard

Despite the importance of Types I–III for our understanding of standardisation in Middle English, it is the fourth of Samuels's types, also termed Chancery Standard, that has proved the most problematic and most controversial. This is perhaps inevitable since it is this variety that has come to be seen by many as *the* standard form of late Middle English, and which Samuels himself offered as the ancestor of the modern Standard English spelling system, endowing Type IV with a prominence greater than each of the others. In this section we will consider in detail the claims made by Samuels for Chancery Standard – both in his 1963 article and in subsequent iterations of the argument – and at the way this concept has been adopted, extended and challenged in subsequent scholarship.

One of the major difficulties in trying to assess the validity of the concept of Chancery Standard as set out by Samuels in 1963 is that, in this original article, he supplied surprisingly few linguistic details, claiming that its differences from the language of Chaucer were well known. As a concession to readers who were not so familiar with the features, he did provide a footnote tabulating a few of the more outstanding differences. The list is as follows:

ITEM	Chaucer	Type IV
GAVE	yaf	gaf
NOT	nat	not
BUT	bot	but
SUCH	swich(e)	such(e)
THEIR	hir(e)	theyre, þeir(e), þair(e), her
THESE	thise	thes(e)
THROUGH	thurgh	thorough, þorow(e)
SHOULD	sholde	shulde

It is surprising that Samuels's claims for the existence of this Chancery Standard should rest on the difference between a handful of common spelling forms. We have already seen how subsequent studies of Samuels's Types I, II and III have drawn attention to the problems presented by the limited data he offered; in each of these instances, the claim for a standard variety crumbled away as more data was analysed and greater variation was identified. With such a small number of spelling forms, it is easy to imagine how similar problems would beset Chancery Standard when subjected to similar extended scrutiny.

The published volumes of *LALME* add little to this discussion. In a short subsection as part of the introduction to Volume I, headed 'The growth of Standard English', the editors simply refer the interested reader to Samuels's accounts of this process discussed above. The section is introduced in precisely the same terms as the 1963 discussion, describing the published survey as providing 'a frame of reference for isolating and classifying those types of language that are less obviously dialectal, and can thus cast light on the probable sources of the written standard English that appears in the fifteenth century' (*LALME* I, 27); the rest of the section simply rehearses Samuels's earlier findings. This is striking, since it shows that the conclusions of Samuels's exploratory 1963 study, based as it was on a small number of features, have now hardened into firmer fact. Although the four types are not explicitly referred to, reference is made to Type IV, identified as 'the so-called "Chancery Standard"'). Since it was Samuels himself who named this variety Chancery Standard, it seems curious for the *LALME* editors to distance themselves from it in this way. The *LALME* discussion does, however, raise the important question of whether Chancery Standard can be regarded a standard language 'in the modern sense', although it makes no attempt to debate this question.

LALME's raising of this question and unwillingness to answer it is surprising, given that Samuels's himself was careful to avoid portraying his types as standards in the modern sense. Despite using the term 'Chancery Standard', it is clear from a careful reading of Samuels's 1963 article that he was concerned not to label his four types as standard languages, with all of the ideological and cultural assumptions that surround this term today (Milroy and Milroy 2012). Instead, Samuels refers to his types as 'incipient standards', that is, varieties which are at an early stage of the process of becoming a standard. A similar distinction has been made by Jeremy J. Smith (1996) in his use of the terms fixed and focused standards: a fixed standard being one which admits no variation (such as Present-day standard written English) and a focused standard allowing a degree of variation (such as Present-day standard spoken English). The four types distinguished by Samuels are therefore standardised, or focused, varieties in that they permit internal variation. But such nuanced distinctions between an incipient standard and a full standard have often been elided in subsequent discussion.

Despite the provisional, partial and sometimes contradictory nature of these accounts, and the incompleteness of the data offered, later scholars have tended to accept Samuels's identification of a Chancery Standard without question. John Fisher (1996), for instance, begins from the assumption that a ruling hierarchy will necessarily implement or adopt a standard language, since this is a requirement of a governmental administration which strives to achieve clarity in its written documentation. Despite having argued that standardisation was a necessary imposition by the centralised state, Fisher claims that it was not imposed as a taught language, but rather developed through an 'unselfconscious "drift"' encouraged by the increasing centralisation and professionalisation of Chancery practice during the first half of the fifteenth century. He likens this process to the apprentice system that lay behind the production and dissemination of the Chancery script: 'this tendency to graphic uniformity produced a corresponding tendency to linguistic uniformity' (1996: 49). The identification of the model for this system was made by Malcolm Richardson (1980), who argued that Chancery Standard was modelled closely on the usage found in the personal correspondence issued by Henry IV. Although not in Henry's own hand, since all such correspondence was dictated to clerks, Richardson argues that the Signet letters are imbued with royal status and authority as 'his official voice speaking "the king's English"' (1980: 730).

Richardson's narrative is closely followed by Nevalainen and Tieken-Boon van Ostade (2006) who draw upon the claim that Chancery Standard originated with the king and his royal secretariat to bolster their view that support by a powerful institution is a requirement for the successful implementation of a standard variety. According to Nevalainen and Tieken-Boon van Ostade, the successful implementation of Chancery Standard within the office of the Chancery was due to its hierarchical structure, which ensured that all the clerks, irrespective of their native dialects, adopted its forms. The authority and prestige of the office of Chancery was central to its dissemination, since Nevalainen and Tieken-Boon van Ostade argue that northern clerks who received their training in that office and subsequently returned to their homes to practise were central to its later adoption: 'These men would have been immensely respected for their knowledge and skills at writing, which in turn invested the work they produced with a kind of "correctness", a stamp of official approval, in the eyes of the local authorities' (2006: 277).

A significant problem with Richardson's claim is that the forms employed by Signet scribes are not exactly those of Chancery Standard and that there remains a degree of variation. Among the differences is the use of **any** rather than **eny**; this is surprising, since for Fisher the use of **eny** was so distinctive and regular as to be a 'Chancery shibboleth'. Elsewhere we find that while Chancery **much(e)** is usual in the 30 Signet letters he analysed, **moch(e)** appears in seven letters; while **shuld** is 'fairly consistent', **should(e)** and **schold** appear in two letters. Variation at this low level is dismissed by Richardson, since otherwise the spelling is fairly consistent with later Chancery practice, 'at least as much as any fifteenth-century spelling is consistent' (1980: 734). This appeal to the general inconsistency of fifteenth-century spelling seems at odds with the basic principles of Richardson's claim. For his claim to be accepted, we need to imagine a scenario in which the language of Henry's Signet letters was so distinctive and regular that other clerks self-consciously adopted and deliberately implemented precisely the same forms in their official writing for the Chancery. It is not easy to dismiss variation of this kind as insignificant within the context of the narrative being offered here. If variation of this kind is typical for Chancery practice throughout the fifteenth century, how can it be argued to represent a standard variety?

In the most searching and important examination of Chancery Standard to date, Michael Benskin (2004) begins by returning to Samuels's early identification of this variety. Confronting the problems discussed above concerning the brevity of Samuels's list of forms, Benskin claims that Samuels's account was intended only to be 'illustrative'. Benskin's caveat serves as the launchpad for a detailed attack on Fisher's account: 'It might be supposed that recognition of a form as "Chancery" or "non-Chancery" would depend on a far-reaching examination of documents initiated in

Chancery and in the hands of Chancery clerks: how else, indeed, could Chancery usage be established?' (2004: 22–3).

This lack of an exhaustive and definitive linguistic account of Chancery Standard does indeed undermine Fisher's claims, but the same criticism might also be levelled at Samuels's definition of Chancery Standard, and its subsequent uncritical adoption in the scholarly literature. While it is true, as we have seen, that Samuels's listing of forms was never intended to be exhaustive, Samuels himself never presented the more comprehensive account to which Benskin refers. Similarly, the fact that Samuels did not include a detailed listing of which documents he analysed in assembling his list makes it very difficult for scholars like Fisher to produce the more exhaustive account which Benskin rightly demands. But, while such an account remains lacking, scholarly discussions of the process of standardisation in this period remain closely wedded to Samuels's 1963 formulation.

An alternative critique of Samuels's claims was published by Laura Wright in 1996. Wright's concern was with Samuels's reliance upon Eilart Ekwall's data concerning immigration patterns into the capital during the fourteenth century. Wright notes that, despite Samuels's citation of this source in support of his claim that the introduction of Midlands and Northern linguistic forms into London was the result of immigration from the Midlands, Ekwall's conclusions were far more tentative than Samuels suggested. Wright further questioned the presumption of social prestige that lies behind his claim that a small group of Midlanders could have prompted shifts in the dialect used by native Londoners. Rather than seeking to explain the shift in the London dialect as a conscious change driven by prestige, Wright suggests that the changes may have happened by a gradual process in which isoglosses for individual items shifted southwards. But while she does challenge the presumptions that lie behind its genesis, Wright does not call into question the concept of Chancery Standard itself.

Another important caveat offered by Benskin and others concerns the process of vernacularisation itself, which did not affect all government offices at the same time. Benskin (2004) showed that, far from switching wholesale to English as implied by Samuels (1963), Chancery documents continued to be written in Latin up to the eighteenth century. Dodd (2011) has noted that, while the switch to English was completed in the second quarter of the fifteenth century in petitions to the crown, in other government offices the switch to English was short lived, with Latin resuming its dominance by 1450. Stenroos (2020) has traced the proportions of English, French and Latin in local documents, finding a tendency for Latin to dominate, alongside a general decline in French, an increase in English and a mixed language that emerged during the period of transition.

Critical to understanding this process is an awareness of the function of the texts themselves. In the fifteenth and early sixteenth centuries, English was adopted in texts where intelligibility to a lay user was important, such as petitions and complaints, marriage agreements, arbitrations and churchwardens' accounts. By contrast, enfeoffments, exchanges, letters of attorney, manorial court rolls, probates of wills and quitclaims, texts which tend to be highly formulaic and used by professionals, are almost always in Latin. The proportions of English and Latin also varied by region, with the shift happening earlier in the northern counties than in the south but then tailing off more quickly. Stenroos's survey of local documents of the fifteenth century finds considerably more variation in legal documents drawn up in Essex and Suffolk, in the fifteenth and even into the sixteenth century, than is suggested by traditional narratives of standardisation of spelling during this period.

In order to consider the extent to which a switch to English in administrative documents had triggered a move towards standardisation of spelling, Stenroos carried out a study of a small number of items as recorded in two regions (the northern counties of Cumberland, Durham, Lancashire, Northumberland, Westmorland and Yorkshire) and two municipalities (Cambridge and London). This survey collected all the variant spellings of five terms, ABOVESAID, LAWFUL, OTHER, SEALS, THESE, chosen for the frequency of their appearance in legal texts. For each of these words large numbers of variants were recorded. ABOVESAID was the most variable with a total of 68 variant forms, LAWFUL appeared in a total of 32, OTHER in 36 and SEALS in 39 different spellings. THESE, used by Samuels to illustrate the development of Type III **thise** to Chancery **these**, is recorded in 49 different spellings. While **thes** and **these** are the most common forms found in these documents, it is striking that the latter form decreases in relative frequency in all the regions over time. Stenroos's study concluded that, even into the early sixteenth century, spelling remained highly variable. Despite this, all five items considered had begun to develop dominant forms, **abouesaid**, **lawfull**, **other**, **seales/seals** and **thes/these**, while more strongly regional forms, e.g. **abounsaid** and **thir**, had died out completely. This loss of certain strongly marked dialect forms is balanced by an increase in others, such as **oder** and **thise/thies**, prompting Stenroos to conclude that, while regional variation does not disappear during this period, the specific variants do alter over time.

It seems evident that the concept of a Chancery Standard has been too easily and uncritically accepted, without a sufficiently exhaustive analysis of a body of government documents. Where its definition has been found lacking, attempts have been made to accommodate it, rather to challenge it. This leaves us with a very partial and inconclusive picture. Samuels characterised his Chancery Standard (although he himself did not always use this label) through the spellings of some eight linguistic items, some of which appear in variant forms. Benskin's subsequent clarifications have stressed that this list should not be considered exhaustive: not all forms will be found in a single text copied in Chancery Standard, nor can a text be considered to be in Chancery Standard simply because it includes all eight. Furthermore, the boundaries between Types III and IV are considerably more fuzzy than might be assumed; documents copied throughout the fifteenth and into the sixteenth century continue to show a mixture of forms from both types. There is also confusion about the extent to which Chancery Standard was adopted in the various offices of state. Despite calling this variety Chancery Standard, Samuels's own listing of its sources suggested that it was used more widely in the government offices. Benskin's subsequent research, however, has shown that there were some offices of State that did not adopt this variety and which continued to copy *literatim*, reproducing the regional forms of their originals.

Despite these many important caveats, the idea of Chancery Standard continues to be adopted and endorsed in the scholarly literature. A more recent sociolinguistic history of English by McColl Millar (2012) begins by recounting what he terms the 'standard account', following Samuels, that schools in London from the 1370s, where boys from the upper social strata were taught, developed 'whether consciously or not, house styles for writing the local English' (2012: 52). As these schoolboys ascended the higher echelons of government service, so their standard English usage was adopted by the administration as a whole. This account takes Samuels's arguments a stage further in tracing the origins of Chancery Standard in London schools; Samuels himself located the origins of Chancery Standard in the government offices themselves. McColl Millar then explains the spread of the standard using the sociolinguistic model of communities of practice, arguing that others would have assumed these spelling forms in order to demonstrate membership of 'the same "club", with assumed values and needs, in a sense a *community of practice*'.

In Lerer (2015: 116) we meet the claim that 'From the 1380s until the 1450s, Chancery taught a house style of spelling, grammatical forms, lexical usage, and idiom that characterized the papers coming out of the royal offices (those of the Signet, the Privy Seal, even of Parliament itself)'. Here we witness a common tendency in later scholarly reappropriations of Samuels's arguments to elide standard English spelling and standard English grammar and lexis. Where Samuels and Benskin noted variation within Chancery documents, Lerer implies a fixity more appropriate to modern standard English. Lerer's account likens Chancery Standard to the modern concept of 'house style', implying a form of codification and policing more associated with modern publishing practices than medieval manuscript production. House style in a modern publishing house refers to a series of preferences codified in an internal document circulated among staff and authors, which dictates the treatment of minor details of orthography, punctuation, abbreviation and referencing. In order to ensure these rules are consistently observed, publishing houses employ proofreaders to check over the final version of a book before publication. No such system appears to have been in place among the medieval scribes of the Chancery; Samuels himself certainly never suggested anything of this kind.

This survey of Chancery Standard has shown the extent to which its significance has been overplayed in histories of standard written English. Returning to Samuels's early identification and labelling of this variety has revealed a much greater hesitancy in its proposal. Since Samuels's promised more extensive survey of the relevant documents was never carried out, the extent to which Chancery Standard is a valid concept has yet to be assessed. Reconsiderations of Types I, II and III have all stressed the extent to which the evidence has tended to crumble when larger quantities of data are brought to bear on Samuels's tabulation. The evidence suggests that similar analysis of the relevant Chancery and other official documents would similarly undermine the evidence for even a 'standardised' or 'focused' usage, let alone the kind of fixed variety often argued to have functioned as an authoritative norm that led to the standardisation of public and private spelling.

Jeremy Smith has proposed an alternative way of approaching this data in future research, suggesting that Samuels's types should be divorced entirely from the history of standard English. Noting that each of the four types presents a distinct set of textual issues, in which aspects of text type, genre, codicology, script and context are all relevant to their linguistic form, Smith proposes that a more fruitful way forward is to consider them as *scriptae*: usages that are 'characteristic of particular discourses and transmitted through the activities of particular communities of practice' (Smith 2020c: 25). Smith's suggestion offers a potential way forward both for reconsidering Samuels's linguistic types and their functions within their textual communities, and for separating that reconsideration from a hunt for the origins of a standard spelling system.

4 Early Modern English

The Early Modern English (EModE) period, from 1500–1750, witnessed a number of far-reaching changes to the English spelling system. During this period, users of English began to be concerned with the relationship between spelling and pronunciation, leading to a number of key reforms to the system itself. Several of these individual reforms will be dealt with more fully in Chapter 11; here we will consider those changes that were more widely adopted. A key concern of this period was the status of English in relation to the classical languages, Latin and Greek. In order to enrich the language's lexicon, large numbers of classical words were borrowed into English. As well as the drawing of vocabulary from Latin and Greek to add status to the English wordstock, the spelling of a number of words was adapted to more clearly signal their classical origins.

We have already noted the way in which Middle English drew many of its neologisms from French. Since French is a Romance language, many of these words are also recorded in Latin, albeit in different forms. The Middle English forms reflected their spelling and pronunciation in the French language from which they were borrowed. Changes were introduced during this period to bring the spelling of some of these words into closer alignment with their Latin etymons, from which the French forms had ultimately derived. This was partly motivated by a desire to raise the status of English by signalling its classical connections, and partly by a belief that a closer link between spelling and etymology aided comprehension. Examples of this process include pairs of spellings like ME **dette** and EModE **debt** and ME **doute** and EModE **doubt**, reflecting the spelling of the corresponding Latin roots (**debitum** and **dubitare**). The letter <c> was added to ME **vitailes** to give **victuals** (Latin **victualia**); the same letter was added to ME **sisours** to give **scissours** (Latin **scissor**; compare modern English **scythe**).

In some cases the etymological re-spelling resulted in an incorrect association, as in the case of AUTHOR. This word was spelled **autor** in ME, reflecting its origin in the Latin word **auctor**. Attempts to re-spell it to reflect its Latin etymology resulted in the spelling **auctour**, as well as **author**, the latter reflecting the mistaken belief that the word was connected with Latin **authenticus**. The modern standard pronunciation with medial /θ/ is a late seventeenth-century spelling pronunciation, reflecting this erroneous etymology.

Other spelling changes deliberately introduced during this period were designed to distinguish homophones. **Whole** derives from OE **hāl**, also the source of PDE **hale**; the spellings with initial <wh> first appear in the middle of the fifteenth century, reflecting a /w/ glide before long open ō, sometimes accompanied by a dropping of the initial /h/. The /w/ glide did not occur in WHOLESOME, where the vowel was short, and consequently this word was spelled without the initial <w>. The spelling was subsequently changed to **wholesome** by analogy with **whole**. For a period, writers employed spellings with and without <w> to distinguish senses relating to health and completeness. While this did not win widespread acceptance, the spellings with <wh> were retained after the loss of the w-, presumably because it was an effective way of distinguishing the word from HOLE (OE **hol**).

This concern with reflecting etymology in spelling was alluded to by Shakespeare in *Love's Labour's Lost*, in which Holofernes, the pedant, insists that all such etymological re-spellings should be reflected in pronunciation: 'I abhor such phanaticall phantasims, such insociable and poynt deuise companions, such rackers of ortagriphie, as to speake dout fine, when he should say doubt; det, when he shold pronounce debt, not det' (*Love's Labour's Lost*, 5.1.17–23). Here Shakespeare is poking fun at the way this concern with etymology had the effect of driving spelling and pronunciation further apart. Holofernes expresses the view that, since words like DOUBT and DEBT are spelled with a medial <b>, this /b/ should be pronounced. To fail to do so is to be considered a racker of orthography: the word here is being used in the sense of 'the pronunciation of words in accordance with their spelling' rather than in the modern sense of correct spelling according to accepted convention.[1] While this extreme view may appear ridiculous, there are instances of words whose spelling was revised to reflect etymology, which subsequently triggered a shift in pronunciation. An example of this is ME **aventure**, which came to be spelled **adventure**; this spelling change prompted the later pronunciation of the additional <d>.

---

1. Oxford English Dictionary, s.v. 'orthography (n.), sense 1.a', June 2024, <https://doi.org/10.1093/OED/5513510512>

4.1 Introduction of printing

The Early Modern English period is marked by a major technological change in the introduction of printing using moveable type, first developed on the continent and brought to England by the merchant William Caxton in 1476. The ability to reproduce hundreds of identical copies of a single text presented an opportunity for standardising written English that was never possible in a manuscript age. But, despite this, scholars differ in the extent to which they consider this technological development to have been a major factor in the standardisation of the spelling system. One reason for the hesitation is that printers continued to be influenced by the spelling systems that they encountered in their exemplars, so that the conflation of systems witnessed in the manuscript age continued to be supported. This situation was more likely to result in a complex mixture comprising different orthographic influences than in the adoption of a single standard system. Another reason for scholarly caution is that the compositors who were responsible for setting the type were recruited from the continent, where the technology was first developed, and consequently English was not their native language. One way of dealing with this challenge was to preserve the spellings of an exemplar intact rather than attempt to impose a single house style. This policy resulted in the survival of a number of idiosyncratic authorial spelling systems, as well as those that would have appeared archaic or dialectal to a metropolitan readership. Printed copies of Sir Thomas More's works preserve some traces of his preferences, such as **hit** over **it**, **myche** rather than **muche** and **thorow** instead of **through**, but not others. In the case of *The Revelation of the Monk of Evesham*, printed in 1482 by William de Machlinia, the north-east Worcestershire spelling system of the scribe responsible for copying the exemplar was preserved by the printer despite its clearly provincial character (Samuels 1988: 86–7).

From this evidence, it is clear that early printers made no attempt to devise a consistent house style, such as have been developed in modern publishing houses, and were evidently content to tolerate a range of variation. This is what led Scragg (1974: 64) to argue that the new technology initially proved to be an obstacle in the movement towards orthographic standardisation: 'Rather than further the stabilising movement of the professional scribes, the printers in effect encouraged lack of conformity in spelling'.

There is another practical reason why compositors would have preferred to retain a more flexible spelling system, which tolerated variation in forms. A key part of the compositor's job was to 'cast off' a text in advance, which required them to estimate the amount of text that would occupy each individual page, and to justify lines of prose, ensuring that the text exactly filled a line of print. The difficulties presented by the requirement to justify lines of print were particularly challenging in cases of books printed in double columns. In order to manage these practical difficulties, compositors typically resorted to tinkering with the spelling, often doubling consonants and vowels, as well as adding or deleting a final <e>, e.g. **had/hadd/hadde**, as space required. It is this flexibility that prompted David Crystal (2013: 137) to suggest that spelling variation was 'a gift for printers trying to make their pages look good to the eye'. However, while scholars have generally assumed that compositors made considerable use of this practical measure when setting type, a study by Rosie Shute (2017) has called this claim into question. Shute analysed the spelling of the two editions of Chaucer's *The Canterbury Tales* issued by William Caxton in 1476 and 1482, and found little evidence of such a practice. Instead of using variation in the spelling of words, Shute found that Caxton's compositors relied more upon the use of contractions and abbreviations, punctuation and the practice of breaking a word at the line end to ensure justification. T. H. Howard-Hill reached a similar conclusion in his analysis of early printed editions of Shakespeare, although in both cases the conclusions are drawn from very limited textual samples. Since Caxton's interests were predominantly commercial rather than literary or linguistic, McColl Millar has suggested that adopting the nascent standard variety was a means for Caxton to both maximise his market and to speed up the process of typesetting (McColl Millar 2012: 53).

We have already noted that Caxton's first compositors were recruited from the Low Countries and thus were not native speakers of English, a factor which also encouraged greater variety in their spelling. While such compositors tended to preserve the spellings of their copytexts when setting type, they did also employ some of their own distinctive preferences. This is equally true of William Caxton himself, whose own usage shows that he had assimilated a number of continental features, especially in his translations. This is well illustrated in his translation of the Middle Dutch *Reynard*, where we find spellings that show the influence of the source language, such as **goed** GOOD, **moed** MOOD and **roek** ROOK, with <oe> instead of <oo> and **vlycche** and **valdore**, with <v> suggesting the voicing of the initial /f/ in **flycche** and **faldore**. N. F. Blake's (1970) study of these spellings led him to conclude that Caxton was influenced both by the printed text from which he was translating and also by his knowledge of spoken Flemish from his time in Bruges. Blake suggests that, in his haste to complete the translation, Caxton frequently imported the Dutch spellings, with which he was very familiar, without thinking; as native Dutch speakers, his compositors did not correct them into the more usual English equivalents. Caxton's long period of residence on the continent may also explain the lack of evidence of recent developments in spelling in his printed books, such as the <ea> digraph, and a general lack of consistency.

Caxton's compositors would have encountered an additional difficulty in the different spelling systems that appeared in their copytexts, since some contain Caxton's original writing (in his prologues and epilogues), accompanied by his translations from other languages, and texts by other authors. The gradual movement towards standardisation among Caxton's followers can be illustrated by N. F. Blake's (1965) study of five editions of *Reynard the Fox*, from Caxton's of 1481 to that issued by Thomas Gaultier in 1550. Blake noted three major developments in the spelling of these editions. In some cases, such as the choice between <i> or <y>, there is no difference in practice at all; in other cases, such as the use of <ck> or <k>, there are marked changes in practice, but these do not reveal any consistent pattern; in others there is a definite move towards consistency, such as the replacement of <wh> with <ugh> in words like **though** and **enough**, or of <e, ee> with <ea> in words like **great** and **break**. Blake concludes that a study of standardisation in this period must take account of the history of each separate grapheme, since consistency appeared in some cases long before it is apparent in others.

M. L. Samuels's (1988: 86–9) analysis of the spelling practices attested by books issued by Caxton's press found a mixture of dialect forms emanating from the printer's Kentish upbringing that continued to be used throughout his career, while others were replaced by equivalents from the London dialect, e.g. the replacement of **axe** with **aske** and **thurgh** with **thr(o)ugh**. Not all forms can be explained this way, however; although he did admit the London and Kentish variants **any** and **eny**, Caxton persisted in employing **ony** throughout his life. This form is typically found in the Central Midlands dialects during the ME period; its appearance in Caxton's usage may be due to changes in the Kentish dialect in this period, or the influence of 'colourless' forms: ones in widespread use that are not tied to a particular dialect (see further Chapters 3 and 12).

During this period, we find allographic distinctions present in ME beginning to be used more systematically. For instance, in ME scribes employed a variety of forms of the letter **s**, the Greek sigma <<σ>>, another shaped like the numeral 8, and a long-s that resembles <f> without a crossbar. In ME these letters were often used interchangeably, but in the EModE period this began to be rationalised. Typically, the long-s appeared at the beginning of words, while a short-s was employed in other positions in early printed texts. This distribution continued until the eighteenth century. A shorter-lived distinction concerned a two-shaped r, resembling the letter <z>, also inherited from medieval scripts, which continued to be employed following <o> and <p> until the sixteenth century.

Texts printed before 1630 retained the Middle English distribution of <v> and <u>, with <v> being used initially and <u> elsewhere. But after 1630 the two letters were used according to phonetic value rather than position, so that **loue** became **love** and **vntil** changed to **until**. The one exception was the upper-case <V>, which was retained until 1700. Also in the seventeenth century, the letter <j> came to replace <i> in words like **jolly** and **judge**. In origin <j> was simply an extended version of <i>, used in Latin in final positions, such as in the genitive of **filius** 'son': **filij**, and in numerals. These same uses were taken over into ME, where it had a disambiguating function in numbers like <iij> THREE and <viij> EIGHT. Because the pronunciation of <g> remained ambiguous, <gu> and <gh> were employed, following French models, as in **guesse**, **guift** GIFT and **guirl** GIRL. Alternatively, a Dutch practice was adopted in spellings such as **ghesse** GUESS, **gherle** GIRL, **ghest** and even **ghuest** GUEST.

4.2 Vowels

An important development in this period was the introduction of a distinction in the spelling of the mid close and mid open vowels. As we saw in the previous chapter, in ME the front vowels, [eː] and [ɛː], were both spelled <ee>, while the back vowels [oː] and [ɔː] were both spelled <oo>. In the fifteenth century, the <ea> digraph was introduced to create pairs of words like **meet** and **meat**; in the mid-sixteenth century the <oa> digraph was adopted by analogy, producing pairs like **boot** and **boat**. Although the <ea> digraph had been used by scriveners employed in the Chancery, it is not widespread in the earliest printed texts. It is, however, firmly established in print by 1550. In the fifteenth century <ie> was taken over from French to represent ME /eː/. This practice is mostly attested in French words, e.g. **grief**, but it later spread to native words like **thief**.

A major change in pronunciation of the long vowels during this period disrupted the patterns of sound-spelling correspondences inherited from ME. This change, known as the Great Vowel Shift, began around 1500 and was completed by 1700. Although there were lots of local differences in the way the changes took place, in broad terms it was a chain shift that saw all long vowel sounds move to a higher position in the vowel space. It likely began with the diphthongisation of the close vowels /iː/ and /uː/, so that ME **wife** (/wiːf/) and **doun** (/duːn/) initially began to be pronounced /weif/ and /doun/ and later as /waɪf/ and /daʊn/. The second stage of this chain shift saw the raising of /eː/ and /oː/, with the result that words like **feet** and **food** began to be pronounced /fiːt/ and /fuːd/. In the northern dialects, this change only affected the front vowel /ɪː/. There is some debate about which of these two shifts was the earlier; did the diphthongisation 'pull' the lower vowels up, or was it a 'push' shift, whereby the raising of the /eː/ and /oː/ vowels forced the close vowels to diphthongise? The next stage in the process was the raising of the low-mid vowels into the space vacated by the raising of the high-mid vowels, so that /ɛː/ and /ɔː/ became /eː/ and /oː/. Hence **meat** was pronounced /meːt/ and **bone** as /boːn/. The final stage saw the low /aː/ vowel in /naːm/ raise to /ɛː/. These changes can be dated by occasional idiosyncratic spellings employed by individuals, such as the spellings **teym** TIME, **mey** MY, **bey** BY, testifying to the diphthongisation of /iː/. But the spellings of these words in the developing standard system remained unchanged. In a later development, words like **meat** and **meet** began to be pronounced identically, as the vowels /eː/ and /iː/ merged. Again, this change was not reflected in the spelling. While this had the effect of making the spelling system even less phonetic, it did preserve a written distinction between homophones such as **meat** and **meet, sea** and **see**. A small group of words was unaffected by this merger and today preserve the earlier pronunciation: **great, break, yea**.

This period also witnessed changes in the functions of final <e>, triggered by the tendency for <e> not to be pronounced at the ends of words. Once it ceased to be pronounced, final <e> was repurposed as a diacritic whose main function was to indicate that the vowel in the preceding syllable was long, e.g. **name, mete, nose**. Once it had become recognised as a marker of vowel length, final <e> was transferred to parallel examples, so that the spellings **life** and **case** replaced ME **lijf** and **caas**. This created potential ambiguity in pairs of words like **writen**, which began to be spelled **written**, and **driven**, which retained its single consonant despite its preceding short vowel. Final <e> was also used to indicate the pronunciation of consonants at the ends of words, where there would otherwise be ambiguity: **prince, plunge, breathe**. Another role it acquired was to prevent certain letters appearing in final position; hence: **lie, toe, glue, love, freeze**. This function, in combination with consonant doubling, has also given rise to the so-called 'short word' or 'three-letter' rule, which serves to differentiate the subsystem of lexical words from that of grammatical words, to which the rule does not apply. According to this rule, the lexical words **bye, bee, inn, too** are distinguished from the function words **by, be, in, to**. In other examples, final <e> is used simultaneously to indicate the quality of the preceding consonant and the length of the vowel, e.g. **grace, mice**. But, while the versatility of final <e> made it a very useful tool, its different functions in similar words can be a cause of confusion. In the case of **love** it is used to prevent <v> appearing at the end of the word; in the similar **grove** it functions as a length marker. The similarity in the spelling of these words might well be considered to indicate that they should be pronounced identically. It is no wonder that Richard Mulcaster (1582) described <e> as 'a letter of maruellous vse in the writing of our tung ... most times it is writen to great purpos, euen where it semeth idle'.

The adoption of a single preferred spelling form was encouraged by the existence of printed spelling books intended to be used in classrooms. An important example is the *Elementarie* (1582), by the schoolteacher Richard Mulcaster, whose career included stints as the headmaster of the Merchant Taylor's and St Paul's schools. Mulcaster's introduction to elementary education proposed a series of comparatively modest spelling reforms (see Chapter 11), but the work was perhaps most influential for its inclusion of a General Table indicating the spelling of the 7,000 commonest words, many of which are identical to those found in standard PDE, e.g. **through**, **such**, **after**, **again**, **against**. However, some of the spellings selected by Mulcaster differ from modern usage, such as the <ie> instead of <y> in **anie**, **verie**, and <k> rather than <ck> in **quik**, **stik**, **pik**.

Case study I: Shakespeare's spelling

Despite the compositors responsible for setting the type for the First Folio copy of Shakespeare's collected works (1623) imposing their own spelling habits on the text, it is possible to discern the conventions employed by the scribes who produced the fair copies from which the folio texts were copied. One such scribe was Ralph Crane. Comparison of the spellings of his own poems, as found in the work he published in 1621 with the title 'The Workes of Mercy, both Corporeall and Spirituall', suggests that he was responsible for producing fair copies of *The Tempest*, *The Two Gentlemen of Verona*, *The Merry Wives of Windsor*, *Measure for Measure* and *The Winter's Tale*. The distinctive features of his spelling practices include a preference for <ei> over <ie> in **feirce** FIERCE, <nck> rather than <nk> in **thinck**, <s> or <sse> instead of <ss> in **profes** PROFESS and **progresse** PROGRESS, <ow> over <ou> in in **lowd** LOUD, <oa> instead of <o> in **doated** DOTED, <ea> in **tearmes** TERMS, and <ique> not <ic> in **heroique** HEROIC.

It is in the early quartos that we are likely to get closest to Shakespeare's own spellings. Since compositors are considered to have been more likely to alter the spelling of high frequency words for which they have their own established preferences, it is in the rarer words that we are most likely to find traces of the author's own habits. For instance, **mobled** and **arint**, words deriving from the Warwickshire dialect of Shakespeare's youth, are likely to have been preserved in his spellings. Another principle is that, the more unusual the spelling, the more likely it is to have originated with the author himself. This would suggest that the three instances of **somnet** SUMMIT, not found elsewhere, represent Shakespeare's spelling of this word; the early quartos contain the spelling **culd** CULLED, which may also reflect an authorial preference. The spelling **scilence**, used in the name of a character in the quarto edition of *Henry IV Part 2*, and also found in the Hand D section of the play *Sir Thomas More*, thought to be in Shakespeare's own hand, may also be his preferred form of the word SILENCE. However, the spelling is not limited to these occurrences, but is found in the works of other dramatists of the period (Crystal 2008a: 62–3).

The increased standardisation of the written language meant that it became more possible to use non-standard conventions to signal a regional pronunciation. We find an instance of this in *King Lear*, where Edgar, disguised as a rustic peasant, adopts a practice of employing voiced initial fricatives, as signalled by the spellings: **vor** FOR, **vortnight** FORTNIGHT, **vurther** FURTHER, **zir** SIR, **zo** SO and **zwaggered** SWAGGERED. Since fricative voicing was a feature of southern accents of this period, this would fit with the location of the scene in Dover. But, despite this, Shakespeare is not attempting a realistic depiction of a local accent, but rather is using a stereotyped feature of a stage dialect, of which these spoken features are an especially useful tool to signal rusticity.

The First Folio attests to the use of <v> and <u> as positional variants, with <v> being used at the beginning of a word and <u> in the middle, irrespective of the sound they represent. But, despite this, we do find occasional spellings that point to the change that was to come, by which <v> came to signal the consonant sound. Crystal (2008a: 45) finds 46 instances of **auoid** alongside a single occurrence of **avoid**, 23 cases of **eu'n** and 3 of **ev'n**. The use of <v> is also present to represent the vowel sound within words in upper case, as in the forms **CATALOGVE** and **IVLIET** found in titles. The latter example shows the use of <i> for [ʤ] which is consistent throughout the First Folio, e.g. **iustifie**; <j> is only found in numerals, e.g. **iij** THREE. This avoidance of the use of <j> runs contrary to recent developments and suggests that the editors of the First Folio were reflecting a more old-fashioned practice.

But in the case of other kinds of variants, the Folio text is more advanced. Words like **truly**, **many**, **bury**, **very** are more commonly found in their modern spellings than in the older alternatives with <ie>: **trulie**, **manie**, **burie**, **verie**. Similarly words ending in a final consonant are more commonly found without the double consonant and final <e>: **had** rather than **hadde**, **bad** rather than **badde** and so on. There is continued variation in the representation of the vowel sound in words like BELIEVE: **beleeue** is much more common than **belieue**. Where the sound follows <c> we find **receiue** more frequently than **recieue**, while **deceuie** and **perceiue** are the only spellings of these words, indicating that the tendency to spell this sound <ei> in this position was well established by the early seventeenth century. The extent to which the spelling of the First Folio pointed forward to the PDE standard system rather than back to that of ME was explored by David Crystal (2008a: 60–1). Surveying the spelling of all words in the opening fifty lines of *Hamlet*, excluding grammatical words, proper names and singular/plural variants, Crystal found that roughly 70% of them are spelled identically with PDE. According to Crystal, over 80% of the spelling differences between the First Folio and PDE can be accounted for by the following five factors: the presence or absence of a final <e>; the replacement of a letter with an apostrophe; the use of <ie> in place of <y> at the end of a word; double rather than single consonants; the use of <ie> or <ee> in words like **neer** NEAR. The most striking difference between the spelling of the First Folio and PDE is not the variety of different forms it incorporates, but the frequent tendency to switch between variants, even in the same line of text.

By the second half of the seventeenth century, it had become the responsibility of compositors to impose standard spelling preferences upon the manuscripts they printed, or to 'discern and amend the bad Spelling and Pointing of his Copy', as Joseph Moxon put it in his *Mechanick Exercises on the Whole Art of Printing* (1683–4). With this shift, the ability to observe external norms of spelling and punctuation had become a feature of professional competence; for those writing purely for their own pleasure, it remained acceptable to use a more personal set of spelling preferences. Salmon suggested that this licence was particularly extended to scholars and gentlemen; that the lower classes were looked down upon for variable spelling is apparent in the criticism directed at the diarist Henry Machyn. But this judgemental attitude is more that of modern scholarship than of his contemporaries, and it remains unclear how others would have viewed his repertoire of forms.

Case study II: Henry Machyn

The diary of Henry Machyn, written in his own hand between 1550 and 1563, offers important evidence for private spelling habits in this period. Machyn's spelling shows considerable variation and a number of unusual forms, such as **sawgyers**, **harodes**, **sogettes**, **pycter**, **reme**. It was these apparently 'ill-educated spellings' that led modern scholars to dismiss his evidence (Salmon 1999: 30). Wyld (1936: 141–7) similarly drew attention to the 'exotic spellings', including **whent, cronnacull, howsswold**, that riddled his diary, and which Wyld claimed would have drawn attention to his lack of education. As such, much of the evidence of Machyn's spelling has been discredited as the idiosyncratic and ill-informed usage of a poorly educated Londoner.

However, subsequent research by Derek Britton demonstrated the extent to which Machyn's spelling could be understood according to his dialect. While Machyn was living in London when he wrote his diary, his spelling reflects an origin in South-West Yorkshire. Features of this dialect preserved in his writing include <–ys> and <–es> as the present indicative plural inflexion, although this form is attested in some varieties of London English from the late fifteenth century, probably as the result of immigration from the north. In the weak past tense and past participle inflexions Machyn generally uses <–yd>, alongside a less common <–ed> variant. In other common items we find a mixture of London forms alongside more prevalent northern alternatives. For instance, for the item MANY we find **mony** (264x), **money** (8x), **many** (13x). The prevalence of the <o> spellings adds strength to the argument that Machyn was not a native Londoner; the **many** spelling may indicate a form that he picked up from his time in the capital, or a variant form derived from his native dialect.

Another Yorkshire feature that Machyn continued to employ is final <–ur> in words like BROTHER, DAUGHTER, MOTHER, NEITHER, OTHER. But while the <–ur> spelling is dominant in NEITHER and OTHER, and largely dominant in BROTHER, it appears alongside <–er> in equal proportions in THITHER, while in DAUGHTER and MOTHER <–er> is the more frequent form. Other Yorkshire features that appear include the minor variant **tho** THE, which appears just once, alongside the additional rare alternatives: **de** and **tho**. However, the dominant forms are **the** and **ye**, as found in the majority of EModE dialects. **She** is the main spelling of the feminine pronoun SHE; alongside it we find minority **sche** and a single instance of the SW Yorks form **sho**. Machyn's usual form of THERE is **ther**, alongside a single occurrence of **her**. This use of **her** for THERE is paralleled by a single instance of **he** for THE; however, the rarity of these forms means that they may simply be mistakes. By far the most common spelling of IT is <yt>, although there are five examples of spellings with initial <h>. These are probably explained by Machyn's tendency to employ an unetymological <h> which, in this particular instance, accidentally produced an etymologically correct spelling.

Although it is possible that these rare forms are simply mistakes, or perhaps even misreadings by modern editors, since <e> and <o> are easily confused in Machyn's handwriting, the fact that they cluster in SW Yorks is highly suggestive. Their rarity in Machyn's output might suggest that he was deliberately suppressing them in favour of more standardised forms, and that he therefore considered them to be more markedly regional features and so less acceptable in London. Alongside these regionally distinctive forms are more unusual features that may simply testify to Machyn's personal idiosyncrasies. For instance, alongside the SW Yorks forms **yche**, **myche** and **syche** in EACH, MUCH and SUCH, we find the following alternatives for SUCH: **shyche**, **shyth**, **shytt**, **shuche**. For MIGHT and FIGHT Machyn has **might(t)** (5x), **mytht** (1x); **fight** (1x), **fythe** (1x) and **feythe** (2x). In words normally written <Vt>, Machyn has <Vth>, as in **aboythe**, ABOUT, **therbowth** THEREABOUT and **shurth** SHIRT (1x).

Study of Machyn's usage shows that a number of the forms attested derive from his upbringing in South-West Yorkshire. The preservation of these forms in his diary after his removal to London indicates that, in his private writings at least, Machyn felt no pressure to discard these provincialisms. However, the fact that they appear more rarely in Machyn's writing may be indicative of a gradual process of replacement which had not yet led to their complete suppression. This theory is supported by the existence in his repertoire of a number of more widely attested spellings which were likely picked up by Machyn during his residence in London. But the persistence of a small number of idiosyncratic spellings throughout his diary, taken by Wyld to be evidence of Machyn's illiteracy and poor education, indicates that he felt little pressure to cast off his more unusual preferences. As such, Machyn's usage stands as a challenge to the scholarly claim that dialect spelling had disappeared by this point in the history of English. This is a view that can be traced back to Wyld (1936: 100): 'The first point to be mentioned is that Regional dialect disappears completely from the written language of the South and Midlands; both from Literature proper, and from private letters and documents'. It is also regularly found in more recent scholarship, such as Görlach (1999: 506), who endorses this viewpoint, despite obvious contradictory evidence cited in his chapter: 'The occasional mis-spellings that are found in later Early Modern English private documents are generally diagnostic of social status rather than of dialect'. Machyn's spelling habits demonstrate the extent to which dialectal spelling continued to be tolerated throughout the EModE period. It is not until the Late Modern English period that dialect spelling begins to be replaced by a standard written form of the language, as we shall see in the following chapter.

5 Late Modern English

The Late Modern English period, from 1750–1900, is the period of standardisation and codification. During this period the emerging standard form of the written language was finally brought to a degree of fixity, and its rules and conventions were codified in the numerous grammar books that issued from the presses. Of particular importance for the development and codification of spelling was the emergence of the dictionary. Although monolingual dictionaries of English can be traced back to Robert Cawdrey's *Table Alphabeticall* of 1604, these were little more than lists of hard words with simple glosses, intended for those without a classical education who would have struggled with the number of Latin and Greek borrowings adopted into English during that period.

A major development in dictionaries of English was the publication in 1755 of Samuel Johnson's *Dictionary of the English Language*, which attempted to define the vocabulary of English on a much more comprehensive scale. The production of such an authoritative list of words for general use offered its compiler the opportunity to fix the orthography of English by settling on a single preferred spelling for each word. In his preface to the published volume, Johnson highlights the desirability of setting in stone a spelling system that had previously been 'unsettled and fortuitous'. But in selecting a preferred form Johnson recognised the pull of tradition. For, while some irregular forms are recent introductions, others have been part of the language for centuries, and thus have a claim to authority. But, while all languages have anomalies, which must be tolerated, Johnson also saw it as the duty of the lexicographer to correct or proscribe any 'improprieties and absurdities'. In accepting the weight of tradition, Johnson resisted any temptation that he may have felt to tinker with historical spellings such as **knight**; although words preserving silent letters like these may be an inconvenience, centuries of use meant that they were now established features of the language.

Johnson considered the variety in spelling to be the direct result of the process of first committing a spoken language, pronounced in a variety of accents, to written form. Although Johnson exaggerated the extent to which every 'penman' invented his own system for recording his spoken language, he correctly recognised the way in which dialectal spelling systems were partly to blame for the unsettled usage of his day. The result of such a process is a series of anomalous derivatives, such as pairs like **long/ length**, **strong/strength**; while it would be possible to intervene to make the connection clearer, this would require considerable interference for comparatively little gain. Johnson was also correct in noting that a particular difficulty in creating a more phonetic system is the large number of different vocalic pronunciations compared with the small number of letters used to represent these. Although Johnson was critical of the causes of such diversity, attributing them to caprice, accident and affectation, he recognised the impossibility of creating a single system that would satisfy this range of accents. But while Johnson appears to have been tolerant of orthographical variety, insisting that such features are 'not errours in orthography', he saw them as 'spots of barbarity', impressed so deeply into the English Language that criticism cannot wash them away. The imagery that Johnson uses here is strongly moralistic, likening spelling variation to stains upon the language that ought to be cleansed as part of a process of purification. Johnson took a strongly prescriptive attitude towards spelling changes, which he considered to have been caused by accident or 'depraved by ignorance', with the pronunciation of vulgar speakers triggering such shifts in usage.

In order to determine a word's 'true orthography', Johnson referred to its 'original language': the language from which a particular word was borrowed. In such cases, etymology was understood to trump usage, even in cases where a word had an established alternative formation. Thus, Johnson preferred **enchant** over the alternative spelling **inchant**, because the word had been borrowed from French **enchanter**. This seems a reasonable principle to follow; however, following etymological precedent does raise problems that Johnson did not confront. In the case of **enchant**, as with all French words borrowed in the Middle English period, the word is ultimately of Latin origin. If Johnson believed that etymology ought to be the major factor in determining the English spelling of a word, he might have chosen **inchant**, reflecting its ultimate origin in Latin **incantare**. That etymology did not always trump usage for Johnson is apparent in his selection of **grocer** rather than **grosser**, from **gross** 'a large quantity' (Latin **grossus**).

One way of avoiding this complication would have been to select the earliest spellings attested in English. In this case, the **enchant** spelling predates the **inchant** form and so would seem to be the preferred usage. However, this is less clear cut in other cases, such as the spelling **entire** which Johnson preferred over **intire**. In this case, both spellings, **entire** and **intire**, are recorded from Middle English onwards and so either might have been chosen. While the principle of etymology led Johnson to select **entire** (from French **entier**), the English spelling was evidently affected by scribes who were familiar with the Latin etymon, **integrum**. So, while these two examples help to set out Johnson's rationale when selecting a preferred spelling, they also highlight some of the complexities in determining what the 'correct' form of borrowed words should be.

Johnson's *Dictionary* codified the distinction between **practice** (n.) and **practise** (v.), although no such distinction was made between **licence** (n.) and **license** (v.), both of which are entered under **license**, despite Johnson correctly noting their derivation from French **licence** and **licencier**. He did, however, introduce a distinction between **council** and **counsel**; up until the publication of his dictionary, there was considerable confusion between these two words and much overlap in their spelling. Although Johnson based his distinction on etymology, the modern distinction corresponds to neither Latin nor French usage. Even though Johnson does employ the spelling **flour** in his definitions ('a composition of fine flour'), he did not observe a distinction between **flower** and **flour** in the headword, so that **flour** is entered as sense 4 ('The edible part of corn; the meal') under the headword **flower**. The spelling **mettle** was a variant spelling of **metal** that was used for all the word's senses throughout the sixteenth and seventeenth centuries. The first dictionary to separate the figurative senses and list them under the spelling **mettle** is Kersey's *New English Dictionary* (1702). By the mid-eighteenth century, it is rare to find this spelling used in non-figurative senses. Johnson included **mettle** as a subsense under **metal** (2. 'Courage; spirit'), but notes that: 'In this sense it is more frequently written *mettle*', for which he includes a separate entry.

In other examples, Johnson accepted the need to sacrifice uniformity for the sake of custom. In the case of words like **convey** and **inveigh**; **deceit** and **receipt**; **fancy** and **phantom**, Johnson recognised that the weight of tradition, combined with the extent to which these anomalies had become accepted, meant that it would have been folly to attempt to standardise them. The degree to which Johnson was willing to accept current practice rather than attempt to interfere is apparent from the way he tolerated inconsistencies in the representation of certain vowel sounds, such as **jewel** and **fuel**, even when they are found in the same word, e.g. **choak/choke**; **soap/sope**. In such cases, Johnson sometimes inserted the word under both spellings, so that readers looking up the word would be able to locate it, whatever their preferred spelling. While the word **choke** is entered under that spelling, there is an entry for **choak** which points the reader to the alternative form. Similarly, there is an entry for **sope** which reads 'see soap'; **compleat** directs the user to the entry under **complete**.

In cases where a word is entered just once, the spelling of the headword reflects Johnson's preferred spelling. A major innovation of Johnson's *Dictionary* was the inclusion of quotations from texts in which a particular word is used. When citing these textual authorities, Johnson left the authorial spelling 'unmolested', so that the reader might compare Johnson's preference with that of the author and judge between them. But, in doing so, Johnson warned, the reader should bear in mind that some authors pay scant attention to such details as sound and derivation, while others have been more influenced by classical learning than the languages from which many English words have been derived.

In general, then, Johnson rejected previous attempts to reform spelling and saw his dictionary as an opportunity to promote greater understanding of the principles of orthography rather than as a chance to correct it: 'It has been asserted, that for the law to be KNOWN, is of more importance than to be RIGHT'. Johnson's inclinations were to preserve the spellings that had been passed down from earlier stages of the language, recognising that any changes, even ones that promote consistency, disrupt the stability and convenience of precedent and tradition. Above all, Johnson believed that constancy and stability in the language should always take precedence over gradual correction and improvement. His desire to retain consistency prompted him to select a spelling that agreed with a word's derivatives, even when this contravened his own preferences. For instance, the headword **beggar** is so spelled despite Johnson noting that 'it is more properly written begger', because this brings it into line with the associated terms **beggarly** and **beggarliness**.

One of the reasons that Johnson could afford to be relatively hands-off in his treatment of orthography was that, by comparison with earlier periods, Late Modern English showed greater consistency and stability in its orthography. But, despite this, some aspects of variation continued to be tolerated. For instance, there remained a choice between the use of <ick> or <ic> in words like **music, dramatic** and **antic**. Johnson's dictionary spelled all these words with <ick>, but the <ic> spellings were widely used in the period, and feature in quotations taken from the works of Sidney, Spenser and Dryden. That Johnson's practice was rather old-fashioned by the mid-eighteenth century is suggested by a search of the Eighteenth-Century Collections Online database, which finds 40,694 occurrences of **music** in books published during this period, compared with just 2,572 of **musick**.

Clipped forms like **shan't, won't, mayn't** and **can't** became widely used during this period, although they are more frequent in the representation of colloquial speech in plays. Alongside these are found the alternative abbreviations **sha'n't** and **wo'n't**, in which apostrophes are used to mark all omitted letters in their contractions of SHALL NOT and WILL NOT, the latter originating in the seventeenth century as a contraction of **wonnot**. These spellings are still found in works printed in the nineteenth century, such as Lewis Carroll's *Alice's Adventures in Wonderland* (1865). Although abbreviations of this kind are sometimes found in formal prose, they were never really accepted in that register. Joseph Addison objected fiercely to this practice, which he considered a clogging of the language with consonants (*The Spectator* 135 (1711)). Swift in *Polite Conversation* (1738) brings together the various fashionable phrases of his day in order to cast scorn upon them. He used the orthography to capture the manner in which these words were pronounced, adding that his readers will be very familiar with many of the examples they will encounter in his book, such as 'can't, hav'n't, didn't, coodn't, woodn't, isn't, e'n't'.

The apostrophe was also commonly used in verbal inflexions like **alter'd**, **walk't**, a system that attempted to convey pronunciation rather than morphology. The use of the apostrophe in possessives was restricted to singular nouns, e.g. **boy's book**, since it was understood to indicate an omission. In the case of plural nouns, such as **boys books**, no apostrophe was felt to be needed, since nothing had been left out. In possessive pronouns the apostrophe was generally not included, although it was sometimes added, even by educated writers like Lord Chesterfield and Robert Lowth, who used **your's** in his private writings. Another use of the apostrophe that has not survived into standard PDE is its addition before an <s> in plural nouns ending in a vowel, such as **opera's**; the modern distinction between **tomato/tomatoes** and **mango/mangos** had not yet become established.

Case study III: James Boswell

James Boswell, Johnson's biographer and a prolific letter-writer, employed a range of idiosyncratic spellings in his private correspondence. Tieken-Boon van Ostade (1996) analysed Boswell's spelling habits in his early letters to his friend John Johnston, finding the consistent use of **always**, **immediatly**, **affraid**, **dissagreable**, **chearfull** and **corespondence**; the only instance of **correspondence** occurs in a quotation from a letter by his father. Adjectives that typically end <ful> are always spelled <full>, such as **beautifull**, while nouns ending in <y> are pluralised by adding an <s> rather than switching to <ies>. A striking feature of this set of preferences is its high degree of consistency; far from being a collection of random variants, Boswell's preferences reflect a systematic set of choices.

Boswell's use of a set of variant spelling forms that do not conform to the preferences found in Johnson's *Dictionary* is paralleled by a number of educated writers from this period. These private usages, what Osselton (1963, 1984) has referred to as 'informal spelling systems', were characterised by the use of a large number of contractions, such as **w^{ch}** WHICH, **y^m** THEM, **y^t** THAT, **tho** THOUGH and **thro** THROUGH. Salmon has similarly noted that, after 1660, the ability to spell and punctuate became a matter of technical skill; the scholar and the gentleman remained free to use their own spelling systems (Salmon 1999: 44).

However, comparison of Boswell's spellings with equivalents in his later correspondence with Johnston reveals changes to his practices over time. Later in his career as a writer, Boswell appears to have rejected his private spelling preferences in favour of those employed by the printers of the time. This switch appears to have happened quite suddenly; it can be dated to soon after August 1767. This period marked a major change in Boswell's life; returning from his nineteen-month tour of the continent, Boswell settled in Edinburgh to begin his career as a lawyer. The focus of this work on the written word in its standard form is argued to have been the impetus for the change in Boswell's personal spelling practices. His interest in spelling is apparent from his passionate defence of his orthography in his *Account of Corsica* (1767). Here Boswell takes issue with the recent fashion to 'render our language more neat and trim' by writing <c> rather than <ck> and <or> rather than <our>. Boswell, however, prefers to follow the 'illustrious' Samuel Johnson, whose *Dictionary* preserves the <k> as a 'mark of Saxon original'. Boswell also follows Johnson in preferring <our> in words borrowed from French, and reserving <–or> for words direct from Latin. Thus, Boswell follows his master in writing **horrour**, **errour**, **superiour**, **terrour**, and goes beyond him in preferring **authour** to **author** and **doctour** to **doctor**. While he concedes that such attention to detail may appear trivial, Boswell is keen to preserve such details as traces of the language's development and its affinity with other tongues. He finishes by noting that, should his work be reprinted in the future, 'I hope that care will be taken of my orthography' (Boulton and McLoughlin 2006: 14).

That Boswell was justified in his fear that a printer might alter his spelling when issuing future editions of his work is suggested by the treatment of Lawrence Sterne's memoirs in print. The manuscript of this work included a number of idiosyncratic spellings, such as **supplyed**, **orderd**, **Arch Bishop**, **small Pox**, **Mony** and **Designe**, all of which were changed to the standard equivalents in a posthumous printed version of 1775.

It became increasingly common for writers to expect printers and compositors to impose standard conventions of spelling and punctuation on their texts. One aspect of authorial practice with which printers routinely struggled was the capitalisation of nouns. In the sixteenth century, capitals, or 'great letters', were used at the beginnings of sentences, as well as after colons. In poetry, capitals were used at the beginnings of lines of verse as a useful means of demarcating lines. This was particularly useful in blank verse, which could otherwise easily be mistaken for prose. In the seventeenth century, the practice of using capitals to mark proper nouns and other important words developed in manuscripts, although it was implemented rather erratically and irregularly. Osselton's (1985) analysis of a corpus of published materials identified two rules: nouns were capitalised when an author wished to make a word more prominent, or when it fitted into a particular semantic category. This semantic category included animate nouns, areas of study or academic disciplines, names of concrete objects, as well as abstract nouns where the writer wished to emphasise their generality, e.g. Ambition, Justice.

Despite the efforts of printers to observe such distinctions, this second category proved particularly problematic, since it was often unclear when words like truth and beauty were intended to be personified and when they were not. This was made even more difficult by the way in which authors' handwritten manuscripts often failed to make a clear visual distinction between upper- and lower-case letters, a difficulty exacerbated by the fact that in many cases a capital is just a slightly larger version of a lower-case letter. In response to the challenge of making such judgements, and the time that was taken up doing so, printers implemented a policy of capitalising all nouns. This consistent practice of marking all nouns with capitals was also felt to look more attractive than an inconsistent practice of capitalising some nouns and not others. This was acknowledged in a grammar of the early eighteenth century, which noted that: "'Tis grown Customary in Printing to begin every Substantive with a Capital ... for Ornament's Sake' (Dyche 1707: 118). Writers, however, were unhappy with this development, since it effectively removed the potential of marking subtle nuances of meaning and expression using capital letters. As a consequence, the policy of capitalising all nouns was dropped in favour of the modern system where it is only proper nouns that are distinguished in this way. This shift in policy is summarised by Joseph Robertson (1785: 137) in his treatise on punctuation:

> It was usual with our ancestors, both in writing and printing, to begin every noun with a capital. But this custom, which was always troublesome, and not in the least useful or ornamental, is now entirely discontinued; and small letters are used in all common words.

While accurate spelling became a marker of learning in eighteenth-century England, poor spelling was indicative of a lack of education.

This is well illustrated in Henry Fielding's novel *Joseph Andrews* (1742), where the written copy of a legal deposition, produced by a Justice of the Peace in the absence of his clerk, contains a mixture of Somerset dialect features and erroneous spellings, as indicated by the document's heading: 'The depusition of James Scout, layer, and Thomas Trotter, yeoman, taken befor mee, one of his magesty's justasses of the piece for Zumersetshire' (*Joseph Andrews*, Book IV, Chapter 5). Variant spellings were also exploited by novelists of this period to signal dialect pronunciations. Such spellings were not used in order to render the dialect with phonetic accuracy or consistency, but rather to give a flavour of regional speech, or as a 'signpost', with the extent to which it is used depending more on the demands of the situation than on the likely behaviour of an actual speaker (see Page 1988: 59). Examples of such spellings are those that signal south-western vowel sounds and voiced initial fricative consonants in Henry Fielding's novel *Tom Jones* (1749): **feace** FACE, **quoat** COAT, **veather** FEATHER, **vind** FIND, **zee** SEE, **huome** HOME.

Prescriptive attitudes towards spelling went hand-in-hand with similar attitudes towards speech. The elocutionist Thomas Sheridan, who toured the country giving lectures on correct pronunciation, was equally censorious of incorrect spellings: 'It is a disgrace to a gentleman, to be guilty of false spelling, either by omitting, changing, or adding letters contrary to custom' (*Course of Lectures on Elocution*, 1763). Jonathan Swift was particularly dismissive of the idea that spelling should reflect pronunciation; he was especially critical of simplified spellings such as **tho** THOUGH, **agen** AGAIN, **thot** THOUGHT, **brout** BROUGHT, and lamented the idea that the spelling standard should be subject to 'the caprice of every coxcomb' (Letter to *Tatler*, 1710).

These attitudes became further enshrined in the following century. For Görlach (1999: 45), spelling became 'one of the most important indicators of social acceptability' in nineteenth-century England. Dickens fictionalised the link between educational opportunities and accurate spelling in *Bleak House* (1853), in which Caddy defends her lover's poor spelling on the grounds that his education had been badly neglected. The anxiety provoked by his awareness of his deficiencies in this area lead him to 'put so many unnecessary letters into short words that they sometimes quite lost their English appearance' (Chapter XIV). Pip's early forays into the written word in *Great Expectations* (1861) are rather an extreme attempt to signal his lack of education by his poor grasp of the conventions of standard orthography: 'MI DEER JO i OPE U R KRWITE WELL i OPE i SHAL SON B HABELL 4 2 TEEDGE U JO AN THEN WE SHORL B SO GLODD AN WEN i M PRENGTD 2 U JO WOT LARX AN BLEVE ME INF XN PIP' (Charles Dickens,

Great Expectations, Chapter 7).

By the eighteenth and nineteenth centuries, however, it is clear that niceties of spelling and punctuation were considered to be the business of the printer, and authors expected non-standard spellings to be corrected at the stage of printing. This led to an increased standardisation of the printed word, but private and informal writing, such as diaries, letters and authorial manuscripts, continued to tolerate a diversity of non-standard spelling forms. Following the lead of contemporary printers, modern editors often emend non-standard spellings found in nineteenth-century manuscripts, giving us a somewhat skewed picture of the state of orthography in this period. For example, in the 1904 edition of the *Complete Poetical Works of Shelley*, the editor Thomas Hutchinson corrected all non-standard spellings with the following justification:

> Shelley was neither very accurate, nor always consistent, in his spelling ... Irregular or antiquated forms such as 'recieve,' 'sacrifize,' 'tyger,' 'gulph,' 'desart,' 'falshood,' and the like, can only serve to distract the reader's attention, and mar his enjoyment of the verse. Accordingly Shelley's eccentricities in this kind have been discarded, and his spelling revised in accordance with modern usage ... In a few cases Shelley's spelling, though unusual or obsolete, has been retained. Thus in 'aethereal,' 'paean,' and one or two more words the *ae* will be found, and 'airy' still appears as 'aëry.' Shelley seems to have uniformly written 'lightening': here the word is so printed whenever it is employed as a trisyllable; elsewhere the ordinary spelling has been adopted. (lv)

There is an interesting contradiction in the editorial treatment of these two groups of spellings. The first are considered to be eccentricities which should be discarded, whereas the second are 'unusual or obsolete' and consequently are preserved. The important distinction here is probably that the second group are classical spellings and therefore ones which belong to a literary tradition; this is confirmed by the *OED* entry for **aery**, which carries the label: 'Chiefly *poetic* and *literary* in later use'.[1] But while there is a whole entry for the spelling **aery**, the **aëry** spelling preserved by the editor is only recorded in a quotation from Shelley and another from a poem by Thomas Dermody (1800). The preservation of such spellings raises the question of whether the other spellings that Shelley used enjoyed a similarly literary pedigree and were intended to be used in that way by Shelley. Might not these spellings have been understood in a similar way by a contemporary reader? By replacing these with modern equivalents,

---

1. Oxford English Dictionary, s.v. 'aery (adj.)', July 2023, <https://doi.org/10.1093/OED/5288639121>

the editor has removed such distinctive spellings from consideration.

That such spellings may have enjoyed wider use is implied by their appearance in a number of literary sources. The spelling **tyger** is well known for its appearance in the eponymous poem by William Blake from his *Songs of Experience* (1794). The poem also includes the spelling **sieze**, which recalls Shelley's use of **recieve**. It is interesting that the examples of **recieve** in the *OED* entry for **receive** (v.) are both in quotations from works by Blake:[2]

> 1804 W. Blake *Let.* 22 June in *Compl. Writings* (1969) 849 I write immediately on recieving [*sic*] the Above Information.
>
> 1789 W. Blake *Night* in *Songs of Innocence* But if they rush dreadful; The angels most heedful, Recieve [*sic*] each mild spirit, New worlds to inherit.

The **desart** spelling discarded by Shelley's editor is recorded regularly in writings from 1500–1800; the *OED* labels it the 'regularly accepted spelling' of the eighteenth century.[3] The accompanying quotations include a number of examples of **desart** from the nineteenth century, including examples in the works of Shelley's contemporary poet Lord Byron.

The manuscripts of Charles Dickens's novels contain many non-standard spellings, which are frequently corrected by modern editors (Mugglestone 2006: 279). The editors of Dickens's letters follow the spelling of the original documents, though they note that the author's spelling preferences changed over the course of his life. In the earlier letters Dickens employed the spelling **inclose**, but changed to **enclose** in the 1840s. Similarly, his preferred spelling **choak** is replaced by **choke** from 1843. The editors also draw attention to a number of alternative spellings favoured by Dickens, including **controul**, **ecstacy**, **expence**, **handfull**, **groupe**, **intreat**, **negociate**, **recal**, **trowsers**, noting that, while these appear archaic today, they were acceptable alternatives in Dickens's day. Given their tolerance of this variation, and their tolerance of the alternative spellings in private writings such as letters in the nineteenth century, it is surprising that the editors label the novelist's preferred spellings of **phenomonon** (or **phænomonon**) and **poney** as 'life-long mis-spellings'. It is not clear why the editors consider one group of spellings to be acceptable alternatives, and another to be erroneous. Perhaps this view was encouraged by the fact that **phenomonon** does not appear among the variant forms recorded in the *OED*. However, a search of the

---

2. Oxford English Dictionary, s.v. 'receive (v.), Forms', June 2024, <https://doi.org/10.1093/OED/8273269571>
3. Oxford English Dictionary, s.v. 'desert (n.2), Forms', September 2023, <https://doi.org/10.1093/OED/1101909442>

Google Books corpus turns up a number of nineteenth-century examples that indicate that it was a common spelling during Dickens's lifetime. Modern editions of Dickens's novels generally iron out such irregularities for the contemporary reader. Some unusual spellings are, however, retained by editors as appearing to have been authorised by the author. The World Classics edition of *Bleak House* preserves the use of –or spellings of **favored**, **parlor** and **humor**, as well as more unusual spellings like **secresy**, **gypsey**, **chimnies**; in other unusual forms, such as **villanous**, editors remain uncertain as to whether these are errors or genuine Dickensian spellings.

Dickens's employment of non-standard spellings is comparatively trivial by contrast with that of the biologist Charles Darwin. In a letter of 1834, Darwin's sister teased him about the numerous erroneous spellings that appeared in his diary; these included forms such as **lose** LOOSE, **lanscape** LANDSCAPE, **higest** HIGHEST, **profil** PROFILE, **cannabal** CANNIBAL, **peacible** PEACEABLE, **quarrell** QUARREL, **berrys** BERRIES, **barrell** BARREL, **epock** EPOCH, **untill** UNTIL, **priviledge** PRIVILEGE. Although she recognised that some of these mistakes are merely the result of a lack of care when writing at speed, she nevertheless felt it worthy of comment. Scholars have used certain patterns of change in Darwin's spelling habits to date entries made in the notebooks he compiled on the *Beagle*. A curious feature of these changes is that they do not always shift in the direction of the standard. In the case of **pacific**, this spelling is replaced by **pacifick** in 1834, while in 1836 Darwin returned to the **pacific** form. Other spellings, such as **thoroughily**, **broard** and **Portugeese**, remained his preferred forms throughout his journal entries.

The nineteenth century also witnessed the publication of the *New English Dictionary* (later the *Oxford English Dictionary*), which replaced Johnson's *Dictionary* as the authority for standard English spelling. In the General Explanations that set out the procedures to be adopted, James Murray, the first editor, explained that every main word is included in its 'modern current or most usual spelling' – thereby signalling the extent to which current usage would dictate the spelling of the dictionary's headwords. In cases where two spellings are current, both are given in the main form, as in examples like **analyse/analyze**; **chemistry/chymistry**; **inflection/inflexion**. This inclusion of variant spellings shows the extent to which the dictionary was willing to tolerate alternative spelling forms and saw its role as reflecting contemporary practice rather than prescribing it. In the case of verbs ending in <–ize> or <–ise>, however, the dictionary adopted the principle of always using <–ize> rather than <–ise>, since the latter is 'only the French spelling of the same Greek ending'. Just as it is entirely appropriate for French to remain consistent in the use of <–ise>

in new formations, so is it correct for English to prefer <–ize>. Where the decision was taken to choose just one form from a variety of spellings with no clear preponderance of usage, recourse was to 'etymological or phonetic propriety'; or 'general analogy with similar words'. The editor is clear that, in such instances, it is no way implied that 'the form actually chosen is intrinsically better than others which are appended to it' (Murray, 'General Explanations': xix–xx)

Lynda Mugglestone (2011: 9) quotes a response by Murray to an enquiry from a member of the public as to the correct spelling of WHISKY: 'when in a hurry you may save a fraction of time by writing whisky, and when lingering over it you may prolong it to whiskey … in matters of taste there is no "correct" or "incorrect"; there is the liberty of the subject'. Although this reply would have been of little help to the enquirer, who was no doubt hoping for something more definitive, it does serve to highlight the extent to which the dictionary tolerated variant usage. In the published dictionary both **whisky** and **whiskey** were given as alternative spellings of the headword. Murray's decisions about the spelling of various headwords in the *NED* was no doubt influenced by his personal views about spelling and the desirability of reforming it. As we will see in Chapter 11, Murray was not a purely objective recorder of orthographic variation; he used his Presidential lecture to the Philological Society to make a case for a set of spelling reforms designed to bring spelling and pronunciation into closer alignment. This example reminds us that even lexicographers and philologists, for whom 'there is no "correct" or "incorrect"', can have strong views when it comes to the preferred way of spelling English words.

6 US English

The origins of US spelling lie in the conventions of the variety of Early Modern English adopted by the first settlers. The employment of this system, based upon the southern English dialect, was reinforced by its appearance in the English books by authoritative writers like John Dryden and Joseph Addison which were imported into the USA. The influence of Augustan writers can also be seen in the aborted attempt of 1780 to establish an academy to oversee and codify correct usage in the USA. Its proposed title, 'The American Academy for Refining, Improving and Ascertaining the English Language', was evidently influenced by Jonathan Swift's 'A Proposal for Correcting, Improving and Ascertaining the English Language' (1712) and its suggestion that an academy consisting of experts be formed in order to advise on matters of English usage.

Despite their shared origins, a number of differences now set the American spelling system apart from that of Britain. In this chapter we will examine a selection of these divergences in detail and consider how they arose. One of the best known concerns the distinction between British English <our> and American English <or> in words such as the following:

British	American
colour	color
honour	honor
favour	favor
flavour	flavor
labour	labor

This group of nouns are of Latin origin but were borrowed into English from French. Those derived from Old French generally had <o> or <u>, as in **onor** and **onur** HONOUR, whereas those from Anglo-Norman were spelled <ou>: **honour, onour**. During the Early Modern period, many of these French borrowings were re-spelled to reflect their Latin etymons; later loanwords tended to follow this pattern, thereby increasing

73

the number of such words spelled <or>. Thus we find words like **error**, **horror** and **tenor** in British English, even though these were often spelled <our>. In the case of ERROR, HORROR and TERROR, the spellings **errour**, **horrour** and **terrour** were common up until the end of the eighteenth century. In most cases, we find <or> spellings from the sixteenth century onwards, although they did not dominate until the eighteenth century, when they began to be selected as the spelling of the relevant headwords in dictionaries. The 1753 edition of Nathan Bailey's *Universal Etymological English Dictionary* is the first to accept **error** as its headword, while Johnson's of 1755 continued to use **errour**.

In the case of HONOUR, the <or> spelling was established in Early Modern English; the spelling **honour** was chosen for the headword in most dictionaries from the seventeenth century onwards. In the eighteenth century, one lexicographer preferred **honor** as 'a modern but correct spelling from the Lat[in]' (Ash 1775), while John Wesley urged Methodist preachers to avoid the 'fashionable impropriety of leaving out the u' in words like **honour** and **vigour**, describing it as a 'mere childish affectation'.

There are parallel differences in words spelled <oul> in British English, which appear as <ol> in US English, e.g. **mould/mold**; **smoulder/ smolder**. But the distinction between <ou> and <o> is not a generalised rule that applies in all relevant instances. In derivatives like **honorary**, British English has the <or> spelling, while in the adjective **honourable** the <our> is preserved. According to the *OED*, the tendency is to use <or> for those derivatives with a more explicit link with the Latin etymon, e.g. **honorary** and **honorific**, and <our> where the connection with **honour** is most obvious, e.g. **honoured** and **honourable**. In the adjective **laborious**, British English adopts the US version without the <u>. The Merriam Webster dictionary lists **saviour** as an alternative spelling of **savior**, **smoulder** as an alternative for **smolder**, while the headword for **glamour** is spelled in the British English manner with <our>, and with <or> listed as a less common alternative. British English is also inconsistent in its use of <our>, since words like **terror** and **squalor** are spelled with <or> rather than <our>, despite the fact that the spellings **terrour** and **squalour** were common in the seventeenth century. The variation is the result of the different origins of the word in English, since **terror** is a borrowing direct from Latin **terror** and **terrour** from the Anglo-French **terrour**.

Where British English has –re, American English has –er:

theatre	theater
fibre	fiber
metre	meter

Once again, we come across inconsistencies and variation between the two sets of correspondences. Variation between **theatre** and **theater** has been recorded in English since the Middle Ages; between 1550 and 1700, **theater** was the more common spelling, especially in dictionaries, although **theatre** is found in the work of a number of prominent writers, such as Milton and Pope. Nathan Bailey's *Universal Etymological English Dictionary* of 1727 offered both spellings; soon after this **theater** fell out of use entirely in Britain. It was, however, retained or perhaps revived in the USA. A similar story concerns the word **fibre**, which was spelled both **fibre** and **fiber** in Britain; by the end of the nineteenth century **fiber** was common in the USA but rare in England. Not all <re> words are spelled <er> in American English; **acre** and **ogre** are spelled in the same way as British English, rather than **acer** and **oger**.

A key principle of the American variants is that they are more phonetic than the UK equivalents. But this comes with certain trade-offs, since it creates additional homonyms. For instance, the US spelling of **tyre** is identical to the verb **tire**, a **cheque** is spelled identically with the verb **check** and a **storey** in a building is spelled **story**, thereby creating the potential for confusion with the term for a narrative.

Words that end in –l in British English are spelled –ll in American English:

distil	distill
fulfil	fulfill
instil	instill

Once again, this group shows variation between both forms in the pre-modern periods. Derived from Latin **distillare**, the word was spelled **distill** or **distille** in the fifteenth and sixteenth centuries. In the seventeenth century the **distil** spelling appears and the two are used alongside each other. The entry in the first edition of the *OED* (dated 1896) gives both spellings in its headword. The *OED* revised entry for **fulfil** gives a lengthy list of earlier forms, going back to Old English **fulfyllan**. Since the word is a compound of **full** and **fill**, the spelling with <ll> dominates for much of its early history. In the 1600s the spelling **fulfil** is introduced, alongside **fulfill**, which the *OED* labels 'now chiefly U.S.'.[1]

When –ful is added to a word ending in –l, British English drops one of the l's while American English keeps both:

skilful	skillful

1. Oxford English Dictionary, s.v. 'fulfil | fulfill (v.), Forms', September 2023, <https://doi.org/10.1093/OED/9980461987>

According to the forms listed in the *OED*, the spelling preserving both l's was first recorded in the 1500s, when it was used alongside that with a single <l>. Both continued to be used in free variation in British English until the 1800s when **skillful** became mostly restricted to the USA.

programme   program

The word **programme** was borrowed from French **programme** and Latin **programma** in the seventeenth century. The spelling **program** was more common in the earliest instances, and remained so in Scots. This spelling, which more accurately conforms to the usual spelling of such words in English, cf. **anagram** and **telegram**, remained the usual form in Scottish writers in the late eighteenth and early nineteenth centuries, even after the borrowing of the sense 'advance notice describing a formal proceedings e.g. an entertainment' from French. In England, the influence from the French word led to the **programme** spelling becoming dominant in the nineteenth century. The **program** spelling remained the sole way of spelling this word in the USA; more recently the US spelling has been adopted in British English in reference to computing, a sense introduced in the 1940s.

Other shorter spellings in American English are:

dialogue   dialog
catalogue   catalog

The word **catalogue** was borrowed from French and that spelling has been preserved in British English; the variant spellings **catholog** and **cataloge** are found up to the sixteenth century, while the **catalog** spelling is first recorded in the 1800s. This spelling did not catch on in British English but became the standard spelling in US English. **Dialogue** was borrowed from Latin **dialogus**, but subsequently reinforced by two different French forms: Anglo-Norman and Old French **dialoge** and Middle French **dialogue**. These two French spellings gave rise to considerable variation in Middle English, e.g. **dialog**, **dyaloge**, **dyalogue**; by the eighteenth century, the **dialog** spelling had become established as the usual form in US and Scottish usage.

disc   disk

Disc was initially borrowed from French **disque** and then again from Latin **discus**. The word is first recorded in English in the spelling **disk**; the **disc** spelling was an eighteenth-century innovation, alongside the alternative form **disch**. The later **disc** spelling came to replace **disk** in British English; however, the earlier **disk** spelling remains the standard spelling in the USA. In a similar way to **program**, **disk** is now standard in computing contexts in British English, as a result of influence from US usage.

Old English **grei** could be spelled a number of ways in Middle English; the variation between spellings with <ey> and <ay> is the result of a merger of these diphthongs in the late ME period. The choice of different alternatives can be seen today in the standard spellings of e.g. **clay** (Old English **clæg**), which is found as both **cleye** and **claye/claie** in Middle English, and **whey** (Old English **hweg**), for which spellings **wei** and **way** are recorded in the fifteenth century. The first edition of the *OED* attempted to resolve the question of which of the two spellings of **grey** should be preferred. An enquiry in November 1893 discovered that **grey** was more common in British usage, despite Dr Johnson and later lexicographers preferring **gray**. For some, the two forms were considered to have different meanings, with **grey** denoting a 'more delicate or a lighter tint than gray'; for others **gray** was a 'warmer colour', with a mixture of red or brown.[2]

An early nineteenth-century borrowing from Urdu, the word PYJAMAS was initially represented in a wide variety of spellings: **paunjammahs, paejamus, paijamahs, piejamahs, pigammahs, pyjamas** – the Standard British English spelling – and **pajamas** – the spelling that is now standard in the USA. **Jewellery** first appears in the fourteenth century as a native derivation based upon a French loanword. As with other examples we have considered, the US spelling **jewelry** is one of a number of alternative early spellings, e.g. **juelrye, iewelrye, iewellrie** and **jewellery**, which has since become the standard form in the UK. SCEPTIC is a borrowing of the French **sceptique**; despite the French word being pronounced with /s/, the English pronunciation adopted the /sk/ of the Greek. With that the spelling **skeptic** emerged and was adopted by Dr Johnson in his *Dictionary*. Despite this, **skeptic** did not win widespread acceptance in Britain, although it has since become the standard spelling in the USA. This is somewhat surprising, since <sc> in British English usually corresponds to /s/, as in **scene** and **scent**; the <sk> spelling would have enabled a clearer distinction between /s/ and /sk/.

Another difference between UK and US spelling is the replacement of <ae> with <e> in scientific terms such as **archaeology** (US **archeology**) and **palaeography** (US **paleography**); the UK spelling of **palaeography** is itself a simplification of an earlier spelling with <æ>. Another scientific term that differs in British and American English is **sulphur**, usually spelled **sulfur** in American English, a variant spelling which was used by

---

2. Oxford English Dictionary, s.v. 'grey | gray (adj. & n.), Etymology', June 2024, <https://doi.org/10.1093/OED/2919413057>

chemists in the 1920s. The word was borrowed into English from a French word **sufere** during the medieval period, which in turn was adopted from Latin, where the word was spelled both **sulphur** and **sulfur**. Usually, English words spelled with <ph> are derived from Greek, where the <ph> represents the Greek letter 'phi', but in this case the ultimate source of the word is Arabic.

Curb is the usual spelling in all senses in British English, while **kerb** is found in the UK specifically in the sense of the edge of a pavement.

Some distinctions appear to have become obsolete. British English **waggon**, a spelling which was dominant in the eighteenth century (despite Johnson selecting **wagon** for his *Dictionary*), persisted into the early nineteenth century, but has since become increasingly less common. There are just 159 instances recorded in the GloWbE corpus; 60 of these are from Great Britain, while 22 are from the US and 18 from Australia. More usual now in the UK is the spelling **wagon**, which is the standard form in the US. The US spelling **airplane** is recorded in the early twentieth century in Britain but is labelled 'rare' by the *OED*; British English is much more likely to use the earlier form **aeroplane**. There are 1,145 occurrences of **airplane** in the British section of the GloWbE corpus, but these include a number of references to the film *Airplane* and to the airplane mode feature on electronic devices. An example of a UK/US difference that has largely disappeared concerns the distinction between **gaol** and **jail**. These reflect two different forms borrowed from French: Old Northern French **gaiole** and Old French **jaiole**. The former reflected a distinct pronunciation which fell out of use in the spoken language, although the associated spelling, **gaol**, continues to be supported as an archaism in official usage. In more general usage the British English preference is for **jail**, the same spelling employed in US English.

The British English distinction between **practice** (noun) and **practise** (verb) is not observed in US English, where both words are spelled **practice**. The UK distinction appears to be disappearing in casual use today, perhaps under the influence of US usage, or perhaps because it is not felt to be necessary. Similar changes have affected the British English spellings **inflexion** and **connexion**, which are now commonly found in their American spellings of **inflection** and **connection**. Another distinction between British and American spelling that is gradually disappearing concerns the silent <e> following <dg> in words like **judg(e)ment**. Both spellings date from the early sixteenth century; by the late seventeenth century **judgment** was the more common of the two. However, the nineteenth century witnessed an increase in uses of **judgement**, particularly in British English, leaving the **judgment** spelling to become the favoured form in US English and in certain specialised legal contexts in Britain.

The inclusion of the <e> goes back to an earlier spelling with <gg>, **juggement**, where it functioned as a diacritic, signalling that the <gg> was pronounced as /dʒ/ rather than as /g/. Today the distinction between **judgement** and **judgment** is one of personal choice; in printed media it is regulated by the set of conventions, or 'house style', laid down by particular publishing houses. In the fourth edition of Fowler's *Dictionary of Modern English Usage* (2015), Jeremy Butterfield observes that, in most varieties of English, **judgment** is much more common than **judgement**, apart from in Indian and Irish English, where the two forms occur in roughly equal numbers. In British English, the use of **judgement** or **judgment** is not a matter of correctness, but merely 'one of convention in various publishing houses' (450).

Another convention that is often considered to be American is the spelling <yze/ize>, where British English often uses <yse/ise>. But this is not simply a feature of American English; recognising that the suffix itself is from Greek <ιζειν> (<izein>), the *OED* took the decision to spell all such words with <yze/ize> and this has also become the policy of Oxford University Press. Another complexity is that there remain a number of such verbs that are always spelled with <–ise> in both British and American English; these include examples such as **advertise**, **supervise**, **compromise** and **televise**. These differ from the rest of the group for a variety of reasons; a key factor is that the <–ise> ending was adopted from French or Latin sources that were never spelled with the <–ize> ending. Although a variant spelling **supervize** is recorded in the 1600s, **supervise** has always been spelled this way, since it is from Latin **supervis–**, the past participial stem of **supervidere** 'to examine'. Similarly, **advertise** is from the Middle French **advertiss–**; historical instances of the spelling **advertize** show how it has been assimilated to the <–ize> ending.

Many of these differences between British and American English are due to the influence of the spelling reformer and lexicographer Noah Webster (1758–1843). Webster began his career writing spelling books which adopted the spellings advocated by Johnson's *Dictionary*. Initially, his approach to spelling was to preserve the traditional forms; Webster was openly critical of reformers who advocated preferring **favor** and **honor** to **favour** and **honour**. While Webster recognised the imperfect relationship between spelling and pronunciation, he did not seek to change it. But his attitude altered under the influence of Benjamin Franklin, who had himself devised a reformed orthography. Webster came to feel that a reformed spelling system would improve the language and raise standards of literacy.

The success of Webster's spelling revisions was largely thanks to his decision to link linguistic reform with national identity. Webster considered a more phonetic spelling system to be a means of fixing pronunciation and thereby creating greater national unity, as speakers of American English would not be divided by different accents. For Webster, a national language is 'a band of national union'; Webster set out to create a language that Americans could call their own and which would inspire them with pride in their national character and a greater desire for independence from Britain and the 'blind imitation of its manners', which he considered to be prevalent among his fellow Americans.

Another factor that enabled Webster to succeed where other reformers had failed was the moderate nature of his proposals. Unlike the reforms of Benjamin Franklin, which involved the introduction of new characters and radically different spellings, Webster introduced a modest number of alterations, most of which were already known in British English, and which also created closer sound-spelling correspondences: removing silent letters like the <u> in **labour** and reversing the last two letters in **fibre**. In doing this, Webster had learned from his experience, since his early efforts included more radical proposals, such as dropping the silent letters in words such as **crum**, **tung**, **giv**, **nabour**, which had failed to win acceptance. But the biggest factor behind the success of these proposals was the publication of his dictionaries, in which he laid out the set of revisions that has since won widespread acceptance throughout the US. It was the 1828 edition of *Webster's Dictionary* that established Webster's preferred spellings in American usage. These spellings were also promulgated by the revised edition of Webster's famous work for schools, *The Elementary Spelling Book* (1829), popularly known as 'The Blue-Backed Speller' because of its distinctive cover. This book built on the success of his *American Spelling Book* (1786); by 1880, Webster's spelling book was outselling all books in America apart from the Bible.

A further series of spelling reforms was proposed by the National Educational Association in 1898, who selected a set of twelve words for adoption: **altho**, **catalog**, **decalog**, **demagog**, **pedagog**, **prolog**, **program**, **tho**, **thoro**, **thorofare**, **thru**, **thruout**. The process of adoption was gradual, with the proposed revisions being initially adopted in official proceedings and in a number of educational journals (Thomas 1902). The plan was to gradually introduce an awareness that 'usage is another name for fashion' and that such fashions are created by the initiative of an individual person or group. The success of this approach is apparent from the adoption of the spellings with <g> instead of <gue>. While the contracted spellings **tho** and **thru** have not been taken up in formal printed text, they are often found in signs or text messages, where space or speed are at a premium.

The US Simplified Spelling Board was founded in 1906, under the patronage of Andrew Carnegie, who felt that the progress of English in its adoption as a world language was being hindered by its erratic spelling system. Its members included the author Mark Twain and Melville Dewey, deviser of the Dewey decimal system of library cataloguing. The Board issued an initial list of 300 proposed revisions, which focused on the replacement of <ed> with <t> in past tense inflexions, so that **blessed** would become **blest**, and the dropping of silent letters in words like **anser, definit, frend** and the simplification of digraphs in scientific words like **encyclopedia**. Since many of these changes had already been proposed by Webster and featured in his dictionaries, they appeared relatively modest. But, despite winning the support of the president, Theodore Roosevelt, who recommended their use to the Government Printing Office, the Board's proposals failed to convince the press and consequently did not gain widespread support. The British press was especially vociferous in its ridiculing of Carnegie's efforts to meddle with the language of Shakespeare. The report in *The Sun* newspaper was especially damning:

> Mr Andru Karnegi (or should it be Karnege?) and President Rusvelt (or is it Ruzvelt?) are doing their (or ther) best to ad to the gaiety of nations (or nashuns) by atempting to reform the spelling of the English langwidge. No dowt their (or ther) intentions (or intenshuns) are orl rite, but their (or ther) objekt is orl rong, not to say silly (or sily).

Roosevelt quickly recognised that the lack of support in the media meant that such efforts were doomed to failure and gave up the battle for spelling reform.

In order to boost its academic credentials and to respond to criticism in the British press, the Board invited a trio of eminent British philologists to join its ranks. Sir James Murray, editor of the *New English Dictionary* (later the *OED*), Joseph Wright, editor of the *English Dialect Dictionary*, and Walter W. Skeat, editor of *An Etymological Dictionary of the English Language*, all accepted the invitation to become members of the Board. Despite this, the Board came to be a source of frustration for Carnegie, who wrote to the Chairman in 1915 criticising its methods and lack of progress. Rather than trying to alter the spelling of a few words at a time, the Board had erred in offering too radical a set of proposals at the outset. When he died in 1919, Carnegie, who had sunk nearly $300,000 into the work of the Board up to this point, left no provision for its activities in his will; the Board was disbanded the following year.

The winding down of the Board's activities coincided with the publication of a *Handbook of Simplified Spelling* (1920), which surveyed the various attempts to reform spelling, criticising these as too radical and too costly. The Board's aim was to eschew radical or revolutionary schemes and instead set about implementing a small series of gradual or 'progressiv' changes. Recognising that these changes would not solve all the problems with the current system, the Board argued that it was better to make some improvements rather than wait for the evolution of a 'perfect sistem'. In response to those who objected to reform on the grounds that a spelling that was 'good enuf for them is good enuf for their children', the *Handbook* argued that 'English spelling at present is not good enuf for anybody – not even for those who would deprive their children of any educational advantage not enjoyd by themselvs' (26). Instead, the *Handbook* proposed a new 'orthografy' that would bring about greater regularity and consistency, and which would favour the shortest and simplest spellings available. Where possible, silent letters ought to be dropped, as in **crum** and **scool**, and more phonetic alternatives chosen, e.g. **enuf** and **rime**. Despite the modest nature of these proposed changes, the *Handbook* claimed that around a hundred million dollars would be saved in teaching children to read and write – a figure based on the assumption that an entire year's worth of education would be saved in basic literacy instruction. But even this vast figure is nothing compared to the incalculable waste of nervous energy expended by both teachers and pupils forced to do battle in the spelling lesson, with its disruption of the otherwise orderly, reasonable and natural course of education.

Another objective of the Board's proposals was to combat the increasingly slovenly standards of spoken English, which they attributed to the failure to clearly signal the values of vowel sounds, especially those in unstressed syllables. According to the Board, the spelling system is the direct cause of the widespread 'tendency to slur over many sounds, to run words together, to adopt passing fads, and to create wide divergences in the English spoken not only in separate parts of the world, but in different sections of each country' (10).

In the published *Handbook*, the Board conceded that the original list of proposed reforms went too far and elected instead to concentrate on a smaller group of changes. Since acceptance of such changes relied upon precedent, the *Handbook* urged its readers to adopt as many of these simplified spellings as possible in their correspondence and, as far as possible, in print. The reforms themselves were set out in two ways: a series of rules followed by a list of dictionary entries containing words in frequent use. The rules consist of a series of changes to particular spelling conventions, such as the simplification of double consonants in words like **cigarette** and **glas** GLASS, the dropping of silent letters, such as the <b> in **det**, **dettour** and **dout** DEBT, DEBTOR, DOUBT and at the ends of **crum**

CRUMB and **thum** THUMB, and the <h> in **caracter, mecanic** and **stomac**. A number of instances involve the removal of silent <e> at the ends of words like **ar** ARE, **activ** ACTIVE, **twelv** TWELVE, **believ** BELIEVE, **wo** WOE, and in past-tense endings like **cald** CALLED and **sneezd** SNEEZED. Silent <e> is also dropped from words like **donky, vally** and **journy**. An attempt to regularise the spelling of words like BELIEVE and DECEIVE led to the re-spelling of the latter with medial <ie>: **deciev, reciev**, a change which would at least have removed the need for schoolchildren to learn the most famous of all spelling rules: 'i before e, except after c'. Other changes involve the use of <f> instead of <gh> in **cof** COUGH, **enuf** ENOUGH and **ruf** ROUGH, and the omission of the <h> in **gost** GHOST and **gerkin** GHERKIN. In words where the <ph> spelling is used to signal the /f/ sound, the *Handbook* proposes to spell them with <f> instead: **alfabet, emfasis** and **fotograf**. Similarly, the <rh> digraph is reduced to <r> in these proposals: **retoric, reumatism** and **rubarb**. The dictionary list that follows the rules contains a list of words to be included in school and desk dictionaries designed to meet the ordinary needs of students, the general public and professional men and women. Scanning this list highlights the lack of impact enjoyed by the Simplified Spelling Board and its published *Handbook*. The inclusion of a list of thirty of the most common words, available as a separate leaflet, was designed to enable supporters to make changes without first having to learn the various rules and the extensive list of proposed revisions. Although the majority of these proposed changes gained little or no traction, it is possible that the Board's proposals were responsible for the widespread adoption of some of the US spellings discussed above. The Google Books Ngram Viewer shows a decided spike in the use of **catalog** in American English in 1920, the year in which the *Handbook* was published. Similar peaks are recorded for other spellings espoused by the *Handbook* in 1920, such as **enuf** and **thoro**, but these tail off almost as suddenly as they appear. A spike in the instances of **telefone** in 1920 is followed by a sharp decline by 1930; a similar trajectory can be seen in the case of **journy**.

6.1 Global Englishes

In this chapter we have summarised the major differences between British and American spelling. But the English language is now used throughout the world; in this final section we will consider where other varieties of English are situated in relation to these British and American spellings.

Comparing instances of **colour** and **color** in the GloWbE corpus reveals a number of clear trends. Irish, Australian and New Zealand

Englishes prefer the British English spelling **colour**. Canadian English, usually thought to be closer to British than American usage, only shows a mild preference for **colour**, with 7,143 instances of this spelling against 5,252 of **color**. A clear preference for the American spelling is apparent in Indian English and in the Philippines, while other varieties show a roughly 50–50 use of both forms.

In the case of **theatre/theater**, most varieties show a preference for the British English spelling. As with the previous example, the British English form is found in Irish, Australian and New Zealand Englishes; in this instance, Canadian English is strongly in favour of this variant too. Even Indian English sides with British English here, with 2,463 examples of **theatre** and 788 of **theater**. Indeed, the only country that shows a preference for the American spelling is the Philippines, where we find 1,346 instances of **theater**, against 420 occurrences of **theatre**.

The British English spelling **catalogue** is similarly preferred by most other Global varieties over the American alternative **catalog**. Indian and Bangladeshi Englishes show a 50–50 split between the two spellings, while Pakistan and Malaysia are the two countries that show a distinct preference for **catalog** over **catalogue**. The American spelling **defense** is less popular than the British English **defence** in most Global varieties. The only exception to this is in the Philippines. In Canada the preference for British English **defence** is only slight, while similar numbers of both spellings are also recorded in Pakistan and Singapore. In the case of **grey/gray**, even American spelling is split, with 5,624 instances of British English **grey** against 7,840 of American English **gray**. Once again, we find most Global varieties of English preferring the British English alternative, apart from the Philippines, which is the one location where instances of **gray** outnumber those of **grey**.

7 Present-day English

Present-day English orthography is highly standardised so that most individual words have a single acceptable spelling. However, there are a number of specific areas in which variation continues to appear, and others in which we are witnessing change. As Stubbs (1992: 221) writes: 'One stereotype of English spelling is that it is highly standardized, has been that way since the mid-1700s, and is now highly stable. In fact, some aspects are undergoing rapid change'.

One ongoing area of uncertainty concerns the correct spelling of words that have been transliterated into English from languages with non-Roman alphabets. An example of this is the word for the thin, round Indian crisp bread which can be spelled **poppadom**, **poppadum**, **pappadam**, **papadum**, or **papadam**. Although it is first recorded in English in the early nineteenth century, the spelling of this word has not yet been fully regularised. The *OED*, while conceding that the word can be found in a large number of different spellings, suggests that the preponderance of usage strongly supports the spelling **poppadom**, which is selected for the headword. This is not supported by the spelling adopted by a leading manufacturer, however, which instead uses the form **pappadum**.

As well as the ongoing variation that is tolerated in a small number of words, there is evidence of change in progress. A good example of this is the word **supersede**, which is commonly spelled **supercede**. This change in usage is presumably driven by analogy with verbs like **precede**, **recede** and **intercede**. The difference in spelling between these two groups, however, reflects a difference in etymology. The origin of **supersede** is Latin **super + sedeo**, whereas **precede**, **recede** and **intercede** are derived from Latin **cedere** 'to go'. While this spelling distinction reflects the ultimate Latin etymology, the spelling **supercede** has been in common use since the seventeenth century. While the word does indeed have a Latin root, it entered English from French, where it was spelled both **superseder** and **superceder**, so that there is no etymological justification for retaining the **supersede** spelling in favour of the increasingly widespread form

supercede. Its increasingly wide usage is recognised by Dictionary.com, which labels it 'a frequent misspelling of supersede'; the Merriam-Webster online dictionary is more accepting, labelling it an alternative spelling.

A further way in which spelling is changing today is the influence of US conventions. One example of this is the way in which the US spelling **program** has replaced the standard British English spelling **programme** in all senses relating to computing. The **program** spelling is the earlier of the two; it was replaced by **programme** under the influence of the French word in the nineteenth century. Since the 1940s, however, it has become usual to use the US spelling **program** when referring to the series of coded instructions that direct a computer operation, while the British English spelling **programme** is used for all other senses of the word. The *OED* quotations given for other senses, however, show variation between **programme** and **program**, suggesting that the US form may be becoming more dominant in other areas as well.

Another example of the influence of US spelling concerns the spelling of **practice/practise**. The source of both words is the verb **practise**, which was derived from a French word **practiser** 'to strive' in the fifteenth century, pronounced with the stress on the second syllable. The noun was derived from the verb and was originally spelled **practise**; it was subsequently given the <–ice> ending to bring it into line with words like **justice**, **cowardice** and **malice**, where the <–ice> ending derives from the Latin suffix <–itia>. While this allowed a written distinction between the two words, the two spellings were effectively interchangeable until the eighteenth century. To make matters more complicated, the pronunciation of the verb also changed, with the stress shifting to the first syllable, so that the two words became interchangeable in speech too. Since the nineteenth century, the single spelling **practice** has been used for both noun and verb in the US, while the distinction between **practice** (n.) and **practice** (v.) has been maintained in British English. The influence of US usage, however, can be regularly seen in the widespread tendency to use **practice** for the verb in British English. An alternative tendency sees the spelling **practise** being adopted for both noun and verb in the UK.

Spelling online

The influence of US English is no doubt the result of its dominance in online usage. Indeed, online communication is the domain where there is the greatest amount of change in spelling in Present-day English. Attitudes towards correct spelling vary greatly depending on the user and the online platform. An online style guide composed in the late 1990s called upon its readers to 'anticipate the future' by adopting neologisms, simplifying spellings, avoiding capitals and removing hyphens from compound words. The guide also exhorts users to 'Be irreverent' by playing around with grammar and syntax and appreciating unruliness. It is striking that this call to irreverence does not extend to spelling and punctuation. Indeed, this call to playfulness and anti-authoritarianism is balanced by a call for caution in light of the global nature of online usage. A later precept refers to this global nature of online usage, reminding users of the importance of correct spelling and accent marks when using foreign words – 'don't be lazy or xenophobic'. This example neatly captures the very different attitudes that users have towards spelling in the online medium. For some, online usage is a platform in which standard spelling rules do not apply, or where they can be freely repurposed in creative ways. For others, however, there should be no such relaxation of rules online; all electronic usage should be subject to the same standards of spelling, with misspellings and typos being treated with the same level of scorn as in the printed medium.

There are a number of ways in which online communication breaks with the conventions of standard English. For instance, a salient feature of early text messaging was its use of abbreviations and logograms, such as the letter <u> to represent the second person pronoun YOU, or the numerals <2> and <4> in place of TO and FOR. Along with these, we find the replacement of syllables with numerals, as in words like **4ever** and **gr8** and **cu l8r** SEE YOU LATER. Also characteristic of this register is the use of contractions in which letters, particularly vowels, are dropped in order to save space and time, as in **pls** PLEASE, **tmrw** TOMORROW, **msg** MESSAGE and **tx** THANKS. Another feature associated with this mode of communication is the deliberate employment of non-standard spellings, such as **coz** BECAUSE, **skool** SCHOOL, **sum** SOME, **thru** THROUGH, **wot** WHAT. In an early study of texting, David Crystal (2008b: 37–52) noted that all these devices could be paralleled in earlier modes of discourse. The use of logograms is part of the lengthy tradition of word play common to the wider European linguistic tradition, while contractions and clippings are employed as standard abbreviations in numerous formal registers, such as in forms of address, e.g. the clipped spellings **Mr** and **Mrs**, **Sgt** and **Lt**, or in weights and measures, e.g. **mm** MILLIMETRE, **oz** OUNCE, **ft** FOOT. Non-standard spellings like **cos**, **wot** and **luv** can be traced back to the nineteenth century, while spellings like **skool** are familiar from graffiti and comic books. Crystal set out to debunk the popular belief that texting had evolved as an entirely new phenomenon, full of abbreviations and deviant uses of language, and which was fostering a decline in literacy, especially among the teenagers who were the most prolific users of this technology. His analysis concluded that distinctive linguistic features were only found in a tiny proportion of text messages (Crystal 2008b: 9). Furthermore, research into children's literacy suggests that the language play represented by the use of logographs and non-standard spellings actually facilitates rather than hinders literacy. A study by researchers at Coventry University, while finding no negative effects from the use of logograms and abbreviations, went on to suggest that playful experimentation of this kind, in a context where standard English is not required, could have a beneficial effect. Texting increases a child's exposure to text at a key stage in the acquisition of literacy, while the employment of abbreviations aids the development of phonological awareness. Research has also found that young adults who report the frequent use of 'textisms' – abbreviations and acronyms – typically do not make any use of such devices in formal or even informal writing (Pan et al. 2021).

Naomi S. Baron (2008: 60–2) subjected the linguistic habits of her students when using Instant Messaging to analysis and received similar results to Crystal. She discovered that abbreviations and acronyms were rarely found, while contractions appeared less commonly than in the spoken language. A striking feature of Baron's findings was the small number of spelling mistakes: only 1 spelling mistake appeared for every 12.8 transmissions. More than a third of these errors involved the omission of apostrophes, while the remainder were usually the result of an omitted or superfluous letter, phonetic spellings or the confusion of homonyms, such as **real** and **reel**. Furthermore, 9% of these errors were self-corrected, suggesting that these students retain a clear sense that Instant Messaging belongs to the formal written mode rather than to the less formal mode of spoken discourse. This led Baron to conclude that, despite its more casual and informal style, Instant Messaging was still associated with the formal domain of written usage and correct spelling.

Sali Tagliamonte and Derek Denis (2008) set out to analyse teenagers' use of non-standard features in Instant Messaging as part of a study called Teen Talk in Toronto, carried out between 2004 and 2006. A novelty of their approach was that the fieldwork and data collection was carried out by two teams of teenagers from high schools within the Toronto District School Board. This enabled it to be a more authentic set of data than those collected by researchers themselves, since it is teens interacting with teens. The survey found that abbreviations, short forms and symbolic uses were much rarer than is usually suggested in the negative portrayal of such usage in the mainstream media. For instance, the standard spelling **you** was far more popular than **u**. However, in contrast, the majority of individuals used the lowercase **i** instead of **I** for the first-person singular pronoun. Having selected one preferred form, however, the teenagers did not vary between the two alternatives. The text messages collected were characterised by numerous typos, misspellings, numeric forms and a tendency to employ lower case, along with swear words and colloquialisms. Also characteristic of this mode of writing was the use of expressive lengthening, in spellings like **aaaaaagh**, as well as abbreviations like **ttyl** and **lol**. The researchers concluded that the discourse of Instant Messaging is best categorised as a hybrid register, comprising a mixture of features drawn from the informal spoken register and those from a more formal one.

In *Language and the Internet* (2006), David Crystal highlighted the way in which chatgroups, blogs and virtual worlds make use of non-standard spellings that reflect pronunciation, e.g. **yep, yup, yay, nope, noooo**, and **kay** or **sokay** for IT'S OK. He also showed how the level of emotional distress, excitement and shock could be expressed quite subtly by varying the numbers of vowels and consonants, e.g. **aaaiiieee** and **yayyyyyy**. Crystal also noted how alternative spellings, such as **phreak** FREAK, **kool, fone** PHONE, have become standard usage in the online world. But, while this may have been true in 2009, a number of such forms, including **d00dz** DUDES, **l0zers** LOSERS and **c%l** COOL, have a distinctly dated feel today. Crystal cites the spelling **k-kool** as evidence of the use of <k> as an emphatic prefix. While *Urban Dictionary* does include an entry for **kkool**, which it defines as 'used to express one's satisfaction or a significant amount of amusement', it also includes the second sense 'used to sarcastically express above emotions', suggesting that it may have reached the end of its lifespan as a positive term. It has been largely replaced today by the abbreviated form **kk**, used to mean 'ok' or 'sure', which *Urban Dictionary* claims 'avoids any suggestion of sarcasm or doubt'. In more specialised chatgroups Crystal found that misspellings quickly attract privileged status, functioning as an in-group language that must be learned by newcomers in order to gain acceptance.

Crystal's analysis of email, where messages are usually planned and proofread more scrupulously, found that creative re-spelling was less common. However, Crystal did conclude that misspellings are a natural feature of the message itself, regardless of the educational background of the writer. This, he claimed, is the natural outcome of a mode of communication that is carried out quickly; usually, the presence of such errors causes little disruption to the message itself. According to Crystal, no reader would make a social judgement about the educational ability of the sender on the basis of such errors; he contrasts this with a traditional letter containing such errors, where such normative attitudes are common. In a footnote, Crystal notes that just two of fifty messages in his inbox contain spelling mistakes. But such data is potentially misleading, since anyone writing to one of the English language's foremost linguists is likely to proofread their message extremely carefully.

McCulloch (2019: 215) suggests that, while email may be a kind of informal writing, addressed to a controllable number of recipients, it is nevertheless usually subjected to a degree of editing. By contrast, text messages are much more informal in their language use and therefore less prone to self-editing. This is a reflection of the speed with which conversations can take place using this medium, and the fact that they are often addressed to a single individual. As well as being more tolerant of typographical mistakes, text messages can even be self-corrected in a follow-up message. If you send a message in which a spelling error might create confusion, a quick follow-up clarification can remove any possible misinterpretation.

McCulloch has also suggested that the widespread adoption of emoji pictograms and gifs has had an impact on the use of abbreviations, acronyms and creative re-spellings intended to express emotions. For instance, the Laughing with tears of joy emoji is now frequently employed as an alternative to the earlier acronyms **LOL** 'laughing out loud' and **LMAO** 'laughing my ass off', as well as lengthened spellings like **hahaaa**.

Similar conclusions were drawn in a study by Jacob Eisenstein and Umashanthi Pavalanathan, who examined a Twitter database containing messages posted between February 2014 and August 2015 to consider how the adoption of emojis affected the use of other non-standard features, such as emoticons, creative re-spellings and alternative punctuation. It found that people who use emojis frequently rely less on emoticons, repeated letters, acronyms and creative re-spellings. All forms of non-standard writing are losing out to emojis. Non-standard spellings can often be used as 'paralinguistic cues', used to replicate non-verbal elements of communication: modifying meaning, conveying emotion and interpersonal attitudes. These include expressive lengthening and capitalisation of spelling to create emphasis or shift tone, along with phonetic spelling to signal a specific pronunciation. Emojis are becoming the dominant mode of signalling attitude and reflecting non-linguistic information. In some cases, this may be simply the process by which a cruder emoticon, such as the heart-shaped <3 or smiling and winking ;) emoticons, are being replaced by their emoji equivalents. But even non-standard spellings, such as the expressive spellings **coooooollll** and **Ahhhh** were found to disappear with the increased use of emojis, even in cases where no obvious emoji equivalent exists. The authors conclude that, if these trends continue, 'emojis may be a socio-technical solution to the "problem" of non-standard orthography'. Despite this, the phenomenon of lengthening words by repeating letters in order to create emphasis appears to be very prominent in electronic communication today. Although it is often considered to be a recent development, it is an expressive tool that has been in use for centuries (McCulloch, 119). Tyler Schnoebelen (2012) explored this phenomenon of 'expressive lengthening' in a study of nearly 4 million tweets posted between January and June 2011. Setting out to study the use of emoticons, Schnoebelen was struck by the frequency with which users repeated the final letters of words such as **aww, hmmm, ohhh, sooo**, noting that such usages tended to be more prominent in private texts than in public posts.

Another, more specialised category of online usage concerns the use of misspellings to create a particular effect or personality. For instance, the Twitter handle @jonnysun, who describes himself as 'an aliebn confused abot humamn lamgauge', employs creative misspellings and acronyms, while shunning capitalisation and punctuation to create his persona. Followers tweet back in 'aliebn-speak', a kind of linguistic game which McCulloch (2019: 60) likens to a familect. The popularity of this mode of communication resulted in the publication of a book called *Everyone's a Aliebn When Ur a Aliebn Too* (2017).

Another specialised example of creative re-spelling which has become a language in itself is Lolspeak. This began life as a website which posted images of cats with text overlaid, typically written using non-standard spelling and grammar. The website took its domain name from one of the early memes: the question 'I can has cheezburger?' with the use of <z> for [z], which is a distinctive feature of the spelling of Lolspeak. We can see this if we look at an extract from the translation of the Bible that was made into Lolspeak. Here is John 3:16, rendered into this mode of communication:

> So liek teh Ceiling Kitteh lieks teh ppl lots and he sez 'Oh hai I givez u me only kitteh and ifs u beleeves him u wont evr diez no moar, kthxbai!'

Here we see a number of features that are common to online usage: **teh** for THE, **u** for YOU and contractions such as **ppl** PEOPLE, **wont** WILL NOT and **evr** EVER, with no apostrophes to signal the omissions. But, alongside these familiar features, are others that are most distinctive to this particular genre of writing. These include the use of <z> in **givez** GIVES and **diez** DIES, the phonetic representing of the diphthongs in **liek** LIKE and **moar** MORE and the single word **kthxbai**, which runs together three words in standard English: OK, THANKS, BYE.

The extent to which spelling has been standardised, and the way in which variant spellings are characterised as errors or deviant forms, has meant that there has been comparatively little study of such variation by sociolinguists. An important exception is the work of Mark Sebba, who has identified two different kinds of variation in spelling: licensed and unlicensed. Licensed variation is found where the conventional forms admit a choice between two acceptable alternatives, as in the case of **judgement** and **judgment**. Unlicensed variation refers to ways in which conventions of correct spelling can be broken in a way that still allows the meaning of the word to be understood, as in **skool** SCHOOL or **woz** WAS. An additional aspect of this unlicensed variation is the conveyance of an additional social meaning which derives from the deliberate contravention of the norms of standard orthography. Central to Sebba's survey of modern spelling habits, in English and in a range of languages, is the notion that 'where there is variation, there is in practice always social meaning' (Sebba 2007: 32).

Sebba offers helpful ways of categorising the most common strategies for employing spelling variation. The first category involves spellings that exploit genuine sound-symbol correspondences, but uses them in environments where they are not usual, as in the examples of **skool** and **woz** cited above. These are termed 'grapheme substitutions' by Androutsopoulos (2000); they include examples like **phreak** and **fone** discussed earlier. This has been a standard feature of much conventional graffiti of the 'I woz here' variety; recently it has become particularly popular among parents keen to give their children unusual names. These are usually re-spelled using this same practice, so that we find Alexander rendered Alexzander, Emily as Emmalee, Chloe as Khloe and Mia as Myah. A similar strategy has been embraced by the food industry in the United States, where brand names are often spelled and punctuated in unusual ways. In a blog post titled 'Phood for Thought', Nancy Friedman cites examples like Cheez-It crackers, Chik'n Wyngz and Kandy Kakes. Friedman suggests that phonetic spellings like these stand out from the competition and give the brand the advantages of 'distinctiveness and memorability'. Employing weird and wonderful spellings in brand names is not a new phenomenon. Louise Pound (1925) traced the prolific use of the letter <k> in trade names and by advertisers in the 1920s, arguing that such simplified spellings were the most significant legacy of the movement to reform spelling. Pound predicted that the widespread use of this gimmick by businesses like Korrect Koats, Kiddies' Koveralls and Keene's Kwality Kandies meant that, in the future, such novelty – or 'klever koinages of kommerce' – would no longer be sufficient to stand out from the crowd. Davies (1987: 48) has noted that, in some instances, unconventional spellings have become a convention in themselves, so that they simply function as a means of flagging its status as a trade name. Attempts to stand apart from spelling conventions reflect a desire to become distinctive as well as a belief that more unusual spellings are more memorable.

A second category comprises re-spellings that reflect non-standard pronunciations. Sebba cites examples from the [h]-less pronunciation of HERE, **ere**, found in informal speech, as well as the spelling **eya**, reflecting a northern English dialectal pronunciation. Recent studies have helped to reinforce Sebba's identification of this category. Despite its global reach, language used on social media has been found to vary according to region. While many researchers have treated this as a single, uniform dialect, Jacob Eisenstein and his co-researchers (2014) discovered that the abbreviation **ikr** I KNOW RIGHT was especially popular in the Detroit area, where it appears six times more frequently than in the United States overall. Similarly, the phonetic spelling **suttin** SOMETHING was found five times more frequently in New York City than in the US data as a whole. This was based on a study of a corpus comprising 107 million messages posted on Twitter, from 2.7 million unique user accounts, between 2009 and 2012.

In a similar way, Rachel Tatman (2015) found that spellings like **awn** OWN, **awlso** ALSO, **becawse** BECAUSE were especially common in Southern American English and African American English, along with r-deletion in **foah** FOR, **yeah** YEAR and **da** and **dat** for THE and THAT. These re-spellings were evidently intended to reflect the local pronunciation more closely. There is also evidence of spellings that reflect a Scots pronunciation, as signalled in messages that make use of **tae** and **dae** for TO and DO, **ye** YOU and **oan** ON (see Corbett and Stuart-Smith 2012).

The third category identified by Sebba includes single letters of the alphabet or non-alphabetic symbols as substitutions. This category comprises the examples we have noted in which the letter **u** comes to stand for the word YOU, **2** for TO, **4** for FOR and the numeral **8** for the sequence [eɪt] in words like **gr8**.

The fourth group is concerned with the use of archaic or pseudo-archaic spellings. Historically, this has been a feature of personal names where the spelling is widely divergent from the current pronunciation. These are usually of Norman French origin and so attest to an ancient lineage that carries cultural capital. Examples include Beauchamp, Cholmondely, Colquhoun and Featherstonehaugh. Today it is more commonly found in the varied attempts to offer quaint spellings of common given names, in an effort to make them stand out. Carney (1994: 449) captures this significance well when he labels surnames 'totem-poles of language' and suggests that it is the pressure of 'distinctive function' that drives the search for unusual and distinctive spellings in personal names.

Sebba concedes that variant spellings drawn from these four categories are largely restricted to marginal literacies, such as graffiti, computer-mediated communication and SMS text messaging. By contrast the world of the authorised media, encompassing printed books, newspapers and official documents, is dominated by the highly regulated standard spelling system. But, in the fifteen years since Sebba's book was published, electronic media have become increasingly central and new platforms have emerged. Just a year after the publication of Sebba's book, the micro-blogging site Twitter was founded, in which these orthographic strategies have become highly visible, especially given the restricted character limit of individual posts. Sebba introduces a distinction between regulated and unregulated spaces within the domain of orthography, locating the unregulated space on the margins, both orthographically and socially. While this seems an appropriate model for understanding the place of graffiti, private letters and diaries, fanzines and dialect literature, it is less satisfactory when considering the role that electronic communication plays in society today.

One final aspect of electronic usage that plays an important role in spelling today is the spellchecker, which identifies errors and proposes alternatives. One obvious potential impact of such tools on spelling today is to make the traditional learning of spelling in schools less important. Why spend hours learning the various irregularities that bedevil English spelling if a computer can do it for you? Recent research has confirmed that spellcheckers have indeed brought about higher standards of spelling, reducing the prevalence of spelling mistakes in student essays. Lunsford and Lunsford (2008) compared their data from a study carried out in 1988 (Connors and Lunsford 1988) and found that spelling mistakes had fallen from the most common type of error recorded to only the fifth most common. However, students were frequently found to have employed a correctly spelled word that was used incorrectly, such as **brake** instead of **break** (Pan et al. 2021). This evidence shows both the benefits of spellcheck in ironing out common spelling mistakes and the pitfalls associated with relying upon it too heavily. If a word is correctly spelled, it is likely that spellcheck will not identify whether it is the correct word for the context. Another study noted various other aspects of writing that are commonly not captured by spellcheck software, including incorrect capitalisation and mistakes using punctuation (Lunsford and Lunsford 2008).

As well as influencing standards of spelling today, spellcheckers may be influencing the spellings we use. Gretchen McCulloch (2019: 46) argues that spellcheckers have brought about a change in the British English use of <–ise> and <–ize> in words like **organise** and **analyze**. Where US English prefers to use <z> in such words, British English has traditionally employed both <–ise> and <–ize> spellings. According to McCulloch, the tendency for spellcheckers to insist on consistency in such words within a single document has prompted an increase in the use of <–ise> endings among British English users. At the same time, the tendency for a squiggly red line to appear under spellings like **analyze** serves to reinforce the sense that this and other <–ize> spellings belong to US English. Anne Curzan has noted how Microsoft Word and other word processing software packages are transparent about which dictionaries their spellchecker draws upon in a way that they are not about their grammar-checking facility (Curzan 2014: 67). But most users are unaware of this information and are unlikely to question the authority of the squiggly red line, or to suspect that there may be more than one correct possibility. As such, it is likely that the preferences of the spellchecker will become more and more significant in the way spelling develops in the future.

8 Spelling Scots

In Present-day Scotland there are speakers of Southern Standard British English, largely English immigrants and members of the Scottish aristocracy, and others who speak Scottish Standard English, essentially Standard English spoken with a Scottish accent. In both cases, the written form of the language is Standard English and follows the conventions of spelling associated with that written variety. The third group of speakers employ Scots, a variety originally in use throughout the Lowlands of Scotland, from where it has also spread into parts of the north-east. It is the history of the spelling of this language that will be the subject of this chapter.

8.1 History

The history of the Scots language is divided into three major periods: Old Anglian, Older Scots and Modern Scots. During the first of these periods the language formed part of the Old English dialect continuum, reflecting many of the same features found in the Old Anglian dialect of Old English (see Chapter 1). This was the variety spoken by the Angles who invaded Britain in the fifth century AD, and who settled in the north, reaching Scotland by the seventh century. The northern counties of England and the lowlands of Scotland were part of a single Anglian kingdom of Northumbria, which became distinct from the Anglian dialect used in the Midland kingdom of Mercia, which is now known as Old Mercian. The distinction between these two dialects was greatly increased by interaction with the Scandinavian language spoken by the Vikings who settled in an area known today as the 'Great Scandinavian Belt' which crossed the north of England (particularly the counties of Lancashire and Yorkshire) and which triggered major linguistic changes (Samuels 1989).

The Norman Conquest that led to the dominance of French in England during the Middle English period had a similar effect in Scotland, with Scottish kings preferring French language and culture. In Scotland, the dominance of French was also at the expense of Gaelic, a Celtic language spoken in the north and on the islands. The suppression of Gaelic created a space for the corresponding expansion of Scots, which became well established as a vernacular in lowland Scotland, later replacing Gaelic in northern parts of the country as well.

Use of the Scots vernacular as a literary language began to flourish in the fourteenth century, as there was a shift from writing in the languages of the elite: French and Latin. During this period prestigious documents, including legal and other official records and literary writings, began to be composed and recorded in a language known at the time as 'Inglis'. This term highlights the extent to which writers in Older Scots considered their language to be part of the same literary language that was used by southern English poets of the period, such as Geoffrey Chaucer. It is not until the late fifteenth century that writers like Gavin Douglas began to refer to their language as a distinct Scottish vernacular, for which they adopted the label 'Scottis'. Up to this point, Scottis was used to refer to Gaelic. Inglis was spoken widely in lowland Scotland and differed strikingly from the Gaelic language that was employed in the Highlands and on the western Isles. As part of its wider elaboration, Scots was used in writing, as the language of record of parliamentary proceedings, and for national literary monuments, such as Barbour's *The Bruce*, composed in 1375. Other major literary writers from the Older Scots period include Robert Henryson and William Dunbar; a further important work is *The Kingis Quair*, composed by James I of Scotland during a period of exile in England.

This language developed out of the Northumbrian dialect of OE, which itself was influenced by practices employed by scribes trained in monasteries in Ireland. Irish influence can be seen in the spelling conventions found in Old Northumbrian, such as in the practice of employing <th> and <u> instead of thorn and wynn, e.g. **uundra, tha**; by the tenth century, Old Northumbrian had also adopted thorn and wynn, in line with southern practice. Another difference in convention from West-Saxon is the use of <ch> instead of West-Saxon <h> to mark the velar fricative /x/, e.g. **lecht, inlichtet**, both recorded in the glosses to the Lindisfarne gospels. The influence of Scandinavian on the Northumbrian dialect is apparent in the use of <ai> to mark [aː], which spread from Scandinavian loanwords to ones from the Old English lexicon. Other differences in spelling that mark off the northern dialect from its southern counterpart include the representation of the reflex of Old English <hw>, which was written as <qu, qw, qwh> from the end of the thirteenth century. Words from OE with <cw> were written with <wh> in this area, so that <qu> and <wh> appear as allographs for both OE /hw/ and /qw/. Intervocalic /f/, usually <u> in ME, is sometimes <f> in the northern dialect, e.g. **luf** LOVE, **gif** GIVE, **haf** HAVE; at other times, the <f> is doubled: **luff, giff, haff**. This development probably represents a voiceless final consonant, distinct from the voiced equivalent attested in southern Middle English **loue** and **yeue**. In initial position, <w> sometimes has the allograph <v>, e.g. **Valter**, while ME /v/ may be represented by <w>: **Prowost**. As a consequence <w, v, u> could represent /u, w, v/, e.g. **wpon, vpon, upon**. This use of <w>, also attested in spellings like **ws** US and **cwmyn** COME, seems to be a peculiarly Scottish development.

Older Scots also made use of the letters thorn and yogh found in Middle English. In the northern dialects of ME and in most varieties of Older Scots, the letter thorn was written identically to <y>. According to Benskin (1977: 507), the only Scots texts that make a distinction are ones that originate in Dumbarton and Glasgow. An exception is the Scone Glosses (c. 1350), a Latin document with vernacular equivalents of names added in the margins, where an attempt has been made to distinguish thorn and <y> by using a superposed dot to mark the latter, although this diacritic has often been misplaced, perhaps indicative of a system that was breaking down. Another text that does make an effort to distinguish <y> and thorn is the manuscript of the *Kingis Quair* (Bodleian Library MS Arch Selden B.24), though the distinction is limited to a restricted set of words. In his study, Benskin notes that the use of a y-shaped thorn was restricted to word-initial voiced contexts, e.g. THEY, THEN, THERE, apart from in medial contexts immediately followed by a suspension; elsewhere <th> is used. After both the y-shaped thorn and the yogh, it was common to add an <h>, e.g. **yhow** THOU, **ʒheris** YEARS.

Since the earliest Scottish printers of the late fifteenth century imported their fonts from abroad, they replaced thorn and yogh with <y> and <z> respectively, e.g. in **ye** THE and the personal name Menzies. As happened in ME, the y-shaped thorn was replaced in all instances by the digraph <th>, although a number of idiosyncratic practices are recorded in the spelling habits of certain individuals. John Knox used <ht> in place of <th> in **pleaseht** PLEASES, while Marion Home employed <tht> in **batht** 'both'.

Older Scots included two consonants that have not survived into Present-day Scots; these are the n-mouillé and l-mouillé which were found in words borrowed from French and Gaelic. The n-mouillé, found today in French words like **ligne** LINE, was represented in spelling by <nʒ, ngʒ, ng, nyh>, e.g. **fenʒeit**. The process of assimilation into Scots meant these consonants became accommodated to more familiar ones; the n-mouillé came to be replaced by /nj/ and /ŋ/. The l-mouillé, /ʎ/, was spelled <lʒ, lʒh, hlʒ>, as in **bailʒe** BAILIFF; it was later assimilated to /lj/ and spelled <ly>.

There are a number of additional features that distinguish the spelling of Older Scots from southern varieties of Middle English. We have already noted a distinction in the representation of the /x/ sound, which came to be spelled in a variety of ways, e.g. <quh, qwh, qh, qhu, qhw>. In words like WHICH and WHO, the spellings show a continuum from Southern ME to Northern ME and Older Scots: **which** (Southern ME), **whilk** (Northern ME), **quhilk** (Older Scots); **who** (Southern ME), **wha** (Northern ME), **quha** (Older Scots). Where the /x/ phoneme was followed by /t/, in words like NIGHT, MIGHT, TAUGHT, it was spelled <ch>, e.g. **nicht, micht, taucht**; this replaced an earlier usage in which the sound was spelled <h>. Where this sound was lost in Middle and Early Modern English, it has been retained in Scots, e.g. **loch**; however, the sound is often replaced with /k/ by younger speakers. The <ch> digraph was also used to represent the sound /tʃ/, as in **wich** WITCH. The influence of words borrowed from Old Norse, showing a pronunciation difference whereby Old English /tʃ/ was pronounced with /k/, means that Older Scots has examples such as **kirk**, where ME has **chirch**. In the earlier period, we find <sc> for /ʃ/, which was later replaced by <sch>, a convention found south of the border, where it came to be replaced by <sh>. In unstressed positions, this sound was also spelled <s>, <ss>, while <s> was used for /s/ in **sall** SHALL and **suld** SHOULD.

In Older Scots the fronted reflex of ME /oː/, pronounced /øː/ and subsequently /yː/, was spelled <u>, as in **fut** FOOT and **buk** BOOK; the same letter was used in French borrowings, like **duk** DUKE. This ambiguity probably led to the introduction of alternative conventions, such as <Ce> in **fute**, and <ui, uy> e.g. **guid**. The <ui> convention is a later development, first appearing at the end of the fifteenth century. Although it is generally perceived to be distinctively Scottish, it spread to Older Scots from the north of England. Both these conventions, the use of <e> at the end of a word and the addition of an <i> after the vowel, were used in Older Scots as methods of indicating a long vowel, e.g. **stane, stain** STONE.

A process known as l-vocalisation was responsible for the creation of long vowels in Older Scots. This can be seen by comparing the earlier spelling **full** with later Scots **fow**, pronounced as /fuː/, showing the loss of the /l/ and a compensatory lengthening process. Although this process began in the fifteenth century, it took some time for the change to be reflected in spelling at the ends of words, so that **hall** HALL and **haw** LIVID, continued to be distinguished in spelling. Another change was the loss of /v/, also with compensatory lengthening, as seen in words like **deill** /diːl/ DEVIL.

OE ā and Old Norse á were fronted to /aː/ in Scots and Northern ME, spelled **stane, baith, lang, auld**; in southern dialects these sounds were raised and rounded, and spelled <o(o)>, e.g. **stoon, ston**. The process of fronting attested by the Northern and Scots spellings probably arose through contact between English and Norse speakers, since earliest examples are found in the Great Scandinavian Belt (See Samuels 1989). An exception to this usual practice is the word **laird**, which is often replaced by the southern spelling **lord**, even when <a> is found in other OE ā words. It has been suggested that this is because the word was in frequent use as a term of formal address. In documentary evidence, where both spellings **laird** and **lord** appear, the two are distinguished semantically.

Kniezsa (1997: 40) includes a table which sets out a comprehensive series of diagnostic orthographic variants in Older Scots, and which effectively summarises the major points discussed above. Alongside this, she includes a list of the following high-frequency variants which can be expected to appear in many types of text and therefore help to distinguish one written in Older Scots: **bot** BUT, **amang** AMONG, **ony/mony** ANY/MANY, **Ingland** ENGLAND, **ane** AN, **sic/mekil** SUCH/MUCH, **cum** COME.

8.2 Standardisation

Just as with its contemporary form of Middle English south of the border, Older Scots showed considerable variation in spelling, some of which, but by no means all, points to differences in pronunciation. The *Dictionaries of the Scots Language* (DSL) entry for the word **stane** STONE includes the following spelling variants, testifying to a range of alternative pronunciations: **stanne, stain, stean, staen, stehn, sten, stein, steen, stene, steinie** and even **steenockie**. Macafee (2002) summarises the position in the following way: 'the spelling system was a perhaps extreme example of a common medieval European type, in which free variation was a prominent and important feature'. Some of this variation was inherited from the northern dialect of ME, while in other cases, such as the large interchangeable group of conventions for marking /xt/: <th, ch, tht, cht>, it was introduced from within the region. The tendency seems to have been towards an increase in variation, with new conventions typically supplementing rather than replacing existing ones. The only significant example of conventions that fell out of use during this period was the disappearance of <yh> and <ʒh> in the sixteenth century. Even southern English variants that were adopted during this period were typically employed alongside, rather than instead of, Scots equivalents, e.g. <sh> alongside <sch> and <gh> alongside <ch>.

As the function of the Middle English vernacular changed, so there was a shift towards the comparatively fixed spellings of PDE. However, Scots spelling never underwent this process of fixing according to educational norms, nor was it regulated in any official manner. This was in part due to the greater status attached to English, which dominated the more prestigious modes of writing from the sixteenth century onwards.[1] Rather than using 'standardisation' to describe this process in Scotland, some scholars prefer to employ the term 'anglicisation'. Thus, while de-anglicisation refers to the divergence from the northern ME dialect in the fifteenth century, anglicisation marks the convergence of these two triggered by the preference for ME variants over those distinctive of Older Scots. But, while these two processes, de-anglicisation and anglicisation, may superficially appear to be merely opposite sides of the same coin, they were motivated by very different factors. Where de-anglicisation had been driven by a desire for political and social independence, anglicisation was governed by functional rather than ideological reasons. The shift towards an anglicised variety focused on the southern English dialect was a response to what Meurman-Solin (1997: 3) has labelled a 'climate of consensus' which supported the rise of a 'multi-purpose regional norm standard'. Unlike south of the border, prestige was not a significant motivating factor; instead, it was socio-political factors that drove the changes in Scotland.

Therefore, instead of witnessing the establishment of a standard form of written Scots, Scotland saw a process of gradual anglicisation. This development was the result of social and political changes which included the Reformation and the Union of the English and Scottish Crowns in 1603, which saw James VI of Scotland ascend the English throne as James I. This led to the merging of the Scottish and English parliaments in 1707. As a direct consequence of these political changes, there was a gradual but clear shift away from a distinctive Scottish orthography to that of English, throughout the seventeenth century. The Scottish Enlightenment of the eighteenth century cemented Scottish Standard English as the prestige variety rather than Scots (Jones 1995).

Where Scots continued to be written during the sixteenth and seventeenth centuries, it was generally restricted to texts intended for a local audience. But, even private letters tended to witness a move away from Scots to English during this period. The spoken language was increasingly focused on the emerging standard associated with England. The diminished status of Edinburgh as a capital led to the establishment of

---

1. For the failure of this process of standardisation in Scotland, see Devitt 1989 and Meurman-Solin 1997.

the English accent as the prestige variety. An Edinburgh schoolmaster called William Perry authored a textbook called *The Only Sure Guide to the English Tongue* (1776), which set out to educate the young in a pronunciation that conformed with the polite speech heard in the city of London (Bann and Corbett 2015: 78).

It is natural to assume that Anglicisation refers to a simple process whereby English forms replaced Scots equivalents. But it was more complex than this, with hybrid forms emerging, in which Scots and southern English forms were merged, e.g. **quhom** WHOM, **quhois** WHOSE, **quheer** WHERE. In other cases, we find Scots forms being mixed with those typical of northern English dialects, e.g. **wha** WHO, **whaim** WHOM, **whilk** WHICH, a reminder that books introduced into Scotland were printed in York as well as London. Such forms are particularly common in high-style poetry, such as *The Kingis Quair*, Gavin Douglas's translation of the *Æneid* and poems by Dunbar and Lindsey.

Also instructive is the treatment of ME forms by the scribe of a significant manuscript collection of ME verse copied north of the border. This manuscript, Bodleian Library MS Arch Selden B.24, was written by a single copyist whose hand has been identified in a number of other Scottish collections: NLS MS Acc.9253, a collection of Latin and Scottish works, and in a copy of a printed edition of Mirk's *Festial*, now St John's College, Cambridge, MS G.19. The Arch Selden manuscript is significant as the sole surviving manuscript witness to *The Kingis Quair*, but it also preserves a complete rendering of Chaucer's *Troilus and Criseyde*, *The Legend of Good Women* and a version of the *Parliament of Foules* with a uniquely rewritten conclusion. In addition to these genuine Chaucerian works are shorter poems by the English writers Hoccleve, Lydgate and Walton, which have been attributed erroneously to Chaucer. Study of the 'Scotticisation' of Chaucer's Southern ME dialect by Boffey and Edwards (1999) has shown the complexity with which this process occurred. The text of Chaucer's *Legend of Good Women* in the Selden manuscript shows a pronounced replacement of Southern ME forms with those current in Older Scots, e.g. <cht> instead of <ght>, **airly** for **erly** EARLY, and **thaim/thame** and **thair** as replacements for **hem** and **hir**. But the text of *Troilus and Criseyde* has been subjected to a less thorough process of translation. Here we find some clearly Scots substitutions, such as the replacement of <wh> with <quh> and **their** for **hyr/her**; however, alongside these are certain ME forms that appear to have been deliberately preserved, e.g. **might** and **nyght** instead of **micht** and **nicht**. The lack of clear data about the distribution of certain forms considered by Boffey and Edwards may complicate the picture. The <sch> variant that they consider, for instance, is not limited to

Scotland in this period, but was in widespread use south of the border (Kniezsa 1997: 32). In attempting to explain this different attitude to the texts of Chaucer's poems, Boffey and Edwards suggest that the patchy distribution of Scots forms in *Troilus and Criseyde* may be explained by its appearance first in the manuscript. As proficiency in translating from one dialect to the other increased, so did the degree of consistency. An alternative possibility is that the different degrees of Scots forms across the texts reflect distinct patterns of transmission lying behind the exemplars employed by the Selden copyist. One further suggestion is that the Selden scribe was conscious of a need to preserve the English flavour of the writings of a ME poet, which acted as a brake on his process of rendering the spelling into Older Scots. Although this does not explain the relative degrees of Scotticisation across the Chaucerian texts in the manuscript, it does fit with the much more thorough-going translations found in later copies. The mixture of Middle English and Older Scots forms attested in Selden is found in copies of other Scots poems, such as the romance *Lancelot of the Laik*, whose spelling system has been characterised as 'neither Scottish nor English, but a curious mixture of the two' (Kniezsa 1997: 46). From such evidence it would appear that the adoption of this linguistic hybrid had become a deliberate choice by poets writing in Scotland during this period.

Variation in spelling remained the norm during this period of Anglicisation, with the particular mixture being determined by personal, diachronic or diatopic factors. The most strongly Anglicised texts were religious treatises, while the other end of the cline is represented by Scottish official papers, which remained most conservatively Scots in their spelling. Private writing continued to be resolutely mixed, and often reflected the upbringing and education of the individual. Most writers did not spell with a single fixed or self-consistent form; variation remained the norm. The tendency for writers to develop their own idiosyncratic spelling systems is apparent from a legal case dated to 1609, in which a writer's spelling habits, including the fact that he 'newir vseit to wrytt ane "ʒ" in the begynning of ony word, sik as "ʒow", "ʒouris", "ʒeild", "ʒea", and siclyk; bot ewir wrait "y" in steid of the said "ʒ", were used to ascribe unsigned five treasonous letters to his authorship' (Macafee 2002).

Legal terms typically show a greater preponderance of English spellings, e.g. **realm**, **seal**, **fee**, suggesting that they may have been borrowed in this form, rather than being the result of the more gradual process of Anglicisation. The distinction between public and private spelling habits is especially apparent in the works of the Scottish reformer John Knox. The printed editions of his works employed a number of English forms that are not attested in his manuscript writings (Bann and Corbett

2015: 59–60). Although these English forms may have been the work of his printers, they could also represent a deliberate decision by Knox to make his work appeal to the widest possible audience. Since the Bible itself was only available in English translations, it may be that English was considered to be the more authoritative vernacular, more suited to the transmission of religious discourse.

8.3 Revival

While Anglicisation was more or less complete by 1700, some Scots forms continued to appear in specific literary genres. At the beginning of the eighteenth century there was a vernacular revival in literary writing, associated in particular with the work of Robert Burns, that sparked a newfound interest in writing in the Scots language. Despite the Treaty of Union marking the transition of Scottish powers of lawmaking to Westminster, Scotland preserved its own legal system, while the General Assembly remained the governing body of the Church of Scotland. The bitter opposition to the Act of Union triggered efforts to express Scottish identity using the Scots language.

Those who continued to use Scots often drew upon historic practices to which they had access through printed versions of Older Scots texts, although some of these were issued with modernised orthography. In some cases, Scots spelling was achieved through the use of archaic features actually borrowed from Early Modern English. An example of this is *The Minstrelsy of the Scottish Border*, a collection of ballads compiled by Walter Scott, published in three volumes in 1802–3. The ballads present a mixture of distinctively Scots forms, e.g. **feir**, **rae**, alongside others, e.g. **foreste**, **manie**, **grete**, that are purely archaic (See Blake 1981: 137).

For others, the representation of their Scottish identity was achieved through the remodelling of standard English spelling to reflect a distinctively Scottish pronunciation. The spellings employed in the more ephemeral works issued as part of this vernacular revival – broadsides, collections of poems, pamphlets, journals and newspapers – established the conventions for writing in Scots in the serious prose works of the nineteenth century. The spellings employed by these texts are a mixture of Older Scots forms and those used in standard English. In many cases the mixture employed does not reflect a single consistent mode of pronunciation, but rather one that draws upon both Scots and English usages. The most celebrated poet of this period was Robert Burns, who drew upon the oral culture to produce collections of poetry in Scots. In the nineteenth century, Sir Walter Scott produced *Waverley* (1814), which included extensive use of Scots.

Although the use of Scots lexis is one way of marking a text out as Scots, this can result in problems of comprehension. To circumvent this problem, authors often resorted to the use of Scots spelling conventions. Although, paradoxically, since these conventions themselves were not well understood outside Scotland, some Scottish writers had to resort to employing English spelling conventions to represent Scots pronunciation if writing for a wider audience. An example of this is the use of spellings like **doon** DOWN, reflecting the use of the English <oo> digraph, as used in **soon**, to represent the Scots pronunciation /duːn/. More recently, writers like Tom Leonard have employed phonetic spellings such as **sumdy** SOMEBODY and **emdy** ANYBODY to convey Glasgow pronunciation to their readers (Macaulay 1991: 281).

In the eighteenth century, the Scottish printer Thomas Ruddiman (1674–1757) produced a critical edition of Gavin Douglas's Older Scots translation of Virgil's *Æneid* (1710), accompanied by a glossary to aid comprehension. The glossary is prefaced by an introduction that sets out to explain the conventions adopted, including the following account of the treatment of spelling:

> It is to be observed in the first place, That throughout the whole, the way of spelling is very far from being uniform; Which was the general fault of those and former times, especially among them who wrote in the Saxon, old Scots, and English Dialects: An imperfection which too much attends all living Languages; notwithstanding all the attempts of learned men to rectify it.

Ruddiman's response to these faults was to set out a series of his own preferred spelling practices, which were in turn influential in Allan Ramsay's treatment of spelling in *The Ever Green* (1723–4), a compendium of medieval Scottish verse edited by Ramsay. Jeremy Smith has compared Ramsay's representation of the spelling of the Older Scots works he prints with the original versions in the Bannatyne manuscript and Ramsay's transcription of them. Corrections in Ramsay's transcription show him gradually becoming accustomed to the Scots forms of his exemplar, so that **litle** is replaced by **lytill**, **she** with **scho** and **shall** with **sall**. Some English spellings, e.g. **again**, remain uncorrected, while others, e.g. **frae**, **tak**, **nowther**, appear in their Scots form in the original transcription. Strikingly, some of Ramsay's Scots forms are not attested by the manuscript exemplar from which he derived his texts at all, but instead appear to be a 'hyper-correction in the direction of a perceived more "authentic Scotticism"'. An example of this is Ramsay's replacement of the manuscript form **diuill** with **deil**, a form later sanctioned by its use by Robert Burns (Smith 2020b: 141–2).

During the twentieth century, there was an effort to create a new form of Scots that could carry prestige, known as 'Lallans', the revival of a term, meaning Lowlands, formerly used of the Scots language. Constructed by Hugh MacDiarmid and other Scottish writers, Lallans was a synthetic brand of Scots, formulated via a blending of various features of Scots, past and present. Despite his evident investment in promoting a constructed Scots, capable of full literary expression, MacDiarmid had little interest in the detail of spelling. Dorian Grieve has noted the inconsistency found in the spelling of MacDiarmid's poetry, where we find **guid** alongside **gude** and **good**; **change** and **cheenge**; **death** and **daith** (Grieve 2011: 31–2). In general, despite a disdain for his predecessor, MacDiarmid employed the spelling conventions adopted by Burns. Lallans remained somewhat restricted in its take-up, featuring only in certain literary contexts, and criticised by some writers for being a 'plastic' variety. Despite this, some of its later exponents attempted to codify its written conventions through the development of a style sheet which sets out a series of specific spelling preferences, such as the spellings **guid** GOOD, **aa** ALL, **nou** NOW and the dropping of apostrophes in words like **fa** FALL, **deil** DEVIL and **fin** FIND.

More recently, Scottish writers have attempted to make use of a more authentic Scots, reflecting actual usage, rather than a constructed version. An example of this is the highly successful novel *Trainspotting* (1993) by Irvine Welsh, which uses spellings such as **nae** NO, **dae** DO, **oan** ON, **wi** WITH, **goat** GOT, to convey the Edinburgh accents of its central characters. For such writers, the concern with spelling which occupied the Lallans movement was an object of ridicule, as in this caption from a cartoon by the Glasgow poet Tom Leonard (quoted in Bann and Corbett 2015: 90): 'Makars' Society Gran' meetin' the nicht tae decide the spellin' o' this poster. Admission: thritty pee (a heid)'. In 1948, the Makars' Club set out to establish a model of orthography that would unite the traditional spellings of Burns and others with the more radical models of contemporary writers. But this had limited impact outside a small, exclusive literary coterie.

Despite this, concern with establishing a standard written form of Scots continues today, especially in the work of the Scots Language Resource Centre, founded in the 1990s under the stewardship of J. Derrick McClure. Here, the motivation is a desire to imbue the Scots language with the level of prestige enjoyed by other national vernaculars, like English, which do have a fixed written form. It is striking that this movement is not concerned with the promotion of literacy in Scots; in fact, Scots publisher Itchy Coo, which produces early reading books for children, does not set out to establish a single set of spellings, believing instead that exposure to written Scots is more important than imposing a single set of correct forms. But, for reformers concerned with the status of Scots as a national language, the desire to establish a standard form is more concerned with promoting the cause of Scottish nationalism and establishing a Scottish identity.

The extent to which the identity of Scots orthography is bound up with its direct opposition to that of English is clearest in the directions issued in the report and recommendations of the Scots Spellin Camatee 1996–1998 concerning the 'Apologetic Apostrophe', which 'shuidna be uised ti shaw "missin" English letters, e.g. he'rt, ca', ha'e, wi' – but is better uised ti shaw missin Scots anes – e.g. 'im HIM, 'e HE, THE, 'is THIS etc. This haes the effect of lattin Scots by-leids be seen as dialects o Scots rather nor English'.[2] As McColl Millar explains, this use of the apostrophe is an unfortunate side-effect of the way Scots spelling developed, intended to make writings accessible to readers who were only literate in English, but which ends up representing Scots as a 'malformed variety of English' (McColl Millar 2018: 208). Like many such attempts to reform the spelling of English, the proposals that were devised have had little effect on wider usage. The withdrawal of the Scottish National Dictionary Association dealt the project a serious blow, and the Scots language remains caught between the conflicting requirements of those who would revive Scots as a vehicle for literary and cultural expression and those concerned to reintegrate it as a language for official administration and governance.

2. Report & Recommends o the Scots Spellin Comatee, November 1996–August 1998.

Part II

Perspectives

9 Prescriptivist attitudes to correct spelling

This chapter will focus on the ideology of standardisation, tracing changing attitudes towards a standard spelling system and attendant concepts of normativity. The beginnings of prescriptivism lie in the eighteenth-century concern with fixing, or 'ascertaining', the English language in order to halt any further change, which was understood to be detrimental to the language's status and utility. Comparing the vernacular with the more prestigious classical languages, Latin and Greek, highlighted the instability of its written form, since, while English was changeable, these two remained fixed. This is of course a false comparison; the reason that Latin and Greek were no longer changing was because they were no longer living languages. Furthermore, the apparent fixity of their written form was due to standardisation and the suppression of the natural variation found in other varieties. The variety with which eighteenth-century scholars were familiar represented an artificial standardised form of these languages, and not the variable forms that were in use during the Classical period.

In addition to the anxiety about the nature of the English language created by comparison with Latin and Greek, there was also a concern that English suffered by comparison with other European vernaculars, such as Italian, Spanish and French, whose use was regulated by academies. The Académie Française, for instance, had been set up in 1635 by Cardinal Richelieu and was tasked with regulating the French language, issuing edicts governing acceptable usage as determined by its body of académiciens, known as the 'immortals'. The French model inspired attempts to set up a parallel body in England to monitor and regulate English usage. In 1664 the Royal Society established a committee tasked with 'improving' the English language. Members of the committee, which included John Dryden and John Evelyn, debated the desirability and remit of an English Academy along the lines of that established in France. Although these discussions did not result in the formation of an academy, the idea of establishing an authoritative body to oversee the development of the language did not disappear. In an essay of 1697 Daniel Defoe called upon King William III to set up an academy 'to polish and refine the English Tongue', and to establish a 'Purity and Propriety of Stile, and to purge it from all the Irregular Additions that Ignorance and Affectation have introduc'd'. Membership of this academy would be drawn from gentlemen and members of the nobility, whose natural authority would discourage the coining of unlicensed words, which would be criminalised in the same manner as false currency.

In 1712, the writer Jonathan Swift directed 'A Proposal for the Correcting, Improving; and Ascertaining the English Tongue' to the Earl of Oxford, who was at that time the Lord Treasurer. Accepting that the Latin language underwent considerable change, Swift argued that it achieved 'great Perfection' before it began to decay. Similarly, despite the way the French had worked to polish their language in the previous fifty years, Swift felt it was then declining: the result of the inconstancy of the French nation and corruption introduced by recent authors. English has yet to achieve a similar 'Degree of Perfection'; if it could be refined to a similar standard, Swift suggested, it might be possible to fix it for ever, ensuring that its authors have a 'Chance of Immortality'. The focus of Swift's tirade is the adoption of new words and idioms, what he called 'affected Phrases and new, conceited Words', along with the tendency of poets to employ abbreviations. But he was also concerned about spelling and especially what he perceived to be the foolish opinion that spelling ought to be guided by pronunciation. Swift rightly recognised that this would obscure a word's etymological relations, that it would require frequent spelling reform to keep track of changes in pronunciation, and that different regions would require alternative spellings to reflect their local accents. Because of this, Swift claimed, it was already difficult to read many recent publications, since the words were 'so curtailed, and varied from their original Spelling, that whoever hath been used to plain *English*, will hardly know them by sight'. Swift called upon the Earl to establish an academy that would set down the rules of correct usage and help prevent further degeneration. The plan nearly succeeded, with the Earl having set aside a sum of money for the purpose of funding such an establishment. However, the publication of a series of grammar books, followed by Johnson's *Dictionary of the English Language*, led to the plan being shelved. For Lord Chesterfield, Philip Dormer Stanhope, a significant man of letters who had shown interest in the scheme, Johnson himself was a one-man academy; in his review of the published work Chesterfield surrendered all his 'rights and privileges' in the English language to Johnson's 'dictatorship'.

The eighteenth century also saw a growing concern with correct pronunciation. The concept of a single prestige accent had emerged gradually;

there are some traces of it in the Early Modern period. Looking back to late Middle English, we can see the emergence of the stigmatisation of certain regional accents. In the late fourteenth century, John Trevisa, translating into English a Latin chronicle called *Polychronicon* by Ranulph Higden, expanded on the negative remarks made by Higden relating to different accents of English. Where Higden merely observed the difficulties southerners have understanding northerners, Trevisa used the opportunity to offer a sustained critique of the northern dialect:

> Al þe longage of þe Norþhumbres, and specialych at 3ork, ys so scharp, slytting [piercing] and frotying [grinding], and unshape, þat we Souþeron men may þat longage unneþe [hardly] undurstonde. Y trowe þat þat ys because þat a buþ ny3 to strange men and aliens þat spekeþ strangelych, and also bycause þat þe kynges of Engelond woneþ alwey fer fram þat contray: For a buþ more y-turnd to the souþ.

Where Higden acknowledged dialect variation, Trevisa displays an intolerance and condemnation of the rough and harsh sounds of the speech of northerners.

But, while Trevisa's remarks suggest the emergence of negative attitudes towards different accents, no standard spoken variety of English had yet emerged. It is not until the sixteenth century that we meet with statements that imply a single accent is more socially desirable than the alternatives. In his *Orthographie*, discussed in detail in Chapter 11, John Hart observes that the 'flower' of speech is that of the city London. The clearest example of this is found in George Puttenham's *Arte of English Poesie* (1589) in which he advises young poets to base their rhymes upon the accent spoken at the London court and its environs: 'the vsual speech of the Court, and that of London and the shires lying about London within lx. miles and not much above'. For Puttenham this accent is not purely a geographical phenomenon; its use also has social connotations, since it is that employed by 'men civill and graciously behavoured and bred'. Despite this, Hart does show a tolerance of regional speech and its reflection in spelling. Since writers in Newcastle or Cornwall cannot be expected to have picked up the London accent, they should be able to devise their own orthography to reflect their native speech, since that is what will be spoken by their neighbours. A Londoner should be no more offended by such writing than if he were present to hear them speak.

Puttenham goes on to specifically warn against adopting the speech of a 'craftes man or carter, or other of the inferiour sort', 'for such persons do abuse good speaches by strange accents or illshapen soundes, and false ortographie'. The condemnation of their 'false ortographie' seems to imply criticism of their written language and specifically their spelling. However, this interpretation is somewhat undermined by the wider context, which is clearly focused on the spoken rather than written language. The reason for this is that Puttenham's criticism of a writer's orthography is focused on the pronunciation of the written word. This use of the word orthography to refer to the pronunciation of words in accordance with their spelling is a development found occasionally elsewhere in the sixteenth century; it also lies behind Holofernes's railing in Shakespeare's *Love's Labour's Lost* against those 'rackers of ortagriphie' who pronounce **doubt** and **debt** without sounding the letter <b> found in their spelling (Act 5, scene i) (see further Chapter 4.). A similar concern with the observation of the proper relationship between spelling and pronunciation is apparent from the preface to Edmund Coote's *English Schoole-maister* (1596), where he explains his mission in the following terms:

> I undertake to teach all my scholers, that shall be trayned up for any grammar schoole, that they shall neuer erre in writing the true orthography of any word truly pronounced … and the same profit doe I offer vnto all other both men & women, that now for want hereof are ashamed to write vnto their best friends: for which I haue heard many gentlewomen offer much.

A striking feature of this stated aim is the implicit recognition that, by this time, poor spelling appears to have become socially disadvantageous. Correct spelling is no longer a concern of printers and compositors, but has also become a necessary skill for the socially-aspirant gentleman or gentlewoman.

It was in the eighteenth century, however, that the concept of orthographic correctness became most clearly linked with social acceptance. In the early decades of this century, the focus was on setting down prescriptions to control grammatical usage, part of a focus on the teaching of English in schools. Where grammar was taught in schools before the eighteenth century, the focus had largely been on Latin. The second half of the seventeenth century did see the beginnings of the teaching of English grammar as an end in itself, with a recognition that this was more useful for most pupils than education in Latin grammar. The eighteenth century witnessed the publication of numerous grammar books, along distinctively normative lines. One of the most successful of these was Robert Lowth's *A Short Introduction to English Grammar* (1762), which became the authoritative reference work for the period. Lowth's approach was to highlight apparent grammatical mistakes in the works of leading writers, an approach which was taken up by numerous imitators.

The eighteenth century also codified the idea of the reference accent as a socially desirable concept. This accent was associated with the elevated and polite social classes, described by Johnson as the pronunciation used by 'people of elegance and taste' (1764: 1). In 1774, John Walker set out his plan for a pronouncing dictionary that would codify the correct forms of pronunciation; his *Critical Pronouncing Dictionary* appeared in print in 1791. In the Preface, Walker situated his work within the recent attempts by distinguished authorities such as Johnson, an intelligent mind and great writer, and Lowth, the 'politest scholar of the age', to cultivate, improve and reform the English language. Walker does, however, set himself apart from Johnson on the matter of the relationship between spelling and pronunciation. Quoting Johnson's claim that the most elegant speakers are those who deviate least from the written words, Walker observes that many preferred pronunciations do differ considerably from their spelling, while words that are spelled identically often have different pronunciations. Indeed, it is precisely difficulties like these that make an authoritative pronunciation dictionary such an invaluable tool. In addition to helping speakers select the correct pronunciation, Walker believed that the availability of such a dictionary would make it possible to correct the various faults used by many speakers, and to eradicate provincial accents, which he believed all carried a degree of 'disgrace'. The pronouncing dictionary provided an authoritative guide to the correct way to pronounce every English word – to which speakers could turn in cases of uncertainty. Walker's dictionary was extremely influential; it was reprinted more than a hundred times and remained the standard work up to the publication of Daniel Jones's *English Pronouncing Dictionary* (1907).

Walker also acknowledges a debt to the work of Thomas Sheridan, who made important advances in the division of words into syllables and spelling out these syllables as they are pronounced. But, while it was a significant advance on previous attempts, Sheridan's dictionary was let down by numerous examples of 'impropriety, inconsistency, and want of acquaintance with the analogies of the language'. Sheridan, in his 1763 *Course of Lectures on Elocution*, was equally censorious of incorrect spellings as he was of erroneous pronunciation: 'It is a disgrace to a gentleman, to be guilty of false spelling, either by omitting, changing, or adding letters contrary to custom'.

The close association between correct spelling and gentlemanly conduct and breeding is apparent in a letter that Lord Chesterfield penned to his son. The letter forms part of a thirty-year period of correspondence, in which Chesterfield wrote some 400 letters offering his son advice on the social mores of the time. In a letter of 1750, he picks up specifically on his son's faulty spelling and emphasises the social consequences of making such mistakes:

I come now to another part of your letter, which is the orthography, if I may call bad spelling orthography. You spell induce, ENDUCE; and grandeur, you spell grandURE; two faults of which few of my housemaids would have been guilty. I must tell you that orthography, in the true sense of the word, is so absolutely necessary for a man of letters; or a gentleman, that one false spelling may fix ridicule upon him for the rest of his life; and I know a man of quality, who never recovered the ridicule of having spelled WHOLESOME without the w.

Helpfully, Lord Chesterfield does not stop at simply castigating his son for his poor spelling and warning him of its dangers. He advises him on how to improve and secure his knowledge of correct orthography. To do this, he recommends reading extensively and carefully. In most cases this will ensure that he encounters a single, authoritative spelling for every word. In the small number of cases where he comes across words that are spelled differently by writers of equal authority, he is free to choose whichever he prefers. Where there is a single correct form, such as in the cases of ENDUCE and GRANDURE, however, it is critical that he adopts that spelling: 'it is unpardonable and ridiculous for a gentleman' to do otherwise. Indeed, Chesterfield suggests, even a woman with a most basic education would ridicule a lover who sends her an 'ill-spelled billet-doux'. As well as directing his son to printed books as a means of determining the correct spelling of a particular word, Lord Chesterfield also advocates Johnson's *Dictionary* as a key resource for the uncertain speller. We have already noted above how Chesterfield saw Johnson as a one-man academy. This extended to his treatment of orthography, with Chesterfield earnestly recommending his fellow countrymen and women to surrender all their 'natural rights and privileges of misspelling, which they have so long enjoyed and so vigorously exerted' (Chesterfield, *The World*, 1754).

   As Lord Chesterfield's remarks make clear, letter-writing is a particularly dangerous pursuit for the insecure speller. Without compositors to correct faulty spelling and replace any authorial idiosyncrasies with standard equivalents, the letter-writer was exposed to ridicule if any errors were allowed to creep in. Such concerns are found even in the seventeenth century, when the standard spelling system was only newly bedded in. For example, Thomas Lye addressed his *A New Spelling Book* (1677) to those who are able to read but struggle to spell and consequently find themselves unable to engage in correspondence: 'Read, they hope they can; but spell they cannot; and therefore to write either to Child, Friend, or Servant, they are ashamed'. William Holder in *Elements of Speech* (1669) testifies to the way in which misspellings, especially those triggered by spelling by sound rather than custom, are viewed as evidence of a poor education and a lack of sophistication, and liable to prompt ridicule: 'We are apt ... to laugh at the uncouth Spelling in the writings of unlearned persons, who writing as they please, that is, using such Letters, as justly express the power or Sound of their Speech; yet, forsooth, we say write not true English' (Holder 1669: 107). That such attitudes remained the norm by the eighteenth century is apparent from how the author of *The London Universal Letter-Writer* (c. 1800) views ignorance in the spelling of a particular word to be a 'mark of ill-breeding, defective education, or natural stupidity'. The advice he offers is similar to that offered by Lord Chesterfield: the consultation of a dictionary and studying the writings of the best modern authors. That dictionaries were explicitly addressed to those unsure of the spelling of certain words is apparent from Nathan Bailey's comments regarding the aim of his work, which was intended to provide assistance to those who 'when they have learn'd the use of a Pen, make such a hideous jumble of Letters to stand for Words, that neither the Vulgar nor the Learned can guess what they mean by them' (Bailey 1727: vol II).

Eighteenth-century attitudes towards correct spelling were consolidated in the nineteenth century, when being able to write and spell correctly became an important marker of educational achievement. Not all writers recognised the importance of spelling to the mastery of written English. The grammarian William Cobbett viewed orthography as 'the very humble business of putting Letters together properly' and dismissed it as 'so very childish a concern' that he would not spend much space describing it (Cobbett 1833: 14). Even the highly prescriptive *Don't: A Manual of Mistakes & Improprieties more or less prevalent in Conduct & Speech* makes no specific reference to spelling. Structured as a series of prohibitions regarding polite behaviour and discourse, the book warns against the dangers of solecisms in pronunciation, such as clipping final consonants, e.g. comin' for COMING, dropping [h] before vowels, e.g. ouse for HOUSE, inserting [h] where it is not required, as in a horange for ORANGE, and dropping the [r] in CARD. What all these examples have in common is the belief that pronunciation should mimic the written language; instead of seeing these as alternative pronunciations of the words in question, they are perceived to be failures to sound letters that are found in the spelling. In this way, spelling became enshrined as a key indicator of correct pronunciation. In order to pronounce a word properly, a speaker must have a proper grasp of its spelling. The importance of literacy is further apparent from the extent to which improper pronunciation, such as [h]-dropping, was viewed as a slight on a person's grasp of spelling as much as accent. Such mistakes are not only made by the ignorant, they can often be heard in the speech of educated people when they are not paying sufficient attention. Appearing to be over-scrupulous in attending to such details, however, was considered to be a further sole-cism. Over-aspirating an initial [h] sound, for instance, was viewed as a significant mark of vulgarity, since it suggests a speaker trying too hard to indicate that he or she is not a member of the common people. For this reason, just as the correct pronunciation of [h] was considered by Henry Sweet to be 'an almost infallible test of education and refinement', so was its correct use in spelling (Sweet 1877: 195). Lynda Mugglestone has described how changes in the role of [h] are bound up with transforma-tions taking place in English society and the role of accent as a social as well as a linguistic phenomenon (Mugglestone 1995: 109–59). These transformations were also important in establishing correct spelling as a badge of social status and poor spelling as an indicator of social and educational disadvantage.

Ridiculing spelling mistakes and using them to make assumptions about a person's education and intelligence remains widespread in the twenty-first century. The major difference from earlier periods is that, while accent remains strongly tied to class, spelling no longer carries such connotations. But the tendency to mock those who are guilty of individual spelling mistakes, even ones commonly made by large numbers of people, remains strong. For instance, during Michael Gove's term as Education Secretary, the Department for Education introduced the SPAG (Spelling Punctuation and Grammar) test, which included examining an eleven-year old's ability to correctly spell a list of 162 words. As his critics were quick to point out, Gove's belief in the importance of accurate spelling was somewhat undermined by a number of misspellings in the White Paper which set out the policy itself. The tendency for politician's lan-guage use, and specifically their spelling, to be policed is apparent from an infamous example of a political career blighted by a spelling blunder. Dan Quayle, former Vice President of the United States of America, famously misspelled POTATO in a spelling bee at a school in New Jersey. When he launched his unsuccessful bid for the presidency in 2001, his largest obstacle was termed the 'potato factor'. In Quayle's case, the appeal of this gaffe to the media may have been as much about the word itself as the misspelling; as Quayle himself later said of the incident: 'it seemed like a perfect illustration of what people thought about me anyway'.

The spelling bee is a particularly American institution, highlighting different attitudes towards spelling in the USA and Britain. The first spelling bees date back to the 1700s, when they constituted an important component of a child's education. By 1800 they were viewed principally as social entertainment. Puritans, opposed to such frivolities, rebranded them as 'spelling schools' in an attempt to re-assert their educational basis. Spelling bees gradually fell out of favour in New England society, but were preserved within a frontier culture for whom correct spelling was still considered an important badge of education and social status. The publication of *The Hoosier Schoolmaster* (1871) led to a craze in spelling contests, following which the term 'spelling bee' was introduced. The use of the word 'bee' to refer to a social gathering of this kind, often with a specific purpose in mind, such as 'apple-bee' and 'husking bee', is based upon the social behaviour of bees. But while spelling bees were indeed social, they also developed into highly competitive encounters, as the alternative name 'spelling fight' makes clear.

The first national spelling bee was introduced in 1925, later becoming the Scripps Spelling Bee in 1941, and continues to be hotly contested today. Over time, the competition has become progressively harder, with recent winners successfully spelling rare, technical words of foreign extraction in order to claim their prize. Frank Neuhauser won the inaugural contest by correctly spelling the word **gladiolus**. Other early winning words include **albumen, fracas, knack** and **torsion**. The 2023 winner, Dev Shah, had to successfully navigate the word **psammophile** in order to take home the trophy. The cash value of the prize, $50,000, a considerable sum for a young child – entrants must be fourteen years old or younger – is relatively small compared to the social prestige and national acclaim attached to winning the Scripps Spelling Bee. The popularity of the spelling bee is far greater in America than it is in Britain. The British equivalent, the BBC's *Hard Spell*, was a short-lived innovation broadcast in 2004. The competition was won by Gayathri Kumar, who correctly spelled an assortment of challenging words, including **apocalypse, mezzanine, troglodyte, claustrophobia, geisha** and **resuscitate**. Apart from being revived as a one-off celebrity contest, Star Spell, the format was not reused. Despite accurate spelling remaining an important badge of achievement in schools, British schoolchildren rarely engage in the competitive spelling bees that are such an integral part of American society.

Another key difference between the teaching of spelling in Britain and America is the availability in the latter of a single, authoritative manual for learning how to spell. This came in the form of Noah Webster's *A Grammatical Institute of the English Language*; Part I was published in 1783, followed by a grammar in 1784 and a reader in 1785. It was Part I, with its focus on helping children learn to read and write by breaking words up into their component syllables, that was the most successful of these publications. During Webster's lifetime, the work went through a total of 385 editions, with its title changing to *The American Spelling Book* in 1786 and *The Elementary Spelling Book* in 1829. To most of its readers, it was known as the 'Blue-Backed Speller', from its distinctive blue cover. Webster's spelling book sold in huge numbers. By the mid-nineteenth century, more than 1.5 million copies were sold each year. In 1880, William H. Appleton, director of the publishing house responsible for issuing Webster's speller, claimed that it enjoyed the largest sales of any book in the world except the Bible. While Webster's speller eventually came to be replaced as the main instructional text in American classrooms, it retained its status as an authority on spelling, since it was for a long time employed as the official rulebook for spelling bees. The Merriam-Webster Unabridged dictionary, which still bears Webster's name, is the official dictionary for the Scripps Spelling Bee today.

A recent survey of spelling skills and how they are taught in British schools makes comparisons with the advice given in a spelling guide published in 1920: 'Begin by pointing out the importance of spelling. Give cases, if possible, where people have been discredited because of spelling errors in letters' (Horn and Ashbaugh 1920: xi). The authors note, however, that in the USA increasing scepticism has been directed at the value of instruction in spelling, given the availability of spellcheckers, the fact that spelling is no longer penalised on standardised tests and the extent to which the concept of correct spelling is being challenged by the tolerance of variation in electronic communication. The authors report interviews with educators who believe that such skills are redundant or with employers who only consider spelling to be necessary when hiring a proofreader.

That even the brightest of students continue to struggle with spelling is apparent from a list of misspellings compiled by an examiner of the Oxford English degree in 1986 and 1995 (Richards 1998). Alongside a number of comparatively specialist words that have been misspelled, such as **pathological**, **Calvinistic**, **paradoxical** and **vacillating**, appear many other relatively common words, including **argument**, **consensus**, **definitely**, **occurs**, **sense** and **labels**. The author of the article claims that, while in theory these students should be some of the best in Oxford University, even in the world, when it comes to spelling, 'the facts prove otherwise'. Since these mistakes were made in examinations, however, when students are writing under pressure of time, it is hard to know how much they tell us about spelling standards among Oxford undergraduates. They are, however, a useful reminder that even some of the highest-achieving students of their generation can continue to struggle with spelling into adulthood. Many of the misspellings recorded by Richards include some of the commonest spelling mistakes found today, e.g. **definately**, **concensus** and **arguement**, so that it is perhaps unsurprising to find them appearing in hastily written exam scripts. The importance of time to check spelling in ensuring accuracy is apparent from the article itself, in which the correct spelling of **encomiast** is erroneously given as **encomamist**.

However, research shows the importance attached to correct spelling in the employment sector, where spelling skills remain highly regarded by recruiters and when assessing applications for promotion. Accurate spelling is seen as a vital skill when it comes to securing employment, since a poorly spelled CV is usually a reason for an application not to be taken seriously. In 2022 employment consultants Adzuna analysed over 147,000 British CVs and found that 62.4% contained at least one spelling mistake. Over a third of the CVs analysed were found to contain five or more mistakes, with more than 5,000 CVs featuring 20 or more. To help applicants ensure that their CVs are accurately spelled, they provided a list of the top ten most commonly misspelt words. The presence on the list of words like **modelling, behaviour, labour** and **practised** suggests that, in many cases, the so-called errors are probably nothing more than the use of the US English alternatives, **modeling, behavior, labor** and **practiced**. A survey conducted by Adecco, a firm specialising in Human Resources, found that 43% of the recruiters that were contacted considered it justifiable to reject an application solely on the grounds of poor spelling (Pan et al. 2021).

There are those who have attempted to question the assumption that a poorly spelled job application and CV should automatically be consigned to the dustbin. In 1960, the Oxford academic and author of the Narnia stories, C. S. Lewis, wrote to the editor of the *Times Educational Supplement* questioning the degree to which common spelling variants should be treated as errors. Instead, Lewis proposed that such simple and widespread errors as **sieze** and **seeze** be deemed equally acceptable as the so-called correct form **seize**.

One reason why correct spelling is so important to a business is that mistakes on a website or in an email can undermine customer confidence, since they are often signs that a site is fraudulent or that an email is an example of 'phishing'. Phishing, the sending of fake emails that purport to be from an authentic institution or individual, can often be identified by the presence of spelling mistakes, since they are commonly written by individuals with a poor command of written English. But spelling mistakes may also be deliberately employed as a means of avoiding spam filters, which are programmed to consign email with particular keywords to the junk mail folder.

One spelling feature that is policed by those concerned with maintaining standards of correctness with particular alacrity is the apostrophe. For instance, Lynne Truss (2003) expressed despair at how apostrophes are inserted incorrectly, as in the case of the 'greengrocer's apostrophe', where the apostrophe is used before a plural –s ending; so called because it is thought to be particularly prevalent in greengrocers' signs advertising **apple's**, **pear's** and **orange's**. She is even more appalled by those who confuse the neuter possessive pronoun **its** with the abbreviation **it's**:

> The rule is extremely easy to grasp. Getting your itses mixed up is the greatest solecism in the world of punctuation. No matter that you have a PhD and have read all of Henry James twice. If you still persist in writing, 'Good food at it's best', you deserve to be struck by lightning, hacked up on the spot and buried in an unmarked grave.

Because it is not a particularly useful device, and because many people do not understand the rules governing it, the apostrophe is increasingly being omitted in written English. There was considerable furore when Birmingham City Council decided to drop the apostrophe from its street signs. The decision was described as 'absolute defeatism' by John Richards, founder of the Apostrophe Protection Society: 'Now children will go around Birmingham and see utter chaos. If you don't have apostrophes, is there any point in full stops, or semi-colons, or question marks? Is there any point in punctuation at all?' Similar outrage was voiced when Devon County Council made a similar decision. Writing in *The Guardian*, Lucy Mangan branded it an 'Apostrophe Catastrophe' which 'captures in microcosm the kind of thinking that pervades our government, our institutions, our times', drawing parallels with the government's handling of the banking crisis, binge-drinking and sexual assault. Such extreme views concerning the importance of the apostrophe to the future of society, combined with the huge popularity of Truss's book, indicate that the prescriptive views that we have traced through the eighteenth and nineteenth centuries are still widely held today.

10 Female spelling

The major collection of family correspondence from the late Middle Ages, the Paston Letters, contains a number of letters from female members of the family. Three generations of women are represented in this large collection, but it is not thought that any of their letters are autograph. Agnes Paston employed several clerks: out of a total of seventeen letters, six are in one hand, two in another and the rest in at least eight further hands. Margaret Paston was responsible for some 104 letters, written by a huge variety of scribes. Some of these scribes wrote up to 20 letters, while others are found in just one. Margery Paston's six letters were written by four separate clerks; Elizabeth Paston's two letters were also copied by different scribes. While it remains possible that any one of these hands is that of the author, the evidence seems against it. In many cases the scribes responsible for copying the letters are identifiable from other documents. Furthermore, the fact that the Paston women employed so many different copyists strongly suggests that they were unable to write, or at least that they preferred not to do so. Norman Davis's assessment of the extensive corpus of letters written by Margaret Paston leads to the conclusion that: 'Margaret's autograph remains elusive; and we may never know whether she wrote down any of her letters, or indeed whether she could write at all' (Davis 1952: 14). It is clear from an instruction to 'schewe ore rede' the contents of a letter to Margaret that she was able to read, but this does not necessarily mean that she could write. Margery Paston had only the most rudimentary grasp of her letters; her signature is appended to the body of all three letters from her, in a hand that suggests a very tentative grasp of basic penmanship. While historical linguists have made extensive use of the men's letters in this valuable collection for evidence of orthographic variation and change, it is not possible to do so with respect to the female letters.

Since women's literacy remained relatively uncommon in the sixteenth century, there are comparatively few holograph letters from this period. Where we do find instances, there are marked differences between female and male spelling. The following instance is a letter written by Lady Katherine Scrope to her father, the Earl of Cumberland, dated to 1536:

> My dewty promised unto your Lordship in my most humbliest maner; advertysyng the same that yesterday the commons off Richmontshir did meat at Richmon, wher undoubtedly they dewydet them in thre partyes … My Lord my bedfellow is this nyght at Helbek Hall & wulbe with your Lordshipe at Skypton in as convenient spead as he can maik, to tak suche parte as your Lordshipe dothe. And I wull come this morning towards Katelwell & tary there off my bedfelowe, and wold come with hym to Skipton, iff ye thynk it good. And this nyght I have sent my litell boy with his nursse unto one poore mans house, to be kept privy there we knowe further. And what your Lordshipes mynd is in the premysses I wull hertly besuche you to send it to Catelwell with this berere. Thus tholy Gost preserve youre good Lordship with my Lady my mother & all youres in comfort. At Bolton, this Setterday before day,

> Your humbliest doughter,
> Kateryn Scrope.

> (Text taken from Nevalainen 2012: 143)

The letter shows a number of non-standard spellings, some of which presumably reflect her regional pronunciation, e.g. **wull** WILL, **forther** FURTHER, **besuche** BESEECH; the spelling **Setterday** is recorded by *OED* as a northern variant form of SATURDAY up to the nineteenth century. There are a handful of additional spellings that seem to be her own idiosyncratic forms, e.g. **humbliest** and the doubling of <s> in **nursse** and **premysses**. But, otherwise, Lady Katherine's spelling shows a sound understanding of many of the conventional features of English spelling, such as the standard use of <gh> in **doughter** and **nyght**, and of <wh> in **wher**, the inclusion of the silent <b> in **undoubtedly**, and the use of the standard spelling of **suche**.

However, Graham Williams (2013) has argued that male and female spelling habits were not as different as has been assumed. His claims are based upon a comparative study of the letters of Bess of Hardwick (1527–1608) and her fourth husband, the Earl of Shrewsbury. Like the Paston women of the fifteenth century, Bess of Hardwick made frequent use of amanuenses to write her letters. The decision to use a secretary may have been driven by purely practical reasons, including a need for knowledge of specialised legal terms and formulae. But, on other occasions, Bess's decision to write to her husband in the hand of a scribe seems likely to have been driven by a desire to maintain emotional distance. While her most personal messages to her husband are written in her own hand, those exchanged during a period of marital collapse were written by secretaries. Despite this, there are a total of seventeen surviving letters that are in her own handwriting. Williams's analysis reveals that both husband and wife used a variety of idiosyncratic spellings which are easily distinguishable from the spelling practices of their secretaries. Bess's own spelling habits comprise a selection of features that appear throughout her correspondence and which are therefore taken to be prototypical of her idiolect. These include **faythefoull** FAITHFUL, **har** HER, **moust** MOST, **latter/later** LETTER, **letyll** LITTLE. A few additional spellings are cited by Williams as providing possible evidence of an alternative pronunciation: **pott oup** PUT UP, **onhabyll** UNABLE, **trousse** TRUST, **reyme** REALM.

But, while it is important not to over-emphasise gender as a factor in understanding spelling variation, Bess of Hardwick's female correspondents do show a range of forms that betray a lack of education. A good example is Lady Frances Cobham, whose letter of 1564 contains idiosyncratic forms such as **wlode** WOULD, **innoufthe** and **innoufe** ENOUGH, **lenthe** LENGTH, **faysshyne** FASHION, **mi self** MYSELF. These spellings reveal a tendency to spell phonetically and a lack of awareness of the conventions of the developing standard. The extent of variation found in the correspondence is well demonstrated by Williams's citing of a selection of different spellings of the word DAUGHTER. Bess herself spells the word **dowter**, while her daughter, Elizabeth Stuart, countess of Lennox, uses both **dafter** and **doughter**, the first of these showing a peculiarly northern dialect form. Bess's daughter Lady Frances Pierrepont uses **dautter** and her step-daughter, Grace Cavendish, uses **daughter**. Thus, just one of these women employs the spelling that became the standard form; her husband, the Earl of Shrewsbury, uses **doughter**. Even the scribal copies are of interest from the perspective of gender, since Bess of Hardwick made use of female scribes as well as professional male secretaries.

At the top end of the social spectrum, we can observe the spelling habits of Elizabeth I (1558–1603), a highly educated woman with a sound understanding of Latin and Greek. The following analysis is based upon an autograph letter addressed to her sister Mary I, written on 16 March 1554, in which she appeals against Mary's house arrest, on suspicion of treason. Written in the Italic hand, a style of handwriting developed in renaissance Italy, the letter uses spellings that are largely in line with the emerging standard. However, despite this, a number of variant forms stand out. These include **verefie** VERIFY, **promis** PROMISE, **profe** PROOF, **tru** TRUE, **trueth** TRUTH, **dy** DIE, **hower** HOUR, **migth** MIGHT. In **parson** PERSON, **hart** HEART, and **harde** HEARD we find evidence pointing to a different pronunciation, although Elizabeth uses **desert** rather than **desart**. In unstressed syllables we find **bettar** BETTER, **lettar** LETTER and **sistar** SISTER. The preterite verb ending is written <id> **provid** PROVED. Confusion appears concerning words with the silent <gh>: in MIGHT, SIGHT, BROUGHT and THOUGH we find **migth**, **sigth**, **brogth** and **thogth**; in HIGHNESS, Elizabeth uses **higthnes** alongside **hithnes** and the emerging standard form **highness**. In her unusual spelling of RHYMES as **righmes**, Elizabeth repurposes the silent <gh> digraph to signal the diphthong that had emerged as the reflex of ME /iː/. While the <wh> is found in **who**, **whatsoever** and **what**, WHICH is consistently spelled **wiche**, showing that she pronounced this word identically with WITCH.

It is instructive to compare Elizabeth I of England's spelling with that of her aunt, Margaret Tudor, who was queen of Scotland from 1503–15, by marriage to James IV. Margaret's writing survives in a substantial collection of correspondence, now held by the British Library, which shows the influence of contemporary features of Scots spelling and pronunciation on her usage, which correlate closely with her individual experiences and the socio-political events in which she played a major role. Graham Williams (2016) carried out an analysis of a corpus of around thirty-five letters from the collection of correspondence, covering different stages in Margaret's life, from her first surviving letter in 1503 until the 1530s. The earliest letter, written when Margaret was just thirteen years old, is addressed to her father Henry VII, partly in the hand of a professional amanuensis and partly 'wrytyn wyt the hand of your hu[m]ble douter margaret'. The spelling of the section authored by Margaret shows a sound grasp of the conventions of EModE spelling, perhaps taught to her by her grandmother, Lady Margaret Beaufort, such as the use of the silent <w> in **wrytyn**, **wryt**, although the silent <gh> is not a feature of the spelling of **douter**. Two striking aspects of her spelling that stand out from this early period are the tendency to drop initial <h> before vowels, e.g. **oulde** HOLD, **erefter** HEREAFTER and **ys** HIS, and a lack of final <e> in **tym** TIME, where it functions as a diacritic to indicate the diphthongal quality of the preceding vowel. Final <e> is also missing in **hau** HAVE, but this is inconsistent, since **haue** is also found.

Regrettably, there are no surviving letters dating from the decade that Margaret spent as Queen Consort (1503–13). However, letters from the period of regency that followed her husband's death show that by this time her usage had been influenced by the conventions employed at the Scottish court. In a letter to her brother, Henry VIII, written in her own hand in July 1514, she employs a variety of Scots spellings, such as **quham** WHOM and **quhilk** WHICH. It is striking that these represent the fully Scots versions of these words, rather than the hybridised spellings, e.g. **quhom** or **whilk**, found in some Scots renderings of English texts in this period (see further Chapter 8). Although it is important not to draw too strong an opinion about pronunciation from such evidence, it is interesting to note that spellings like **vnknawne** UNKNOWN, **lange** LONG, **bathe** BOTH imply a pronunciation with the unrounded reflex of OE ā, typical of Scots and northern ME accents at this time. Similarly, the spelling **gud** suggests that Margaret had adopted the raised pronunciation of this vowel, spelled **good** in southern varieties of ME.

During a period of political instability in Scotland, Margaret fled to England in 1516, where she remained until the following year. Letters written during this period demonstrate a shift back to southern English conventions, with **both** appearing instead of **bathe**, **vysche** replacing **quhilk** WHICH and consistent use of <sch> instead of <s> in SHALL and SHOULD. A further change of fortunes that resulted in a second period of regency from 1521 can be linked with a return to the Scots spellings observed above. Letters written during this period of Margaret's life show **vylke** WHICH, **syk** SUCH, **mykyl** MUCH, **tway** TWO, **tyl** TO, along with spellings showing the unrounded reflex of OE ā. These clear shifts in spelling preferences across these different phases in Margaret's life suggest that she was deliberately adjusting her habits to reflect those of the political group with which she wished to align herself. This evidence indicates a strong awareness of the different conventions associated with English and Scots spelling at this time, and an awareness of how minor orthographic differences can help to express political allegiance and to foster a sense of personal and national identity.

Margaret Tudor was no doubt unusual in having such a subtle understanding of the nuances of spelling variation at this time. By the end of the sixteenth century, Coote directed his *English Schoole-maister* (1596) at all grammar school children, 'that they shall neuer erre in writing the true orthography of any word'. He also addressed the work to 'both men & women, that now for want hereof are ashamed to write vnto their best friends: for which I haue heard many gentlewomen offer much'. It is apparent from this remark that, while Coote viewed his audience as comprising both men and women, it is the latter that he believed would have most need of it.

According to a handwriting manual titled *The Pen's Excellencie* (1618), women in the seventeenth century were taught to write using the Italic rather than the Secretary script, since it took less time to acquire: 'Therefore it is vsually taught to women, for as much as they (hauing not the patience to take any great paines, besides phantasticall and humoursome) must be taught that which they may instantly learne'. During this period, the gap widened between male and female spelling, which continued to be influenced by phonetic principles. Lady Brilliana Harley was the third wife of Sir Robert Harley, a politician who supported parliament against the king in the Civil War. The two married in 1623; Lady Harley lived at Brompton Castle, in what is now Brompton Bryan in northern Herefordshire. She wrote letters to her son, beginning after his commencing his studies at Oxford University, during his period at Lincoln's Inn and then ending at her death in 1643, when he was serving in the parliamentary army. Lady Harley was evidently an intelligent and educated woman. The majority of the letters were written in her own hand and employ a clear and controlled prose style. Her spelling system is of considerable interest in the way it shows an awareness of the conventions associated with the emerging standard, but frequently blends these with attempts to reflect her own pronunciation.

The dropping of the initial /w/ in **writing** is reflected in her spelling of **ryteings** WRITINGS; however, in other instances, Lady Harley adds the <w> after the <r>, as in **rwite**, demonstrating an awareness of the convention of including a silent <w> but a lack of certainty concerning its correct placement. A further example of such confusion is apparent in the spelling **enoufg** ENOUGH. Here we can see a half-consciousness of the standard spelling in which the final /f/ is spelled <gh>, alongside a phonetic rendering in <f>. In **boouckes** and **whous** we can see an awareness of the standard spelling in <oo> combined with a consciousness of the raised pronunciation of /oː/ to /uː/ that was the consequence of the Great Vowel Shift. Further evidence of the way in which Lady Harley's pronunciation influenced her spelling is found in the spelling **gareded** GUARDED, in which the intrusive <e> after <r> indicates an attempt to render a rhotic accent, in which the postvocalic /r/ was sounded.

Evidence of regional pronunciation in her spelling system is apparent from her use of the spelling **meathe** MEAD. This form with a medial /ð/ is first attested in Middle English; later instances are largely restricted to the western dialects, where they are probably influenced by the Welsh **medd**. Another spelling that reflects a sound change is **sugsess** SUCCESS; the spelling with medial <gs> is not recorded in the *OED* but appears to show the voicing of /ks/ before a stressed syllable. Lady Harley's use of **biusnes** may reflect the western pronunciation, although it is possible that it also reflects an attempt to accommodate two different conventions: the western spelling with <u> and an eastern form with <i>. In the spellings **saruis** SERVICE, **presarue** PRESERVE and **saruants** SERVANTS we can see evidence of a dialectal pronunciation which is still found in the standard English pronunciation of **clerk**.

Scholars have generally claimed that women's spelling was more erratic than men's in the seventeenth century, a view that gains support from contemporary comments. But modern scholarly assessments of relative spelling standards have typically compared private writing by women with men's public writing. This is not a fair comparison, however, since it overlooks the way in which these two genres of writing differ in the extent to which they demanded observance of an external standard. A comparison of the manuscript writings of Lady Brilliana Harley and those written by William Cavendish, 1st Duke of Newcastle (1592–1676) by Margaret J.-M. Sönmez (2000) allowed consideration of two instances of informal writing by members of the aristocratic class, born within a few years of each other and therefore likely having learned to spell at the same time. This comparison is based upon a number of different aspects of their spelling practices. A quantitative examination of the number of variant spellings recorded for common words reveals that, while both attest different proportions of variants for individual items, the Duke of Newcastle uses slightly more words with irregular spellings than Lady Harley. Similarly, both the male and female writers were found to employ phonetic spellings, despite this having traditionally been thought to be a largely female characteristic. Lady Harley shows a greater tendency to use <ar> in words like CERTAIN and SERVANT, <i> in EMPLOY and DESPAIR, and <e> instead of <i> in CABINET and DELIVER than the duke. But the duke has a higher frequency of instances of spellings showing the loss of the final dental consonant, e.g. **forwar** FORWARD.

The treatment of etymology in spelling threw up similarly unexpected results. Consideration of the spelling of affixes revealed some instances where Harley used more variants than Newcastle, but others revealed the opposite. Assessment of the relatively restricted group of words whose spellings were revised to reflect etymology in this period was similarly inconclusive. Both writers were found to spell ADVANTAGE with <ad> and AUTHOR with <aught>. Whereas Newcastle almost always included the silent <b> in DOUBT, Harley never did. But Harley always included the <c> in PERFECT, whereas Newcastle uses the older form without <c> on two instances. But the different number of occurrences call such comparisons into question. There are just four instances of PERFECT in Lady Harley's letters and 161 occurrences in the Duke of Newcastle's writings. This study concluded that Harley did not make more use of phonetic spellings than Newcastle, and that there was no significant difference in their use of classical affixes or etymological spellings, as one might have expected from their different education and upbringing. Where the two writers do differ concerns the greater use by Harley of spellings that significantly alter the appearance of a word, such as those with double vowels e.g. **beeg** BEG and **geet** GET, and thus are more marked, and so more likely to be commented upon by contemporary and modern readers.

Women continued to be viewed as poor spellers at the beginning of the eighteenth century. J. K.'s *A New English Dictionary* was addressed to 'young scholars, Tradesmen, Artificers, and the Female Sex, who would learn to spell truly'. This recalls Robert Cawdrey's *A Table Alphabeticall* (1604), which saw its audience as made up of 'ladies', 'gentlewomen' and 'other unskillfull persons'. Görlach (2001: 297) prints a private letter of 1705 from Lady Wentworth to her son, Lord Raby, the Earl of Strafford. This letter includes a number of non-standard spelling features, including **billding** BUILDING, **furneture** FURNITURE, **strang** STRANGE, **unusyell** UNUSUAL. Görlach notes that the 'erratic spelling conventions' found in this letter are typical of a female member of the nobility, in an age before correct spelling began to be regarded as a social requirement. But the conventions are not as erratic as this suggests, since a number of her spellings are widely recorded in the written English of an earlier period. **Wensday** is a common variant from Middle English up to the eighteenth century, while **fower** FOUR remained common in the Northern, Midlands and East Anglian dialects in the nineteenth century. In the case of **ritch** RICH, the *OED* shows that it was widely used in the sixteenth and seventeenth centuries, while **thear** THERE was common in sixteenth-century dialect.

Female spelling standards were raised throughout the century; there is evidence from the career of Lady Mary Wortley Montagu that spelling habits improved within an individual's lifetime, e.g. switching from **allwaies, allways, alwaies** to **always**, largely the result of extensive reading of the latest printed novels (Tieken-Boon van Ostade 2009: 45). Analysis of the approximately 8,000-word corpus of private letters written by Sarah Fielding revealed almost 100 unusual spelling forms. While some of these (e.g. unique instances of **buidings, critism** and **illustrous**) are dismissed as errors, others are attested in the work of other writers of the period, e.g. **chusing, desart, intirely, shewing** and **surprize**. Some of these variants (e.g. **inclose, sence** and **your's**) appear alongside more numerous instances of standard equivalents (**enclose, sense** and **yours**), revealing a set of preferences in line with the majority usage. An interesting observation that emerged from this study was the recognition that Fielding varied the extent to which she capitalised nouns depending on the recipient of the letter. When writing to Mrs Montagu, with whom she had a comparatively close relationship, she capitalised 41% of the nouns; when writing to her friend, the printer Samuel Richardson, 60% of the nouns begin with a capital letter. However, when addressing James Harris, whom she addresses in terms of respect and formality, 80% of the nouns are capitalised. This association of capitalisation of nouns with more formal usage was probably influenced by the practice of printers. A similar tendency has been identified in Sarah Fielding's use of <'d> in past tense and past participle forms of weak verbs, which became part of her more formal style later in her career (Tieken-Boon van Ostade 1998).

The influence of Johnson's *Dictionary* upon female spelling has been shown by Tieken-Boon van Ostade and Bax's (2002) study of the habits of Mrs Hester Thrale. Her letters to Dr Johnson show a change in her spelling of words ending in <–ic>/<–ick>. Her early letters reveal a tendency to switch between the two alternative spellings in words such as PUBLIC, ENTHUSIASTIC, FROLIC, LETHARGIC and MUSIC. However, in the course of June 1775, she switches towards invariable use of the more old-fashioned spellings ending in <–ick>. This shift is puzzling, since it runs counter to the general tendency of the time. That Mrs Thrale was concerned about the niceties of spelling and took pride in her own accuracy, and that of her children, is apparent from her comment in one of her diaries: 'My children write very prettily, spelling as exactly as myself'. The preference for spellings ending in <–ck> is found in Johnson's *Dictionary* and Tieken-Boon van Ostade and Bax postulate that it was Johnson's influence that prompted the shift in Mrs Thrale's habits. Since the two corresponded with each other, Mrs Thrale would have been familiar with Johnson's preferred spellings from his own practice, as well as the model offered by his dictionary. Since Mrs Thrale belonged to Johnson's London circle, as hostess of a literary salon at which he was a central member, her decision to accommodate her usage to Johnson's practice may have been due to his influence. It is striking that this change in habits is not found in her letters to other correspondents, nor in her journals or commonplace books. By contrast, Johnson's spelling preferences do not appear to have influenced the habits of James Boswell, despite the closeness of their relationship and his clear admiration for Johnson.

The teaching of spelling in the eighteenth century would have taken place in the home. According to Fairman (2006), grammar schools accepted pupils who could already spell, although it is unclear exactly how this took place. Spelling books of this period generally taught spelling by breaking words down into their component syllables, beginning with two letter combinations, e.g. 'ab', 'eb' and 'ob', termed 'Easie Syllables' in *A Spelling Book for Children* (1707), and then building up to words of one syllable and up to six syllables. At this early point there is no evidence of the devising of spelling rules and their use to teach children to spell. By the end of the eighteenth century, this aspect of teaching spelling had become more developed; Lindley Murray's grammar of 1795 includes three pages of spelling rules: 'The orthography of the English language is attended with much uncertainty and perplexity … a considerable part of this inconvenience may be remedied, by attending to the general laws of formation'.

In Edinburgh, a ladies' club, The Fair Intellectual Club, founded as a riposte to the all-male Athenian Club, held regular meetings at which its members received instruction in spelling from James Robertson, a Glasgow schoolmaster and author of *The Ladies Help to Spelling* (1722). The dialogue structure adopted by *The Ladies Help* gives an insight into how the master delivered his instruction in orthography. In the opening exchanges, the Lady admits her lack of training, which was otherwise focused on specifically feminine pursuits, and her anxiety at being ridiculed for her poor command of written English:

> I know nothing of these Rules, for my Education was too like to that bestowed on most of my Sex; viz. Sewing, Dancing, Musick, Paistry, &c, mean while, ignorant of our Mother tongue, not daring to speak in company lest we blunder; much less to communicate our thoughts to an absent Friend, or Commerade, lest our bad Spelling afford matter of Laughter to the Reader. (Robertson 1777: 2–3)

The raising of standards of spelling and the enforcement of a national standard meant that female spelling habits were especially singled out for censure and ridicule in this period. Scragg (1974: 89) cites an article in *The Guardian* from 1713 in which the author describes his discovery of an anonymous poem, which he claims to be able to identify as the work of a female poet on account of its 'peculiar Modes in Spelling, and a certain Negligence in Grammar'. Jonathan Swift (1727) attributed the low levels of literacy among the daughters of gentlemen to be the result of poor education; since they are not taught to spell in their youth, they never properly acquire the skill. For Swift there was a clear division between male and female standards of spelling. He commended Mrs Whiteway for having 'neither the scrawl nor the spelling of your sex' and noted that her letter was sufficiently well written that he thought it must have been written by a man. In his correspondence with his friend Esther Johnson, whom he called Stella, Swift drew attention to her poor spelling and corrected it on numerous occasions: 'R*e*diculous, madam? I suppose you mean r*i*diculous: let me have no more of that; 'tis the author of the Atalantis's spelling. I have mended it in your letter' (14 December 1710). In a letter dated 23 October 1711, Swift listed a series of spelling mistakes which Stella had employed in her letters, questioning the extent to which these are the result of ignorance or of slips of the pen. These include **dineing** DINING, **intellegence** INTELLIGENCE, **houer** HOUR, **merrit** MERIT, **secreet**

SECRET and **immagin** IMAGINE. The extent to which a lack of classical education affected a woman's ability to spell is suggested by her spelling of PAMPHLETS as **phamphlets**, a spelling which indicates an awareness of the convention of using <ph> in the word, but an uncertainty as to where it appears. Stella's spelling of **bussiness** BUSINESS is widely attested in the sixteenth and seventeenth centuries. It is ironic that, just a few weeks later, Swift found himself unable to recall the correct spelling of the same word, although he blamed his uncertainty upon his exposure to Stella's mistaken spelling (Aitken 1901):

> Pray let us have no more *bussiness*, but *busyness*: the deuce take me if I know how to spell it; your wrong spelling, Madam Stella, has put me out: it does not look right; let me see, *bussiness, busyness, business, bisyness, bisness, bysness*; faith, I know not which is right, I think the second; I believe I never writ the word in my life before; yes, sure I must, though; *business, busyness, bisyness.*–I have perplexed myself, and can't do it. Prithee ask Walls. *Business*, I fancy that's right. Yes it is; I looked in my own pamphlet, and found it twice in ten lines, to convince you that I never writ it before. Oh, now I see it as plain as can be; so yours is only an *s* too much.
>
> (1 Dec 1711)

The association of non-standard spelling with a low intelligence and poor education was exploited by Tobias Smollett in Clarinda's letter to Mr Jackson in his first novel, *The Adventures of Roderick Random* (1748):

> Deer Kreeter,
>
> As you are the animable hopjack of my contemplayshins, your aydear is infernally skimming before my keymerycal fansee, when Murfy sends his puppies to the heys of slipping mortals; and when Febus shines from his merrydying throne: Whereupon I shall canseif old whorie time has lost his pinners, as also Cubit his harrows, until thou enjoy sweet propose in the loafseek harms of thy faithfool to commend. (Chapter XVI)

Here we see a variety of devices being exploited: spellings that show the influence of pronunciation, lack of classical learning (e.g. **Febus** PHOEBUS) and spellings that produce revealing puns (such as **faithfool** FAITHFUL). A similar technique appears in a letter written by Miss Tabitha Bramble in *The Expedition of Humphry Clinker* (1771), whose spellings show traces of her Monmouthshire dialect as well as a lack of education and include suggestive puns (see further Blake 1981: 117, 121).

These associations were still socially significant in the nineteenth century, as can be seen in Fanny Squeer's letter to Ralph Nickleby in Dickens's novel *The Life and Adventures of Nicholas Nickleby* (1839) (see further Brook 1970: 107). Here we find an assortment of non-standard spellings designed to brand the female writer as poorly educated and illiterate. These include **brooses** BRUISES, **goar** GORE, **kimpelled** COMPELLED, **langwedge** LANGUAGE, **pollewt** POLLUTE, **certifiket** CERTIFICATE, **feury** FURY, **sasiated** SATIATED. Some of these reflect a lack of familiarity with the conventions of Latin spelling and thus an inability to correctly spell learned formulations like **compelled**, **language**, **certificate** and **satiated**. This focus on classical conventions is especially apparent in the way Fanny signs off her letter: 'I remain yours and certrer', where the misspelling of ET CETERA especially highlights her lack of classical learning.

11 Reforming spelling

There have been numerous attempts to reform English spelling through-out its history, primarily driven by a desire to restore a closer relationship between spelling and pronunciation. But, while the early Middle English period witnessed local or individual attempts to repurpose spelling con-ventions to reflect regional pronunciation (as we saw in Chapter 2), it was not until the sixteenth century that attempts were made to produce a reformed version of standard English spelling. The earliest spelling reformers emerged from the controversy over the correct pronunciation of ancient Greek, initiated by Erasmus, which promoted a reformed system instead of that of contemporary Greece. This was met with consid-erable opposition from the Chancellor of Cambridge University, Stephen Gardiner, who issued a decree banning use of the reformed system within the university. Those who were discovered to have adopted it would be subject to ejection from the university's Senate. Despite this, two distin-guished Cambridge scholars, Sir John Cheke, Regius Professor of Greek, and Thomas Smith, Regius Professor of Civil Law, remained committed to the reformed system, which in turn prompted them to a reconsidera-tion of English orthography.

11.1 Sir John Cheke

Sir John Cheke devised a new spelling system which he used in the manuscript copy of his translation of the Gospel of St Matthew, accom-panied by a further rendering of part of the first chapter of St Mark's Gospel, thought to have been undertaken ca. 1550. Since Cheke did not publish an account or explanation of his system, we are reliant entirely upon the evidence of its use to reconstruct its principles. One of Cheke's chief considerations concerned the representation of long vowels, which he indicated using double vowels, as in **gaat** GATE, **stoon** STONE, **feest** FEAST and **swijn** SWINE. But this was not carried through with complete consistency; in the case of FRUIT, Cheke used **fruut**, **fruit** and

frute in roughly equal measure. Similar variation can be observed in the spelling of VERY and EVERY, which appear with final <i, ie, y>.

In the treatment of consonants, Cheke's most significant innovation is a form of <g> with a looped ascender like that on the letter <d>, used to represent [dʒ]. Cheke used **yᵉ** and **yᵗ** to represent THE and THAT; **yᵉⁱ**, **yᵉᵐ** and **yᵉʳ** are used alongside **yei**, **yem** and **yeer**. We sometimes find <y> with an acute accent in words like **fayer** and **broyer** FATHER and BROTHER, but in other instances we find <th>, e.g. **throw**, **thow**, **thijn**. We see that /j/ is spelled both <i> and <y>, as in **vijniard** and **vijnyard**. The indication of a long vowel in the opening syllable is probably due to influence from the word VINE, rather than evidence of a lengthening. Two stray occurrences of **hijs** HIS are harder to explain. Dobson (1968: 45) suggests that they are attempts to render the plural form of the possessive pronoun **hise** using Cheke's system. This suggestion may help to explain the distinction between singular and plural HIS in **his wijf hijs childern** (but it may also be that the spelling **hijs** is simply a mistake triggered by the earlier spelling **wijf**).

While <v> and <u> are used as positional variants, as was conventional in this period, Cheke also employs <u> in initial position, so that we find both **vnto** and **unto**. In medial position we find only <v> for the consonant in a handful of words, e.g. **love** and **above**. This lack of consistency sets Cheke apart from other sixteenth-century reformers, one of whose prime concerns was to associate each sound with a single letter and vice versa, as well as to create a system where each word had a single standard spelling form.

Some more idiosyncratic spellings of specific words may derive from his own East Anglian dialect, since Cheke was born in Cambridge. Examples include **sich** SUCH and **mich** MUCH, which appear in small numbers (11 of **sich** and 1 of **mich**) alongside the more widespread equivalents **such(e)** and **much(e)**. The metathesised spelling of THIRSTY as **thrusti** may also derive from this source; John Palsgrave (of Norfolk origins) gives the spelling **thrust** in the entry for **Soyf** in his *Lesclarcissement de la langue francoyse* (1530). The form **hunderd** HUNDRED, more usual in Cheke's text than the occasional **hundred**, is scattered across a number of Middle English dialects, with a cluster of attestations in East Anglia.[1] This dialect form is also recorded in Cheke's **hunderder**, a native coinage offered as an alternative for the more usual Latinate **centurion**. The single instance of **ien** for the demonstrative YON is cited under the b forms in *OED* **yon** adj. and pron., along with examples from other East Anglian

---

1. *A Linguistic Atlas of Late Mediaeval English*, Dot Map 177.

texts.[2] These include *The Castle of Perseverance* from the Macro Plays, *Philotimus* (1588), written by Cambridge-educated Brian Melbancke, and a nineteenth-century vocabulary of East Anglian dialect. The regular spelling of the present participle ending in <–eng> is not due to dialect, however, but is an attempt to avoid <ii> in instances like **criing**, which would otherwise imply a long vowel.

Cheke's phonetic principles are disrupted in a few instances where his spelling is influenced by etymology, as in the spelling of ACHES as **aχes**, no doubt reflecting a false etymological connection with Greek αχοσ. However, in other instances, he rejects the silent letters designed to reflect Latin roots introduced by his contemporaries. Thus he spells DEBT and DEBTOR **det** and **dettor**, and FAULT as **faut**. The inclusion of variants and irregular forms indicate that Cheke had not worked through his system with complete consistency. The presence of spellings showing the influence of his own regional dialect suggests that he was not aiming at creating a standard system that could be adopted on a national basis. This is further supported by the fact that he never published an explanation of his system, while the translations of the Gospels in which it was used also remained in manuscript.

Cheke's system did appear in print, however, in a letter dated July 1557 which he wrote to Sir Thomas Hoby, and which was included at the end of the 1561 edition of Hoby's trans of Castiglione's *Il Cortegiano*, 'The Courtier'. In it Cheke praises his friend's translation and offers a defence of his own practice of avoiding borrowed words in his Bible translation in order to keep our own tongue 'cleane and pure, unmixt and unmangeled with borrowing of other tunges'. Here he uses many of the same distinctive features of his earlier translations of the gospels, although there are some differences. For instance, the word GOOD is always spelled with <oo> to indicate its long vowel in the gospels, but here it is **gud**, a form that suggests a shortening, albeit alongside the traditional spelling **goodness**. An important difference from the spellings employed in the earlier Bible translation may suggest a subsequent development in the system. In the letter to Hoby, Cheke makes use of <oa> in **aloan** (earlier **aloon**) and **boath** (earlier **booth**), indicating an attempt to distinguish /oː/ and /ɔː/, which were both spelled <oo> in his earlier Gospel translations. The Hoby letter also shows the discarding of some of Cheke's more dialectal spellings, perhaps by the compositor of the printed text rather than by Cheke himself. Here we find **suche** rather than **siche**, **she** not **sche**. Other distinctive features of his manuscript translation are not preserved because of the limitation of the printed medium; hence we have **iudgment**, spelled with the conventional <dg> rather than Cheke's own invented letter. There is no sign here of Cheke's version of the letter thorn, which is always replaced by <th>.

This letter reads somewhat oddly as an encomium for Hoby's translation, since it by implication casts some doubt upon Hoby's use of foreign loanwords. Cheke addresses this potential criticism, but notes that Hoby has 'scarslie and necessarily used whear occasion serveth a strange word so' and only when it 'seemeth to grow out of the matter and not to be sought for'. He reassures his friend that he offers such a view only 'for mijn own defens', since he might be considered 'overstraight a deemer of thinges'. Cheke's sense that he needs to defend himself in this context, combined with the potential accusation of his overly narrow and restrictive attitude, suggests that Cheke's aim was to supply an apology of his own views rather than praise of his friend. Cheke's letter ends with a somewhat offhand reference to the 'praise and exhortacion' he would have offered if time had been granted him; instead Cheke has been 'called awai'. The letter was written in July 1557, shortly after Cheke's release from prison and the award of a grant in compensation, following his public recantation in October 1556. Jeremy Smith (2020a) has suggested that Cheke's decision to use the reformed spelling system that he had employed earlier in his Bible translation may have been a coded statement of defiance towards the tyranny of Mary's reign. Such a view does help to explain Cheke's otherwise surprising decision to use this letter to defend his own practice of coining native words in opposition to those of Latin origin, the language of the Catholic Bible.

11.2 Sir Thomas Smith

Sir Thomas Smith was born in Saffron Walden, Essex, in 1513. It was in 1543–4 that Smith was appointed Regius Professor of Civil Law at the University of Cambridge. In 1542 he wrote a volume on the correct pronunciation of Greek, which was published in 1568. In this work Smith argues that the standard for the classical languages should be based upon the usage of the greatest writers, such as Cicero, which was subsequently corrupted. Smith believed that this restoration of the standard classical forms of Latin and Greek by scholars should be extended to their pronunciation. He followed up his publication on Greek pronunciation with a sequel dealing with English: *De recta et emendata linguae anglicae scriptione, Dialogus* (1568). In this work, Smith advocates using as many letters as 'voyces or breathes in speaking and no more, and neuer to abuse one for another'. For Smith, writing is a means of imitating speech, in the same way that a painting attempts to represent a human face on the page. In order to reflect the spoken system accurately, Smith employed a system of marks, including the diaresis, circumflex, macron and hyphen, to indicate vowel length instead of silent letters.

In some of his proposed changes Smith returns to earlier conventions, such as his suggested use of <c> for [tʃ], as in **cop** CHOP; Smith observes that <c> had this use in Old English and in Italian. Given that <c> can signal /s/, Smith argued that <ch> should really be used for [ʃ]. Another innovation that returns to earlier usage is the introduction of the Old English insular <g> for [dʒ]; this is distinguished from <g> which is used for /g/. Smith also re-spelled words like SIGH with an <h>: **sih**. Along with the insular <g>, Smith introduced a number of further innovations, such as a new letter for [v], which resembles a thorn with an angular bowl and no tail, to distinguish it from <u>. Smith employs a variant of <s> with angular lines, like a back-to-front Z, for [ʃ]. He rejects the use of <h> to 'soften' the preceding letter, in digraphs such as <th>, <sh>. Instead of these, he advocates the reviving of the Old English, or 'Saxon', letters: 'thorn d', i.e. <ð> and <þ> for /Θ/, e.g. **ðin** THIN and **þik** THICK; as an alternative solution he also proposes the use of Greek delta <Δ> for [ð], **Δöu** THOU and **Δër** THERE, and Greek theta, <Θ>, for /Θ/. Smith became familiar with the Old English letter <ð> from having seen it in an old manuscript at Ely, from which he quotes several illustrative forms. While it may seem contradictory to offer variants in a new system, Smith saw his work as issuing a series of proposals for implementation, offering users a choice from which they could select.

11.3 John Hart

John Hart was born in Northolt, near London, ca. 1501; he died in London in 1574. His family were tenant farmers, but Hart appears to have been well educated and may have attended Cambridge University, given his links with the Cambridge scholars Thomas Smith and John Cheke. Hart had a successful career in court, initially as a diplomatic courier, then as an official of the court of wards and liveries, later a herald pursuivant and finally being elevated to the position of Chester herald of the College of Arms in 1567. His first treatise on spelling reform survives in a single manuscript dated to 1551 (British Library MS Royal 17 C.vii). This was later expanded, taking account of Smith's recent work, and published as *An Orthographie* (1569). In a further publication, *A Methode or Comfortable Beginning for all Vnlearned* (1570), Hart set out to instruct learners how to adopt the phonetic alphabet that he had constructed. A planned fourth work offering a simplified alphabet was never completed.

As well as being influenced by Smith, Hart was inspired by a contemporary attempt to reform French orthography: Loys Meigret's *Traité touchant le commun usage de l'escriture* (1545). Hart's motivation in proposing his reformed orthography was to raise standards of literacy, as part of his Protestant agenda to encourage more of the laity to read the Bible. Hart was dismayed by the lack of regularity in English spelling, lamenting the disorder and confusion which makes the system a 'kind of ciphring, or such a darke kinde of writing' unfit for recording the spoken language. Hart saw the complexity, lack of regularity and consistency as a handicap to literacy, even going as far as blaming the schoolteachers for putting up with the system so as to gain financially from the extended period of education required to master it.

As well as claiming that his system would accelerate the acquisition of literacy, Hart argued that it would save printers, time, paper and ink. There were also benefits for foreign learners of English, who would not only acquire literacy more efficiently, but would also to come to grasp how the sounds themselves were articulated. One of Hart's reasons for a reform of spelling was to help foreigners and dialect speakers to acquire the most desirable accent: 'for straungers or the rude countrie English man, which may desire to read English as the best sort vse to speake it'.

Hart stands out among the early spelling reformers in having a more nuanced understanding of phonetics. His spellings indicate his awareness of spoken features such as elision, assimilation, stress and intonation. But it is important not to make too great a claim for Hart's phonetic awareness. Lass (1980) has shown how scholars have suggested greater precision in Hart's description than the evidence allows. His claim that the 'a' sound is produced 'with wyde opening the mouth, as whan a man yauneth', can hardly allow us to be precise about the exact quality of the vowel itself. Hart clearly did not recognise the distinction between front and back vowels, despite Dobson's claim that he did (1968: 73).

The main goal of Hart's reforms was to bring spelling and pronunciation closer together, so that each sound was represented by a single letter. In pursuing this objective, he was influenced by the classical grammarians who believed that each letter should correspond to a single sound. Classical writers, such as the Roman grammarian Quintilian, viewed *litterae* as part of a universal alphabet, within which each *littera* mapped on to a single *potestas*. This understanding is apparent from Quintilian's comment about the lack of a *littera* to represent the /w/ sound in words like **seruus** and **uulgus**. Hart adopted a similar approach to his proposed reforms of English spelling. Where English lacked an appropriate letter, Hart chose to devise new ones, rather than 'abusing' other letters by making them represent multiple sounds. Hart objected to the tendency towards 'superfluity': the spelling of a word with more letters than it has sounds, such as in the word PEOPLE. He also opposed unnecessary variation, such as between **sunne** SUN and **sonne** SON, advocating for a phonemic system rather than one that is logographic. Hart argues against the principle of keeping the spellings of borrowed words intact on the grounds that, since foreigners living in England are not required to wear a mark to indicate their origin, so should English words be encouraged to enjoy complete integration.

Some of Hart's innovations are clearly influenced by Smith, such as the proposed introduction of insular g for [dʒ]. However, for [ð] Hart devised his own letter: a variant of <d> with an extra loop, while [Θ] is represented by a <t> with an added loop. Other idiosyncratic adaptations devised by Hart include a form of <s> with a loop to signal [ʃ] and <c> with a loop for [tʃ]. He also introduced a looped version of <l> for the velar /ɬ/ for words like FABLE. Since <g> was only employed for [g], there was no need to use the <gh> in words like **ghost**. Hart's spelling of WHAT, WHEN and WHERE as **huat, huen** and **huer** suggests that these words retained an initial aspiration; Hart describes this letter as having 'no sounde but as you woulde blowe to warme your handes'. His usually careful analysis of pronunciation fails to identify the separate phoneme /ŋ/. While he does observe the [ʒ] sound in words like LEISURE, he does not assign it a separate letter.

These early forays into spelling reform show a number of shared concerns, despite the different solutions proposed by the reformers. Each of these reformers was concerned with making the system more phonetic, with every sound having a single character and with no silent letters. There was also a shared concern with the accurate representation of vowel length, with some reformers advocating a consistent use of double letters, and others the use of dots or diacritics to indicate length.

But, while there was general agreement over these shared concerns, others rejected them and the basic principle of reform altogether. Strong opposition came from the Headmaster of Merchant Tailors' School, Richard Mulcaster, author of *The Elementarie*. Mulcaster considered that the large degree of variation found in English pronunciation meant that it was unsuitable as the basis of a reformed spelling. Although the unreformed system is far from perfect, its establishment and widespread use meant it should not be replaced: '[t]he vse & custom of our cuntrie, hath allredie chosen a kinde of penning, wherein she hath set down hir relligion, hir lawes, hir priuat and publik dealings'. While Mulcaster does make some minor adjustments to this system, such as rejecting superfluous letters and doubling of consonants, his preference is to stick 'to reason and custom' over sound. Mulcaster was also against the introduction of new letters, preferring instead to stick with both the number and use of the traditional alphabet. Where he did propose changes, such as the use of <ss> rather than <zz>, these were driven by the convenience of writing, since <ss> goes more 'roundlie to the pen'.

The tension between phonetic accuracy and usability can be seen in the career of Alexander Gil, who succeeded Mulcaster as the High Master of St Paul's school. Gil published the *Logonomia Anglica* in 1619, in which he set out his proposed system whereby the sounds [ʃ] [ʍ] [Θ] [ŋ] were all represented by single letters. Since the printer lacked the required type for the special characters devised by Gil, these had to be added by hand, either by the author himself or under his close supervision. A second edition was issued in 1621 in which Gil dropped these letters, instead falling back upon the digraphs <sh, th, wh, ng>. While this undoubtedly weakened its phonetic value, it had the benefit of making the work much more practical and easier to use. Gil viewed the current 'cacography' to be the fault of the early printers, beginning a long tradition of blaming foreign compositors for the weaknesses of the English spelling system. In attempting to reform spelling along phonetic lines, Gil was clear that the pronunciation that should form the basis of such a reform ought to be that of the learned, rather than that employed by 'ploughmen, maidservants, and porters'. But, despite that highly prescriptive attitude, Gil is tolerant of spelling variation that reflects regional usage: 'there need not be one fixed way of spelling a word; the spelling may vary if the "dialect" does' (1619: 137). For Gil the basic principle of a reformed system should be that each single element of the voice should be represented by a single character, and that single characters should map on to a single, unique sound. Nothing is more ridiculous, in Gil's view, than a silent letter. It has been suggested that Gil's principles of spelling reform influenced his most famous pupil, John Milton (Darbishire 1931). There are indeed similarities between Milton's spellings of **suttle**, **prisner**, **buis'nesse**, **fiery** and Gil's equivalents, **sutl**, **prizner**, **biznes**, **fjer**; the poet also observes a distinction between **me** and **mee** that conforms to Gil's teaching on the effect of rhetorical stress on vowel quantity. Milton makes careful distinctions in his spelling of the <–ed> ending of past tense and past participle forms of verbs. In examples such as **linked**, **overarch't** and **darken'd** it is clear that the poet intends to distinguish instances where the unstressed vowel is elided from those where it is sounded. However, such spellings are not unique to Gil, and can be paralleled in the work of other contemporary poets. Perhaps it was the impulse to use more phonetic spellings that came from Gil, rather than the individual forms themselves.

The seventeenth century witnessed the publication of a number of additional treatises on spelling reform, especially ones written by schoolteachers for their pupils. Works like Richard Hodges's *English Primrose* (1644) and Edmund Coote's *English Schoole-maister* offered transition scripts and simplified spelling systems, which could be used by pupils acquiring literacy as a stepping-stone to the more complex standard system. Teachers were also concerned with the desirability of a more fully standardised system of both spelling and pronunciation, what Hodges calls greater 'uniformitie, both in our speaking and writing'. These spelling books were supplemented in the eighteenth century with the publication of a number of spelling dictionaries, such as John Newbery's *An Easy Spelling Dictionary* (1745) and Daniel Fenning's *The Universal Spelling-Book* (1756). As we saw in Chapter 5, the eighteenth century was concerned more with stabilisation of spelling than with its reform. Far fewer proposals for reform were published than in the previous century. One exception was an anonymously published work, *The Needful Attempt* (1711), which was concerned with bringing about greater consistency in the relationship between letters and sounds. Another came from the Scottish schoolmaster James Elphinston, author of *Inglish Orthoggraphy Epittomized* (1790), a system in which the use of double consonants to indicate preceding short vowels is rigorously observed. Since 'orthoggraphy iz dhe just Picture ov Speech', Elphinston aimed to make the system more phonetic for fellow Scots who were attempting to gain impeccable English accents.

The nineteenth century witnessed a rise in the scientific study of the English language and with it a deeper, scholarly engagement with the question of spelling reform. James Murray, whom we met in Chapter 5 as the editor of the *New English Dictionary* (later the *Oxford English Dictionary*), confronted this topic in his Presidential lecture to the Philological Society in 1880. In this address, Murray claimed that philologists who once looked askance at proposals to alter spellings whose 'picturesque "irregularities" spoke to them of the dilapidations of centuries' have come to recognise the importance of 'truthful representation' in handing down 'true history'. Murray countered the argument in favour of tradition by observing that a number of valuable reforms to English spelling had already been implemented, such as the seventeenth-century regularisation of <u> and <v>, though he regretted that, in making <v> a consonant, the redundant final <e> was not dropped. Another missed opportunity, according to Murray, was the loss of long-s, which might have been repurposed to represent /ʃ/. The first stage of reform advocated by Murray would be the dropping of letters which are both 'unphonetic and unhistoric', that is, letters for which no etymological justification can be offered. This would include the silent <e> where it does not indicate vowel length, in words like **heavd**, **potatos**, **eatn**, **doctrin**, **favorit**. Other simplifications include dropping the <ue> in **catalogue** and removing the double consonants in words like **traveller** and **reveller**. Murray was aware that such changes were in line with those currently being adopted in the USA; as such they would create greater unity among users of English around the world. A number of the changes urged by Murray are offered on the basis that they restore features of Shakespeare's usage, such as the historical <t> in **fetcht, blusht, pickt**. Appeals to history also involve returning to a stage in the history of English before the Norman Conquest and the interference of French spelling practices. For instance, Murray argues that the introduction of printing means that there is no longer any need for <o> for historical <u>, so that **sum, cum, tung, luv, abuv, wunder** can be 'restored to their native English form ... before Norman cacographers spelled them with o'.

As well as these more systematic changes, Murray's proposals were intended to do away with some of the language's 'worst individual monstrosities': particularly unphonetic spellings such as **foreign, sovereign, scent, island, scythe, rhyme, scissors, ache, debt, doubt, people, parliament, court, would, sceptic**. Under Murray's stewardship, these would become **foren, sovren, sent, iland, sythe, rime, cisors** or **sisors, ake, det, dout, peple, parlament, cort, woud, skeptic**. Anticipating objections that such spellings preserve etymological links, Murray argues that his experience as a lexicographer has taught how such appeals to etymology 'utterly break down upon examination':

> The etymological information supposed to be enshrined in the current spelling is sapped at its very foundation by the fact that it is, in sober fact, oftener wrong than right, that it is oftener the fancies of pedants or sciolists of the Renascence, or monkish etymologers of still earlier times, that are thus preserved.

Deliberate changes that were introduced in the Renaissance mean that the true history of many words has been concealed. As a consequence, etymological spellings are the 'direst foes with which genuine etymology has to contend; they are the very curse of the etymologist's labor, the thorns and thistles which everywhere choke the golden grain of truth, and afford satisfaction only to the braying asses which think them as good as wheat'.

Murray ended his lecture by recognising that spelling will inevitably lag behind speech. As a consequence, it is futile to attempt to devise a system that is fully phonetic. In urging the adoption of a more phonetic system, Murray avoids the problem of diversity of accents, conveniently focusing on just one: the 'ideal of speech to which all educated Englishmen approximate', rather than the 'slurred or imperfect utterance of the average Londoner'. This focus on the educated southern accent recalls George Puttenham's injunction in *The Arte of English Poesie* (1589) that his readers use 'the vsuall speach of the Court, and that of London and the shires lying about London within lx. myles, and not much aboue'.

By the end of the 1870s, there was an increasing appetite for a group to lobby parliament for the appointment of a Royal Commission of Inquiry to determine whether a reform of the English Spelling system was, in the in first instance, desirable, in the second, practicable. This led to the constitution of an association for promoting reform, with an office in London, which comprised many leading philologists, literary figures, scientists, as well as prominent schoolteachers and educationalists. The English Spelling Reform Association was established, with a series of principles shared by all of its members. These involved a belief that the present system was hindering the acquisition of literacy and that a better system could be developed on rational grounds which would greatly reduce the time taken to learn to read, freeing up school time for other educational pursuits. Beyond these practical benefits would come the more widespread adoption of the Received Pronunciation accent and the universal use of the English language throughout the world. In a tract published in 1880, a member of the Association, J. B. Rundell, set out the progress made in achieving its goals of collecting and distributing literature on the subject, instituting experiments in the use of reformed systems in classrooms and holding lectures and large-scale events to publicise the work. While progress was being made with regard to each of these objectives, Rundell accepted that lack of funding and the lack of a regular periodical were hindering the Association's work. Rundell also acknowledged that it was much easier to get a pamphlet printed than it was to circulate it widely and ensure that it was read and fully digested. The Association was not concerned with advocating for a particular reformed system to replace the traditional one, but rather with raising public awareness of the costs in terms of 'time, money, temper and brains' in sticking with the status quo.

Not all nineteenth-century men of letters were enthusiastic about the potential offered by spelling reform. In 1847, Thomas De Quincey published a lengthy critique of the numerous such proposals, suggesting that an entirely new dictionary would soon be required to keep track of all the alternative spellings that have been suggested. Despite Isaac Pitman being knighted for his efforts on behalf of the English spelling system in 1894, his efforts to inculcate a reformed system had little traction. When compulsory primary education was introduced with the Education Act of 1870, the curriculum showed no interest in adopting his proposals, even though they were formulated specifically to facilitate the acquisition of literacy. Indeed, much of the debate about the desirability of a reformed spelling system was conducted in learned periodicals read by the middle classes – the *Westminster Review, Nineteenth Century* and the *Saturday Review* – and had little engagement with those responsible for primary education.

While those concerned with advocating for spelling reform argued for its benefits for the acquisition of literacy, others objected to its tendency towards elitism. By requiring working-class children to learn an entirely new spelling system, they would be denied access to the classic works of English literature which were all composed in the historical system. Even if publishers did eventually re-issue editions of classic works in the new spelling, these would remain beyond the reach of the poor, who typically accessed such works in second-hand copies. Other contributors to the debate in the London journals advocated a more etymological spelling, while still others pointed out the fallacy of attempting to return to a single historical point in the evolution of the language. It was in part this lack of agreement as to the most desirable reforms and their rationale that hampered the reformers' agenda. In a report on letter E of the *New English Dictionary*, Henry Bradley reflected on the difficulties thrown up by the large number of classical derivatives found in this section. Since in each case it would be possible to argue in favour of a variety of different pronunciations on etymological grounds, Bradley concludes that the best pronunciation is 'that which most effectually and promptly suggests to the mind the written form of the word' (Bradley 1891–4: 164).

Difficulties of this kind lead Bradley to observe how many serious objections there are to a phonetic spelling system, and how little its proponents have managed to address them. Bradley notes that a phonetic system would be highly desirable if the function of writing was merely to represent speech, and if the first task of any reader was to read a text aloud, but neither of these is in fact true. Instead, Bradley notes the ideographic value of many combinations of letters, which are processed without being rendered phonetically at all. Bradley responds to the objection that spelling reform would obscure the etymology of words by noting that this is of little significance to most readers and is irrelevant for all colloquial words. However, for those words derived from the classical languages, whose meanings are often closely linked to their etymological roots, this would be a severe hindrance. While Bradley does admit that some slight gains could be made by the gradual introduction of minor changes in the phonetic direction for some words, he concludes that there is no practical way of substantially lessening the burden upon children learning to read.

As Daniel Jones noted in 1869: 'No individual or society under present circumstances would have sufficient influence to introduce an improved system of orthography; if done at all, it must be the public generally'. In the end, one of the most important factors in the failure of the spelling reform campaign was the reluctance of the printers to embrace change. Having underestimated the difficulties that his Glossic system would cause printers, with its new letterforms, A. J. Ellis (1870) introduced a reformed version. But neither was taken up as an alternative to the traditional spelling system, although they were widely used for the study of regional accents by Ellis himself and others.

In 1908 the Simplified Spelling Society was founded in order to campaign for reform in various pamphlets and a regular journal. The Society counted a large number of distinguished academics and writers among its members, including the etymologist Walter W. Skeat, the phonetician Daniel Jones and the writer George Bernard Shaw. This was something of a turnaround for Skeat, who had previously published a letter in *The Athenaeum* highlighting the flaws in trying to devise a phonetic system modelled on a constantly changing pronunciation. Shaw was a fierce critic of the English spelling system, with its numerous inconsistencies and unnecessary letters. A more phonetic system would mean shorter words with huge savings for children learning to spell and for writers: 'Shakespear might have written two or three more plays in the time it took him to spell his name with eleven letters instead of seven' (see Carney 1994: 484). To fix this problem, he left a considerable sum of money to be awarded to the winner of a competition to devise an alternative system, which should have the same number of symbols as there are sounds and with related sounds being represented by related letters. The judging panel eventually selected the system devised by Kingsley Read to be the official 'Shavian' alphabet; Read's system was closely based on contemporary shorthand systems, such as that devised by Isaac Pitman, which Shaw himself used. But, while Shaw adopted Pitman's system for his own personal use, he considered that its unsuitability for printing made it unacceptable as the basis for an alternative spelling system. The new Shavian alphabet was used for the publication of Shaw's play *Androcles and the Lion* in 1962, with a preface written by James Pitman, the grandson of Isaac Pitman, advocating on behalf of the system and its benefits.

James Pitman was himself a spelling reformer and a member of an exclusive club of reformers whose proposals were actually implemented. Pitman was the deviser of the Initial Teaching Alphabet (or I.T.A.) which was a simplified system intended to be used in the instruction of young children, who were then introduced to the full system at the age of seven.

The alphabet employed the basic set of letters alongside ligatures in which digraphs like <th> and <ch> were written as a single symbol. Reversing letters, e.g. the <t> in <th> or the <z>, signalled when the sound was voiced. Ligatures were also devised to represent long vowels and diphthongs, with the intention of producing the 42 symbols needed to represent the full set of English phonemes. I.T.A. was adopted in a number of English schools in the 1960s, spreading to the United States and Australia. The biggest drawback associated with its use was the difficulty children found transitioning to the standard system, often meaning a delay in their acquisition of full literacy; other pupils exposed to the I.T.A. recall being unable to read at the age of seven.[3]

Even some modern scholars have felt inclined to support calls for spelling reform. In 2008, the eminent phonetician John Wells, president of the English Spelling Society, proposed relaxing spelling rules, accepting variants such as **thru** and **lite**, and ceasing to distinguish between **they're**, **their** and **there**. In his speech to the Conservative Party conference in October 2008 David Cameron attacked Wells's proposals, reformulating them as a direct assault upon educational standards: 'He's the President of the Spelling Society. Well, he's wrong. And by the way, that's spelt with a "W"'. In the chapter on 'Standardization and Spelling Reform' in his compendious account of English spelling, Edward Carney cannot resist the urge to advocate for a re-spelling of **woman** as **wummen** and **women** as **wimmin**:

> Had this not been a strictly neutral study of English spelling conventions, I might have been tempted to say that both <woman> and <women> are really quite ridiculous spellings and that *<wummun> and *<wimmin>, with their flowing minim strokes are both phonetically apt and graphically pleasing. (Carney 1994: 470)

It is interesting that Carney's argument for the change is not simply based on phonetic suitability but extends to include graphic appearance.

A co-author of the recent, comprehensive historical survey of English spelling, *The History of English Spelling*, Christopher Upward, was editor-in-chief of the *Journal of the Simplified Spelling Society* and deviser of Cut Spelling, a system of reducing the number of unnecessary letters in English spelling. As well as removing silent letters, like the <b> in DOUBT or DEBT, Cut Spelling proposed dropping unstressed vowels and simplifying double consonants, e.g. **ad** ADD and **add** ADDED. While the result is a shorter and simpler system, a number of additional

---

3. See further 'Educashunal lunacie or wizdom?', 5 September 2001, <http://news.bbc.co.uk/1/hi/uk/1523708.stm>

homonyms are formed which could lead to confusion, e.g. the spelling of both PEACE and PIECE as **pece**. The contemporary arguments in favour of spelling reform remind us that the spelling system is a tool for communication and not an inherent feature of the English language itself. Yet these same reformers must also recognise the universality of this system and thus the great difficulty and expense of attempting to change it.

12 Creating your own research project

This chapter is intended to offer an overview of a selection of resources that are available for the study of English spelling and to suggest ways in which they could be used to carry out original research.

12.1 Analysing Middle English spelling

The *Middle English Dictionary* is the primary resource for studying the ME lexicon, but it also includes valuable data for the analysis of spelling variation in this period.[1] Each entry comprises a headword followed by a list of forms, which includes a representative list of relevant spellings identified during the process of assembling the entry. While these can be extensive and detailed, it is important to recognise that these lists of forms are not, nor are they intended to be, exhaustive. Another limitation of the *MED* form list is the lack of labelling, so that it is not always apparent what the different spellings represent. Since ME covers four centuries of language use, some of the forms will belong to early ME and others to later ME, thereby reflecting diachronic change. In Chapter 2, we saw the extent to which ME dialectal variation was reflected in the written mode. While there is evidently much useful data for the study of ME dialectology in these form lists, it is not always clear which dialects the forms represent, nor are the documents from which they are drawn easily discovered. Below is a sample entry, relating to the adjective **swich** SUCH:

> **swich** adj. Also *swiche, swihche, swhiche, sqwiche, swilc, swilk(e, swiulc, swil, swik, swhi(l)k, squilk(e, swech(e, schwe(s)che, swelk, squech, swoch,* (K) *zuich(e, zueche* & *s(c)hich, shoch, scoche, shuch(e, schusche, schuich, schuilk,* (N) *schilke* & *sich(e, sech(e, sec, soch(e, soiche, souche, such(e, sucche, suc, suich(e,* (chiefly N or NM) *silk(e, sik(e,* (N) *silc, sulk,* (K infl.) *sucher* &

1. <https://quod.lib.umich.edu/m/middle-english-dictionary/dictionary>, accessed 29 August 2024.

(early) *swicche, swic(e, swics, svich, swilch(e, swilce, suwilk, swecche, suweche, swulc, sug,* (SW or SWM) *swuch(e, swucche, swuc, swuhc, swulch(e, swulke, shwuche, schuch(e, schuc, schuuich, scuche, sulche, sulc, sulke, secc, selk* & (early infl., chiefly dat.) *swilcen, swilcere,* (SWM) *swulc(c)here, swulcere, sulchere, soc(c)here, solchere* & (early acc.) *swichne, suicchne, swilcne,* (SW or SWM) *swuchne, swulcne, swulne, sulcne, sochne* & (?errors) *shch, sywch,* (error) *swedche*; pl. (early) *swilcen,* (SWM) *swulchen* & (early infl.) *swilcere,* (dat.) *swicum.* For forms *schch, sche(ch(e, scht, schut(e, scwche, selk, sewyche, sic, squike, sswiche, suchet, sucht(e, suhc, suhe, sutche, syge*

This is a rich list of forms which offers an extensive selection of relevant spellings, but with little labelling to guide the researcher as to the significance of the different forms. In a few cases there are indications of likely dialect provenance, e.g. **zuich(e**, which is given as Kentish (K), and **swulchen**, which is labelled South-West Midlands (SWM). In other cases, the dialect labelling is kept relatively broad: SW [i.e. South-West] or N [North]. More problematic is the large number of spellings that have no dialect provenance at all.

One way of making up for the lack of information about the source of a particular spelling is to search the quotations in the entry in order to find examples, from which one can get a sense of its likely provenance. For instance, **swech** is found in four quotations drawn from different texts written by John Capgrave. Capgrave was an Augustinian friar from Bishop's Lynn in Norfolk; given that the three manuscripts from which these four quotations are drawn are autograph copies, ones in the author's own hand, it seems highly likely that this represents his own preferred spelling for this item. The Norfolk provenance of this spelling is further reinforced by its appearance in quotations from other manuscripts from this area. For instance, the spelling is also recorded in a quotation from the Book of Margery Kempe, BL MS Additional 61823. Since Margery Kempe was also from Bishop's Lynn, this instance adds further support to the theory that it is a form associated with that town. But there are also other instances that it is not possible to localise with the same degree of precision. One example is listed merely as a variant of the form **swiche**, recorded at line D451 of Chaucer's Wife of Bath's Prologue. Since we are not even told in which manuscript the **sweche** spelling is found, it is difficult to trace the source and determine whether this supports the Norfolk provenance, or calls it into question.

Another shortcoming of this evidence is the lack of information concerning relative frequencies, so that we get no sense of which are the most commonly used forms, and which are comparatively rare. The spelling **squech** is only recorded in a single quotation, a Paston Letter dated to

c. 1461; was this a common form in Norfolk, one that may have been used alongside **sweche**, or is this idiosyncratic form found only in the output of this single writer? In the case of the spelling **schuuich**, there are no quotations that include this form, so we have no way of tracing its use nor establishing how widely it was employed. That some spellings were only found in early ME usage is suggested by the label (early), which is added to **swicche**, a spelling only recorded in the early thirteenth-century BL Cotton Cleopatra C.VI manuscript of the *Ancrene Riwle*. Another tricky category are those spellings that are labelled errors: **shch**, **sywch**, **swedche**. While these are indeed unusual spellings that do not conform to the usual pattern of spellings of this word, it is difficult to know how to identify an error with certainty in a period in which spelling was so variable.

A useful way of extending the analysis of the *MED* entries is to search the Corpus of Middle English Prose and Verse that is offered as part of the integrated Middle English Compendium.[2] A search for the spelling **sweche** in that resource returns 22 relevant records with a total of 179 matches. This data helps to reinforce and extend the suggestion above that this spelling was particularly associated with the Norfolk dialect, since 60 of these occurrences appear in Cambridge University Library MS Gg.4.27, a manuscript containing Chaucer's *Canterbury Tales*, *Troilus and Criseyde* and other works, which is thought to have been copied in East Anglia. But this manuscript does not account for all the instances of this spelling in the corpus. A further 37 occurrences are found in *The History of the Holy Grail*, translated from French by the London skinner Henry Lovelich, while a further 11 instances appear in a vernacular version of the French *Merlin*, also by Henry Lovelich. Since we know that Lovelich was a Londoner, this evidence may call into question the suggested Norfolk/East Anglian provenance proposed above. But since there was considerable movement between London and East Anglia during this period, it is not difficult to imagine this spelling travelling between the two places. Its presence in the repertoire of a Londoner like Lovelich is a reminder of the variety that was tolerated in the London dialect in the middle of the fifteenth century, further questioning the existence of a Chancery Standard, as debated in Chapter 3.

The *MED* and its associated corpus are thus very useful ways of surveying the variation found in ME spelling. But there are some limitations, since the corpus is skewed towards literary texts and is taken from old editions of texts in which the spelling may have been emended in some way. This kind of editorial intervention was particularly common among early editors of medieval texts, who would frequently supplement gaps in

---

2. <https://quod.lib.umich.edu/m/middle-english-dictionary>, accessed 29 August 2024.

a manuscript by drawing upon an alternative witness, thereby conflating the spelling systems of different scribal outputs. This can be very misleading when used as the basis of studies of a single scribe's spelling system; this problem undermined a study of Chaucer's spelling by Larry D. Benson, who used the nineteenth-century Chaucer Society transcripts as the basis for his analysis (Horobin 2003).

A useful supplement to the *MED* corpus is offered by the corpus of Middle English Local Documents (MELD), assembled by a team at Stavanger University, Norway, under the direction of Merja Stenroos.[3] The texts included in this corpus are administrative documents rather than literary texts. Since they were transcribed direct from the documents themselves, they preserve the actual usage of the documents, without any editorial interference. Since these texts cover the period 1399–1525 and include precise information about their date and place of copying, they are especially valuable for our understanding of late ME dialect variation. This project is still ongoing; the current version (MELD 2017.1) comprises 840 texts from the eastern and southern counties of England. When complete, the corpus will consist of 2,000 texts covering the whole of the country. The corpus can be searched as a complete collection of texts, or as smaller, representative selections. Since these are administrative, non-literary documents, they have the benefit of having internal evidence by which they can be clearly associated with a particular location. As an example, we can use texts from this corpus to supplement our earlier discussion of the dialect of Bishop's (now King's) Lynn. One relevant example is the following document, which is a notary record now held by the King's Lynn Borough Archives (KL/C7/4 fol. 97v). One of the striking aspects of this document is how standardised its spelling appears. There are fewer distinctively regional features than might have been expected, with spellings such as **not, whiche, yet, other, suche, right, against,** although a number of regional forms continue to appear alongside these, e.g. **afore, tofore, moche.** Carrying out small-scale studies of particular regions, supplementing the more diverse literary evidence of the *MED* with localised documents in MELD, helps to build up a clearer picture of the ways in which regional orthographies shifted towards more a standardised usage during the ME period.

12.2 Analysing the spelling of printed books

As we saw in Chapter 3, scholars have long believed that the decisive factor in the standardisation of written English was the introduction of

3. <https://www.uis.no/en/research/meld-corpus-files>, accessed 29 August 2024.

printing using movable type by William Caxton in 1476. The importance of this date for linguistic history is apparent from its use as the dividing line between Middle English and Early Modern English by the *Cambridge History of the English Language* volume 2 (1066–1476) and volume 3 (1476–1776). Where Middle English is characterised by great diversity in the written mode, the introduction of printing ushered in a new era of regularity and consistency that formed the basis of our modern standard system. The most recent historical survey of English spelling emphatically affirms that printing was the means by which a standard system was established and that Caxton's role in the process was 'crucial' (Upward and Davidson 2011: 84).

There has, however, been no systematic study of the spelling of Caxton's printed output in order to determine the extent to which he did indeed impose a consistent orthography across his works, and, if such a 'house style' can be identified, whether it reflects a nascent London standard. One of the reasons why these claims have remained largely hypothetical, and why examination of the spelling of early printed books has been limited to small-scale, exploratory studies, is the vast amount of linguistic data involved. However, the availability of fully searchable SGML/XML-encoded texts of the books collected in the Early English Books Online Database[4] makes a large-scale study possible, allowing the detailed investigation of Caxton's entire output. In Chapter 3 we saw that M. L. Samuels argued that Caxton's usage showed a 'gradual tendency to discard Kenticisms in favour of standard forms'. But, searching the corpus reveals that the Kentish spellings identified by Samuels continued to appear in printed books issued throughout Caxton's career, revealing a more complex situation than Samuels suggests. In order to account for this variation, we need to analyse their distribution across Caxton's printed books and within the works themselves. Only then can we determine whether they reflect compositors carrying over spellings from their exemplars, the different preferences of individual compositors, or spellings associated with an incipient standard variety.

The availability of the EEBO database means that we can begin to address these questions. For instance, in support of his claim that Caxton discarded Kentish dialect forms in favour of a London Standard during the fifteenth century, Samuels cited the examples of the words ASK and THROUGH. He argued that it is possible to trace a movement from the Kentish dialect spellings **axe** and **thurgh** to the Chancery equivalents **ask** and **through**. But if we look at the data provided by the Early English

4. <https://textcreationpartnership.org/tcp-texts/eebo-tcp-early-english-books-online>, accessed 29 August 2024.

Books online for these spellings, we can see that, while there is evidently a gradual reduction in the use of **axe** and **thurgh**, and a corresponding increase in **ask** and **through**, it is hardly decisive and cannot be explained as Caxton consciously shedding his regional features in favour of those of the standard. In the case of ASK, it is not until the sixteenth century that the standard **ask** spelling becomes the dominant form, while the **axe** spelling continues to appear throughout this century. In the case of THROUGH, we find a significant increase in use of the standard **through** in the 1490s, although the **thurgh** form remains dominant; once again, it is only in the sixteenth century that the shift becomes most evident. But these are just two variant spellings relating to two linguistic items; for a meaningful analysis, it would be necessary to consider a much more extensive list of items and to examine the full range of variant spellings. A key problem that bedevils much analysis of this kind is the difficulty of knowing which variant spellings are likely to appear in order to search for them. Because this corpus is not lemmatised, it is not possible to search for all variants of the item SUCH; instead, one is left searching individually for variant spellings such as **swich**, **swech**, **swuch** and so on. This method means that it is quite possible that minor or unexpected variants will be missed. But, while this was a significant problem in the assembly of *A Linguistic Atlas of Late Mediaeval English*, for which the editors had to assemble a list of items on a questionnaire and then analyse the manuscripts by hand, it is less problematic when using a corpus. For the *LALME* researchers the assembly of the questionnaire was key, since it would not be possible to add to it once the process of data collection had begun. When using an electronic corpus, it is always possible to add items to a questionnaire during the process of data collection, so that the selection of items at the outset is less crucial. This means that, if one begins searching for a set list of items, e.g. **swich**, **swech**, **swuch**, and then comes across another alternative, **swoch**, it is possible to add this to the list of items and carry out a set of searches accordingly. This method of searching the Early English Books Online Database has the potential to shed new light on the process of standardisation of spelling in early printed books. Surveys could be carried out on specific chronological ranges, or on the works of particular printers. These smaller-scale studies will help to build up a much clearer and more detailed picture of the way in which printers and compositors began to standardise the spellings used in their printed books.

Tracking informal spelling practices I: the Paston Letters

Tracing the development of a standard spelling system in printed books only accounts for part of the evidence for the process of standardisation in that it overlooks the substantial body of informal spelling practices from this period. An important resource for tracing the standardisation of spelling in private writing is the substantial collection of letters written by members of the Paston family, which range from the fourteenth to the sixteenth centuries. John Fisher (1996: 61) has drawn on the evidence of the two Paston brothers known as John II and John III as support for his claim that the adoption of Chancery Standard spellings was closely linked to social advancement. According to his account, the two brothers used Norfolk dialect spellings in their early letters but began to replace these with their Chancery Standard equivalents in the 1460s, once they had moved to London and taken service in the royal court.

The availability of electronic transcriptions of the relevant letters,[5] supported by high-resolution digital images of a substantial set of their correspondence,[6] makes it possible to re-examine Fisher's claims in greater detail. The British Library has digitised four volumes of letters covering the period 1440–1489 (British Library Additional MSS 43488, 43489, 43490, 43491) and a volume containing material from the second half of the fifteenth century, along with letters dating from the later sixteenth century (British Library Additional MS 33597). What emerges from such a reconsideration is a much more complex situation than the simple narrative constructed by Fisher. If changes in the brothers' spelling habits were indeed motivated by the prestige of Chancery Standard, and a corresponding devaluing of their own regional usage, we would expect to see the brothers' habits moving in the same direction at a similar rate. But, in fact, the two brothers often show opposing sets of preferences.

For instance, John Paston II consistently employs the spelling **such**, associated by Samuels with Chancery Standard – there is just one example of a variant spelling **syche** in a letter of 1473. John Paston III, however, never uses the **such** form, preferring to use **sych(e)** throughout his correspondence, with a single exception of **sich** in 1500. John II uses **myche** in his first letter of 1461, switching to Chancery **moche** for the remainder. But if this were a conscious switch from a provincial spelling to a more prestigious equivalent, then it seems odd that John III should have used **myche** throughout his entire correspondence. This is not because he was unaware of the **moche** spelling – he used it himself just once in 1474 – but evidently he simply did not consider it necessary to alter his preferences. Furthermore, if John II's switch to **moche** was prompted by its perceived prestige, it seems strange that he should have introduced

5. <https://quod.lib.umich.edu/c/cme/Paston>, accessed 29 August 2024.
6. <https://blogs.bl.uk/digitisedmanuscripts/2015/04/the-paston-letters-go-live.html>, accessed 29 August 2024.

the marked East Anglian spelling **meche** on two occasions, a form never employed by his brother.

John II used **any** throughout, with no instances of **eny**, the spelling of this word that is apparently so typical of Chancery documents that Fisher considered it to be a 'Chancery shibboleth'. John III's letters, on the other hand, have 5 instances of **ony**, which appear in just three letters written between 1462 and 1464; all other instances are spelled **eny**. This may perhaps be indicative of a shift in preference, although it is hard to square with the lack of instances of the spelling in his brother's correspondence.

So, while there are indeed changes in spelling habits across the brothers' correspondence, these are hard to square with a simplistic narrative in which the two men discarded their native forms in recognition of the greater prestige attached to those used by members of the court. It is by no means clear that the brothers perceived their own Norfolk forms to be socially disadvantageous, nor is it apparent that they were anxious to adopt a single socially prestigious alternative. More detailed interrogation of this extensive corpus of letters, drawing upon these valuable primary resources, will enable us to assemble a much more nuanced picture of the development of private spelling habits among an upwardly mobile gentry family in fifteenth-century England.

Tracking informal spelling practices II: John Clare

There is much research still to be done on informal spelling practices of the Late Modern period; this period has been particularly neglected by scholars on the assumption that the spelling system was entirely fixed by this period in its history and that there is therefore little variation to be investigated. A further reason for its neglect is the presumption that the spelling of contemporary printed books is that of compositors rather than their authors. Where variation can be recovered from printed books, it is considered to be of little interest. But this attitude ignores the variation that is attested in authorial manuscripts of this period, which was generally removed by compositors in favour of the standard system. Modern editors of these works have generally taken a similar approach, removing spelling variation found in authorial manuscripts in favour of the PDE standard spelling system. A good example of an author whose spelling is worthy of more detailed examination is the poet John Clare (1793–1864), whose decidedly irregular spelling practices have been recently considered by Philip Durkin (2016). Since Clare had little formal education, previous editors have tended to ignore his unusual forms; however, more recent editions present his spellings as they appear in the originals, providing a fascinating insight into his practices. While spellings such as **neeghbour**, **chusing**, **wether** WHETHER, **colledge**, **heir long** HEIRLOOM, and **tha** THE are unusual, they are not all unique to Clare; some are found in other non-professional writing of the period and in published writings from the preceding century. Seen against this background of informal spelling practices, Clare's usage no longer seems so idiosyncratic.

But what about those spellings that cannot be easily paralleled in other sources? Should they be dismissed as Clare's personal oddities, or might it be that it is our lack of comprehensive sources that means they only appear to be unique to him? Might Clare simply be offering evidence of the continuity of such older forms in the Northamptonshire dialect, for which he is an important source in both the *OED* and the *English Dialect Dictionary*? While a spelling like **pregudice** may not preserve any interesting phonological data, it does offer a link to the pre-1700 spellings with <g> listed in *OED*, and it points forward to the large number of examples that can be found on the Internet or on social media sites like Twitter today. While Clare's spelling **surcumstance** is extremely rare, it is not unique to him. *OED* records **surcomstance** from the 1500s and Google books throws up a number of later instances, including one from a New York petition of 1776. More analysis of the spellings of Clare's manuscripts will likely reveal additional examples of his non-standard forms, while wider consideration of the spelling systems employed by authors in their manuscripts will undoubtedly reveal a greater degree of variation than that found in printed text of this period.

The *English Dialect Dictionary*, edited by Joseph Wright, was issued between 1898 and 1905 in parts intended to be bound into six volumes; the final volume also includes an English Dialect Grammar. It has recently been digitised by a team at the University of Innsbruck, under the direction of Professor Manfred Markus.[7] As noted above, the *English Dialect Dictionary* preserves a variety of primary spelling data which has yet to be harnessed in a study of regional spelling variation and which would offer a useful supplement to the assessment of the spellings of individual authors like John Clare. For instance, an entry like that for BRAMBLE begins with a listing of the various alternative forms accompanied by a record of the counties in which they are attested:

> **BRAMBLE,** *sb.* and *v.* In *gen.* dial. use in Sc. Irel. and
> Eng. Also in forms **bramley** Wm.; **brammle** e.Yks.1;
> **bremble** Dor.; **bremel** Nhb.1; **brimble** Chs.13 Shr.1 Sur.

---

7. English Dialect Dictionary online: <https://eddonline-proj.uibk.ac.at/edd>, accessed 29 August 2024.

Dor. Cor.; **brimel** Wxf.1; **brimmel** Nhb.1: **brimmle** Wm.1
w.Som.1; **broomle** Cum.; **brumble** e.An.1 Nrf.1 Suf.1;
brumley Cum. Yks.; **brummel** n.Yks.12 ne.Yks.1 m.Yks.1
Hmp.1

Searching the dictionary database as a whole reveals a number of additional examples, which extend and refine the dialect evidence given above. For instance, the **brummel** spelling appears to be quite strongly indicative of a Yorkshire provenance. This is reinforced by the Yorkshire expression **brummel-nooas'd** BRAMBLE-NOSED (referring to having a purple nose like a drunkard); however, in Aberdeenshire we find the term **brummel brod**, to refer to a thorn on a bramble, indicating a more extended provenance than suggested by the list of spellings given in the entry. Research of this kind would enable a greater sense of the regional diversity of spelling during the period 1700–1900 covered by the *English Dialect Dictionary*.

12.3 Analysing the spelling of Present-day English

In Chapter 6 we considered the differences between British and US spellings, although we also noted the complex patterns of affiliations found in other Global varieties of English. To trace these patterns of use we employed the GloWbE corpus: a collection of text comprising 1.9 billion words from twenty different countries.[8] By searching GloWbE for pairs of spellings such as the British and American English variants of COLOUR, we can trace their use around the world. In this particular instance, the GloWbE corpus shows strong preferences for the **color** spelling in countries like India, the Philippines and Hong Kong, while Canada, Australia, New Zealand and Zimbabwe have more instances of the British spelling. Others, like Nigeria, Ghana, Sri Lanka and Jamaica, are quite evenly split between the two spellings.

Not all spelling variation maps on to geography: it is notable that there are a substantial number of supposedly US spellings in the British corpus and vice versa. What do these represent? Is this evidence of change in progress? The fury provoked by the appearance of **favor** as an answer to the *New York Times* puzzle Wordle would suggest the British are unlikely to be adopting **color** in the near future. But, despite this, searching the GloWbE corpus is a useful way of gauging the extent to which US spellings are becoming more popular in the UK. For instance, in Chapter 6 we noted the difference between the British spelling **fulfil** and the US

---

8. <https://www.english-corpora.org/glowbe>, accessed 29 August 2024.

alternative **fulfill**. But while dictionaries like *OED* present this as a clear distinction in preferences, the evidence is not quite so clear cut. Searching the GloWbE corpus for both spellings reveals that, while **fulfil** is indeed the dominant form in the UK, with a total of 3,517 occurrences, the US equivalent, **fulfill**, is recorded in 1,965 instances. Browsing through these instances of the **fulfill** spelling suggests that it is most commonly found online, such as in personal blogs or in comments added to newspaper articles. A feature of these forums is that writing is usually more informal and has not gone through any formal procedures of checking or editing. But whether this is influence of the Americanisation of English spelling remains debatable. As we saw in Chapter 6, the **fulfill** spelling was widespread in earlier varieties of English; furthermore, it is a logical way of spelling a word whose second element is the word **fill**, so that it may be triggered by a process of analogy that assumes that it will be spelled accordingly. Although the spelling **fullfill** is much less frequent, with just twenty-eight instances in the UK component of the GloWbE corpus, its appearance in comments posted on websites shows a similar process of analogy at work in unmediated spelling practices.

The GloWbE corpus is also a useful tool for tracking the emergence of variant spellings, as they begin to become more widely accepted into general use. The word **minuscule** is derived from Latin **minusculus**, meaning 'somewhat smaller', and the earliest recorded spelling is accordingly **minuscule**. The original pronunciation had stress on the second syllable and consequently the vowel was clearly and distinctly pronounced. A later development saw the stress shift to the first syllable, leading to confusion concerning the identity of the unstressed vowel. This, combined with the false association with the **mini** in words like MINIMUM and MINIATURE, led to the emergence of an alternative spelling **miniscule**. This spelling has its own entry in the *OED*, with the earliest examples dating from 1874, suggesting that this is now an acceptable alternative spelling of MINUSCULE. Such a view appears to be supported by the *Oxford A-Z of Better Spelling*, which reports that **miniscule** now accounts for 52% of total occurrences of this word in the Oxford English Corpus, a database of over 2 billion words representing English of the twenty-first century. However, it is not as straightforward as these figures suggest, since the Oxford guide also warns that, despite having now overtaken the standard spelling in terms of usage, the **miniscule** spelling has 'not yet become accepted as standard English', advising its readers to treat it as an error to be avoided. The GloWbE corpus shows that this spelling is in use in all Global varieties of English represented in that corpus. The largest number of occurrences is in the USA (607), although Great Britain (473) and Australia (301) also return substantial numbers; in each case the number of **miniscule** spell-ings surpasses the number of instances of the earlier form **minuscule**. Tracing the emergence of such variant forms, their distribution and the process by which they become accepted offers valuable insights into the way spelling is changing today.

References

Primary sources

Anon, *The London Universal Letter-Writer* (1800)

Anon, *Minutes of Several Conversations between the Rev. John Wesley, M.A., and others, from the year 1744, to the year 1789* (London, 1827)

Anon, *The Needful Attempt* (1711)

Anon, *A Spelling Book for Children, with a short Catechism* (1707)

Ash, John, *The new and complete dictionary of the English language Volume I* (1775)

Bailey, Nathan, *An Universal Etymological English Dictionary* (1727)

Billingsley, Martin, *The Pen's Excellencie, or, The Secretaries delight* (1618)

Bunce, Oliver Bell, *Don't: A Manual of Mistakes & Improprieties more or less prevalent in Conduct & Speech* (1884).

Butler, Charles, *English Grammar* (1633)

Cawdrey, Robert, *A Table Alphabeticall* (1604)

Cobbett, William, *A Grammar of the English language, in a series of letters* (1833)

Coote, Edmund, *English Schoole-maister* (1596)

Daines, Simon, *Orthoepia Anglicana* (1640)

Dyche, Thomas, *A Guide to the English Tongue* (1707)

Elphinston, James, *Inglish Orthoggraphy Epittomized* (1790)

Fenning, Daniel, *The Universal Spelling-Book* (1756)

Gil, Alexander, *Logonomia Anglica* (1619, 1621)

Hart, John, *A Methode or Comfortable Beginning for all Vnlearned* (1570)

——— *An Orthographie* (1569)

Hodges, Richard, *English Primrose* (1644)

Holder, William, *Elements of Speech* (1669)

Johnson, Samuel, *Dictionary of the English Language* (1755)

Jones, Daniel, *English Pronouncing Dictionary* (1907)

Kersey, John, *New English Dictionary* (1702)

Lowth, Robert, *A Short Introduction to English Grammar* (1762)

Lye, Thomas, *A New Spelling Book* (1677)

Meigret, Loys, *Traité touchant le commun usage de l'escriture* (1545)

Moxon, Joseph, *Mechanick Exercises on the Whole Art of Printing* (1683–4)

Mulcaster, Richard, *The first part of the Elementarie which entreateth chefelie of the right writing of our English tung* (1582)

Murray, Lindley, *English Grammar* (1795)

Newbery, John, *An Easy Spelling Dictionary* (1745)

Perry, William, *The Only Sure Guide to the English Tongue* (1776)

Puttenham, George, *Arte of English Poesie* (1589)

Robertson, James, *The Ladies Help to Spelling* (1722)

Robertson, Joseph, *An Essay on Punctuation* (1785)

Sheridan, Thomas, *Course of Lectures on Elocution* (1763)

Smith, Thomas, *De recta et emendata linguae anglicae scriptione, Dialogus* (1568)

Sweet, Henry, *Handbook of Phonetics* (1877)

Swift, Jonathan, *Polite Conversation* (1738)

———— *A Proposal for Correcting, Improving and Ascertaining the English Language* (1712)

Walker, John, *Critical Pronouncing Dictionary* (1791)

Webster, Noah, *The American Spelling Book* (1786)

———— *The Elementary Spelling Book* (1829)

Secondary sources

Aitken, George A. (ed.), (1901), *The Journal to Stella*, London: Methuen & Co.

Anderson, John and Derek Britton (1999), 'The orthography and phonology of the *Ormulum*', *English Language and Linguistics* 3:2, 299–334.

Androutsopoulos, Jannis (2000), 'Non-standard spellings in media texts: the case of German fanzines', *Journal of Sociolinguistics* 4, 514–33.

Bann, Jennifer and John Corbett (2015), *Spelling Scots: The Orthography of Literary Scots, 1700–2000*, Edinburgh: Edinburgh University Press.

Baron, Naomi S. (2008), *Always On: Language in an Online and Mobile World*, Oxford: Oxford University Press.

Benskin, M. (2004), 'Chancery Standard', in Christian J. Kay, Carole Hough and Irené Wotherspoon (eds), *New Perspectives on English Historical Linguistics: Selected papers from 12 ICEHL. Volume II: Lexis and Transmission*, Amsterdam: Benjamins, 1–40.

———— (1982), 'The letters þ and y in later Middle English, and some related matters', *Journal of the Society of Archivists* 1, 13–30.

———— (1977), 'Local archives and Middle English dialects', *Journal of the Society of Archivists* 5:8, 500–14.

Benskin, Michael and Margaret Laing (1981), 'Translations and *Mischsprachen* in Middle English manuscripts', in Michael Benskin and M. L. Samuels (eds), *So meny people longages and tonges: Philological essays in Scots and mediaeval English presented to Angus McIntosh*, Edinburgh: Middle English Dialect Project, 55–106.

Black, Merja (1999), 'AB or Simply A? Reconsidering the Case for a Standard', *Neuphilologische Mitteilungen* 100, 155–74.

Blake, N. F. (1965), 'English versions of Reynard the Fox in the fifteenth and sixteenth centuries', *Studies in Philology* 62:1, 63–77.

————— (1996), *A History of the English Language*, Basingstoke: Macmillan.

————— (ed.) (1970), *The History of Reynard the Fox*, Early English Text Society OS 263, London: Oxford University Press.

————— (1981), *Non-Standard Language in English Literature*, London: André Deutsch.

Boffey, Julia and A. S. G. Edwards (1999), 'Bodleian MS Arch Selden B.24 and the "Scotticization" of Middle English verse', in Thomas A. Prendergast and Barbara Kline (eds), *Rewriting Chaucer: Culture, Authority and the Idea of the Authentic Text, 1400–1602*, Columbus: The Ohio State University Press, 166–85.

Boulton, James T. and T. O. McLoughlin (eds) (2006), *James Boswell, An Account of Corsica: The Journal of a Tour to that Island*, Oxford: Oxford University Press.

Britton, Derek (1991), 'On Middle English she, sho: a Scots solution to an English problem', *Nowele* 17, 3–51.

Brook, G. L. (1970), *The Language of Dickens*, London: André Deutsch.

Brunner, K. (1950), *Die englische Sprache*, Halle.

Butterfield, Jeremy (ed.) (2015), *Fowler's Dictionary of Modern English Usage*, Fourth Edition, Oxford: Oxford University Press.

Campbell, Alistair (1959), *Old English Grammar*, Oxford: Clarendon Press.

Cardwell, Margaret (ed.) (2008), *Charles Dickens, Great Expectations*, Oxford: Oxford University Press.

Carney, E. (1994), *A Survey of English Spelling*, London: Routledge.

Connors, R. and A. A. Lunsford (1988), 'Frequency of formal errors in current college writing, or Ma and Pa Kettle do research', *College Composition and Communication* 39:4, 395–409.

Cook, Vivian (2004), *The English Writing System*, London: H. Arnold.

Corbett, J. and J. Stuart-Smith (2012), 'Standard English in Scotland', in Ray Hickey (ed.), *Standards of English: Codified Standards around the World*, Cambridge: Cambridge University Press, 72–95.

Crystal, David (2006), *Language and the Internet*, Cambridge: Cambridge University Press.

————— (2013), *Spell It Out: The Singular Story of English Spelling*, London: Profile Books.

————— (2008a), *Txtng: The Gr8 Db8*, Oxford: Oxford University Press.

————— (2008b), *'Think on my words': Exploring Shakespeare's Language*, Cambridge: Cambridge University Press.

Curzan, Anne (2014), *Fixing English: Prescriptivism and Language History*, Cambridge: Cambridge University Press.

Dance, Richard (2003), 'The AB Language: The Recluse, the Gossip, and the Language Historian', in Yoko Wada (ed.), *A Companion to Ancrene Wisse*, Woodbridge: D. S. Brewer.

Darbishire, Helen (1931), *The Manuscript of Milton's Paradise Lost Book 1*, Oxford: Clarendon Press.

Daunt, Marjorie (1939), 'Old English sound changes reconsidered in relation to scribal tradition and practice', *Transactions of the Philological Society* 38, 108–37.

Davies, Eirlys E. (1987), 'Eyeplay: on some uses of nonstandard spelling', *Language and Communication* 7, 47–58.

Davis, Norman (1952), 'A Paston Hand', *Review of English Studies* 3, 209–21.

De Saussure, Ferdinand (1916), *Course in General Linguistics*, New York: Columbia University Press.

Devitt, Amy (1989), *Standardizing Written English: Diffusion in the Case of Scotland, 1520–1659*, Cambridge: Cambridge University Press.

Dobson, Eric (1968), *English Pronunciation 1500–1700*, Oxford: Clarendon Press.

Dodd, Gwilym (2011), 'The rise of English, the decline of French: supplications to the English crown, c. 1420–1450', *Speculum* 86, 117–50.

Durkin, Philip, (2016), 'Spelling variation as documented in historical dictionaries: the *OED* as a test case', in Vivian Cook and Des Ryan (eds), *The Routledge Handbook of the English Writing System*, London: Routledge, 163–74.

Eisenstein, Jacob, Brendan O'Connor, Noah A. Smith and Eric P. Xing (2014), 'Diffusion of lexical change in social media', *Plos One*: <https://journals.plos.org/plosone/article?id=10.1371/journal.pone.0113114>

Eisenstein, Jacob and Umashanthi Pavalanathan (2016), 'More ☺, Less :) The competition for paralinguistic function in microblog writing', *First Monday* 21:11.

Ellis, A. J. (1870), *Glossic: A New System of Spelling*, London.

Fairman, Tony (2006), 'Words in English Record Office documents of the early 1800s', in Merja Kytö, Mats Rydén and Erik Smitterberg (eds), *Nineteenth-Century English: Stability and Change*, Cambridge: Cambridge University Press, 56–88.

Faulkner, Mark (2020), 'Quantifying the consistency of "Standard" Old English spelling', *Transactions of the Philological Society* 118:1, 192–205.

Fisher, John (1996), *The Emergence of Standard English*, Kentucky: Kentucky University Press.

Friedman, Nancy (2011), 'Food for thought', 25 August: <https://www.vocabulary.com/articles/candlepwr/phood-for-thought>

Gill, Stephen (ed.) (2020), *Charles Dickens, Bleak House*, Oxford: Oxford University Press.

Gneuss, Helmut (1972), 'The origin of Standard Old English and Æthelwold's school at Winchester', *Anglo-Saxon England* 1, 63–83.

Godden, Malcolm (ed.) (1979), *Ælfric's Catholic Homilies: The Second Series*, Oxford: Oxford University Press.

Görlach, Manfred (2001), *Eighteenth-Century English*, Universitätsverlag: C. Winter.

——— (1999), 'Regional and Social Variation', in R. Lass (ed.), *The Cambridge History of the English Language*, Cambridge: Cambridge University Press, 459–538.

Grieve, Dorian (2011), 'MacDiarmid's language', in Scott Lyall and Margery Palmer McCulloch (eds), *The Edinburgh Companion to Hugh MacDiarmid*, Edinburgh: Edinburgh University Press, 23–35.

Hanna, Ralph (2005), *London Literature, 1300–1380*, Cambridge: Cambridge University Press.

Harris, Roy (trans.) (2013), *Course in General Linguistics*, London: Zed Books.

Hogg, Richard (1992), *A Grammar of Old English. Volume 1: Phonology*, Oxford: Blackwell.

Horn, Ernest and Ernest J. Ashbaugh (1920), *Horn-Ashbaugh Speller: For Grades One to Eight*, Philadelphia: J. B. Lippincott Company.

Horobin, Simon (2003), *The Language of the Chaucer Tradition*, Chaucer Studies 32, Cambridge: D.S. Brewer.

Horobin, Simon and Linne R. Mooney (2004), 'A *Piers Plowman* manuscript by the Hengwrt/Ellesmere Scribe and its implications for London Standard English', *Studies in the Age of Chaucer* 26, 65–112.

Howard Hill, T. H. (2006), 'Early Modern printers and the standardisation of English spelling', *Modern Language Review* 101:1, 16–29.

Hudson, Anne (2017), 'Observations on the Wycliffite Orthography', in Simon Horobin and Aditi Nafde (eds), *Pursuing Middle English Manuscripts and their Texts: Essays in Honour of Ralph Hanna*, Turnhout: Brepols, 77–98.

Humphreys, Arthur (ed.) (1991), *Joseph Andrews and Shamela*, London: J. M. Dent & Sons.

Hutchinson, Thomas (ed.) (1904), *The Complete Poetical Works of Percy Bysshe Shelley Volume I*, Oxford: Oxford University Press.

Jones, Charles (ed.) (1997), *The Edinburgh History of the Scots Language*, Edinburgh: Edinburgh University Press.

———— (1995), *A Language Suppressed: The Pronunciation of the Scots language in the 18th century*, Edinburgh: John Donald.

Kniezsa, Veronica (1997), 'The origins of Scots orthography', in Jones (1997), 24–46.

Lass, Roger (1980), 'John Hart *Vindicatus*? A study in the interpretation of early phoneticians', *Folia Linguistica* 1, 75–96.

Lerer, Seth (2015), *Inventing English: A Portable History of the Language*, Columbia University Press: New York.

Lunsford, Andrea A. and Karen J. Lunsford (2008), 'Mistakes are a fact of life: a national comparative study', *College Composition and Communication* 59:4, 781–806.

Macafee, Caroline (2002), 'History of Scots to 1700', *Dictionaries of the Scots Language*: <https://dsl.ac.uk/about-scots/history-of-scots>

Macaulay, Ronald (1991), 'Coz it izny spelt when they say it: displaying dialect in writing', *American Speech* 66:3, 280–91.

Machan, Tim William (2005), *English in the Middle Ages*, Oxford: Oxford University Press.

McColl Millar, Robert (2012), *English Historical Sociolinguistics*, Edinburgh: Edinburgh University Press.

—— (2018), *Modern Scots: An Analytical Survey*, Edinburgh: Edinburgh University Press.

McCulloch, Gretchen (2019), *Because Internet: Understanding How Language is Changing*, London: Vintage.

McIntosh, Angus, M. L. Samuels and Michael Benskin (eds), (1986), *A Linguistic Atlas of Late Mediaeval English*, Aberdeen: Aberdeen University Press.

Meurman-Solin, Anneli (1997), 'Differentiation and standardisation in Early Scots', in Jones (1997), 3–23.

Milroy, J. and L. Milroy (2012), *Authority in Language: Investigating Language Prescription and Standardisation*, London: Routledge.

Mugglestone, Lynda (2011), *Dictionaries: A Very Short Introduction*, Oxford: Oxford University Press.

—— (2006), 'English in the nineteenth century', in L. Mugglestone (ed.), *The Oxford History of English*, Oxford: Oxford University Press, 274–304.

—— (1995), *Talking Proper: The Rise of Accent as Social Symbol*, Oxford: Clarendon Press.

Murray, James (ed.) (1884), *A New English Dictionary on Historical Principles Volume I Part I*, Oxford: Oxford University Press.

Nevalainen, Terttu (2012), 'Variable focusing in English spelling between 1400 and 1600', in Susan Baddeley and Anja Voeste (eds), *Orthographies in Early Modern Europe*, Berlin: Mouton De Gruyter, 127–44.

Nevalainen, Terttu and Tieken-Boon van Ostade (2006), 'Standardisation', in Richard Hogg and David Denison (eds), *A History of the English Language*, Cambridge: Cambridge University Press, 271–311.

Osselton, N. (1963), 'Formal and informal spelling in the eighteenth century', *English Studies* 44, 267–75.

—— (1984), 'Informal spelling systems in Early Modern English: 1500–1800', in N. F. Blake and C. Jones (eds), *English Historical Linguistics: Studies in Development*, Sheffield: CECTAL, 123–36.

—— (1985), 'Spelling book rules and the capitalisation of nouns in the seventeenth and eighteenth centuries', in M-J. Arn and H. Wirtjes (eds), *Historical and Editorial Studies in Medieval and Early Modern English*, Groningen: Wolters-Noordhoff, 49–62.

Page, Norman (1988), *Speech in the English Novel*, Basingstoke: Palgrave Macmillan.

Pan, Steven C., Timothy C. Rickard and Robert A. Bjork (2021), 'Does spelling still matter – and if so, how should it be taught? Perspectives from contemporary and historical research', *Educational Psychology Review* 33, 1523–52.

Peikola, Matti (2003), 'The Wycliffite Bible and "Central Midland Standard": Assessing the manuscript evidence', *Nordic Journal of English Studies* 2:1, 29–51.

Pound, Louise (1925), 'The kraze for "K"', *American Speech* 1:1, 43–4.

Raw, Barbara (1978), *The Art and Background of Old English Poetry*, London: Edward Arnold.

Richards, Bernard (1998), 'Oxford Spelling', *The Oxford Magazine*, Hilary Term, 11–12.

Richardson, Malcolm (1980), 'Henry V, the English Chancery, and Chancery English', *Speculum* 55:4, 726–50.

Salmon, Vivian (1999), 'Orthography and punctuation', in R. Lass (ed.), *The Cambridge History of the English Language Volume III: 1476–1776*, Cambridge: Cambridge University Press, 13–55.

Samuels, M. L. (1989), 'The Great Scandinavian Belt', in M. Laing (ed.), *Middle English Dialectology: Essays on Some Principles and Problems*, Aberdeen: Aberdeen University Press, 106–15.

——— (1963), 'Some applications of Middle English dialectology', *English Studies*, 44, 81–94; reprinted in Margaret Laing (ed.), *Middle English Dialectology*, 64–80.

——— (1988), 'Spelling and dialect in the late and post-Middle English periods', in M. L. Samuels and Jeremy J. Smith (eds), *The English of Chaucer and his Contemporaries*, Aberdeen: Aberdeen University Press, 89–96.

Schnoebelen, Tyler Joseph (2012), *Emotions Are Relational: Positioning and the Use of Affective Linguistic Resources*, PhD dissertation, Stanford University.

Scragg, D. A. (1974), *A History of English Spelling*, Manchester: Manchester University Press.

Sebba, Mark (2007), *Spelling and Society: The Culture and Politics of Orthography Around the World*, Cambridge: Cambridge University Press.

Shute, Rosie (2017), 'Pressed for space: the effects of justification and the printing process on fifteenth-century orthography', *English Studies* 98:3, 262–82.

Sisam, Kenneth (1953), *Studies in the History of Old English Literature*, Oxford: Clarendon Press.

Smith, Jeremy J. (1996), *An Historical Study of English: Function, Form and Change*, London: Routledge.

——— (2020a), 'Godly vocabulary in Early Modern English religious debate', in E. Jonsson and T. Larsson (eds), *Voices Past and Present – Studies of Involved, Speech-Related and Spoken Texts, in Honor of Merja Kytö*, Amsterdam: John Benjamins.

——— (2020b), 'Methodising Scots: the cases of Allan Ramsay and Thomas Ruddiman', *Studies in Scottish Literature* 46, 127–47.

——— (2020c), 'On scriptae: correlating spelling and script in Late Middle English', *Revista canaria de estudios ingleses* 80, 13–27.

——— (2024), 'On "standard" written English in the later Middle Ages', *Speculum* 99:3, 762–79.

Smollett, Tobias, *The Adventures of Roderick Random*, eds. James G. Basker, Paul-Gabriel Boucé, Nicole A. Seary and O. M. Brack Jr (2017), Athens: University of Georgia Press.

Solopova, Elizabeth (2017), *The Wycliffite Bible: Origin, History and Interpretation*, Leiden: Brill.

Sönmez, Margaret J.-M. (2000), 'Perceived and real differences between men's and women's spellings of the early to mid-seventeenth century', in Dieter

Kastovsky and Arthur Mettinger (eds), *The History of English in A Social Context: A Contribution to Historical Sociolinguistics*, Trends in Linguistics Studies and Monographs 129, Berlin and New York: Mouton de Gruyter, 405–39.

Stanley, E. G. (1969a), 'Laȝamon's antiquarian sentiments', *Medium Ævum* 38:1, 23–37.

——— (1969b), 'Spellings of the Waldend Group', in E. B. Atwood and A. A. Hill (eds), *Studies in Language, Literature, and Culture of the Middle Ages and Later*, Austin: University of Texas, 38–69.

Stenroos, Merja (2020), 'The "vernacularisation" and "standardisation" of local administrative writing in late and post-medieval England', in Laura Wright (ed.), *The Multilingual Origins of Standard English*, Berlin: Mouton de Gruyter, 39–86.

Stubbs, M. (1992), 'Spelling in society: forms and variants, uses and users', in R. Tracy (ed.), *Who Climbs the Grammar-Tree?*, Tubingen: Max Niemeyer Verlag, 221–34.

Swift, Jonathan (1727), *A Letter to a Young Lady on her Marriage*. London.

Taavitsainen, Irma (2005), 'Standardisation, House Styles and the scope of variation in Middle English scientific writing', in N. Ritt (ed.), *Rethinking Middle English*, Frankfurt: Peter Lang, 89–109.

Tagliamonte, Sali and Derek Denis (2008), 'Linguistic ruin? LOL! Instant messaging and teen language', *American Speech* 83:1, 3–34.

Tatman, Rachael (2015), '#go awn: sociophonetic variation in variant spellings on Twitter', *Proceedings of the 31st annual NorthWest Linguistics Conference*: <https://journals.uvic.ca/index.php/WPLC/issue/view/859>

Thomas, Calvin (1902), 'The amelioration of our spelling', *PMLA* 17:3, 297–311.

Tieken-Boon van Ostade, Ingrid (2009), *An Introduction to Late Modern English*. Edinburgh: Edinburgh University Press.

——— (1996), 'Social network theory and eighteenth-century English: the case of Boswell', in Derek Britton (ed.), *English Historical Linguistics 1994*, Amsterdam: John Benjamins, 327–37.

——— (1998), 'Standardization of English spelling: the printers' contribution', in Jacek Fisiak and Marcin Krygier (eds), *Advances in English Historical Linguistics*, Berlin: Mouton de Gruyter, 457–70.

Tieken-Boon van Ostade, Ingrid and Randy Bax (2002), 'Of Dodsley's projects and linguistic influence: the language of Johnson and Lowth', *Historical Sociolinguistics and Sociohistorical Linguistics*: <https://www.let.leidenuniv.nl/hsl_shl/johnson%20lowth.htm>

Tolkien, J. R. R., '*Ancrene Wisse* and *Hali Meiðhad*', *Essays and Studies* 14 (1929), 104–26.

Truss, Lynne (2003), *Eats, Shoots and Leaves: The Zero-Tolerance Approach to Punctuation*, London: Profile.

Upward, Christopher and George Davidson (2011), *The History of English Spelling*, Wiley-Blackwell: Oxford.

Venezky, Richard (1967), 'English orthography: its graphical structure and its relation to sound', *Reading Research Quarterly* 2:3, 75–105.

Williams, Graham (2013), 'The language of Early Modern letters: a reader's guide', in Alison Wiggins, Alan Bryson, Daniel Starza Smith, Anke Timmermann and Graham Williams (eds), *Bess of Hardwick's Letters: The Complete Correspondence, c. 1550–1608*, 14 March 2024: <https://www.bessofhardwick.org/background.jsp?id=168>

———— (2016), 'Written like a 'gwd' Scotswoman: Margaret Tudor's use of Scots', *Scottish Language* 35, 89–95.

Wright, Laura (1996), 'About the evolution of standard English', in Elizabeth M. Tyler and M. Jane Toswell (eds), *Studies in English Language and Literature: 'Doubt Wisely', Papers in Honour of E. G. Stanley*, London: Routledge, 99–115.

Wyld, H. C. (1936), *A History of Modern Colloquial English*, Oxford: Blackwell.

Index

AB Language, 20, 28, 29–31
abbreviations, 23, 24, 48, 52, 65, 87–90, 93, 112, 122
Academy, 73, 111–12
accent, 16, 17, 57, 62, 80, 96, 102, 106, 112–15, 117–18, 127, 128, 140, 143–5, 147
acronyms, 88, 90–1
Addison, Joseph, 65, 73
Ælfric, 4–5, 18, 21
Alfred jewel, 16
Anglicisation, 101–3
Anglo-Norman, 40, 73
anxiety, 68, 111, 132
apostrophe, 58, 65, 107, 121–2
Arabic, 1, 78
archaism, 31, 78

back mutation, 29
Bailey, Nathan, 74–5, 117
Baron, Naomi, 88
Bede, 16
Benedictine reform, 20, 22
Black, Merja, 29–30
Blake, N. F., 20, 52–3
Blake, William, 70
borrowing, 27–8, 73–4, 137
Boswell, James, 65–6, 131
Bradley, Henry, 146
Butler, Charles, 5
Butterfield, Jeremy, 79

Cædmon, 16
Cameron, David, 148

capitalisation, 67, 90, 91, 94, 131
Carney, Edward, 148
Caroline minuscule, 15
Carroll, Lewis, 65
Caxton, William, 23–4, 51–3, 154–5
Central Midland Standard, 39–40
Chancery Standard, 36, 38, 41–8, 156
Chaucer, Geoffrey, 37, 41–2, 52, 97, 102, 152, 153
Chesterfield, Lord, 65, 112, 115–17
Clare, John, 157–8
Cobbett, William, 117
complementary distribution, 16, 27
Coote, Edmund, 114, 127, 143
Crystal, David, 52, 57, 58, 87, 89
Cut Spelling, 148–9

Daines, Simon, 5
Darwin, Charles, 71
Davis, Norman, 123
Dickens, Charles, 68–9, 70–1, 133–4
Donatus, 4–5
Dryden, John, 64, 73, 111
Durkin, Philip, 157–8

Early English Books Online, 154–5
Ellis, A. J., 147
emojis, 90–1
emoticons, 90–1
etymology, 9, 49–50, 62, 63, 85, 129, 137, 144, 146

Faulkner, Mark, 21–2
Fielding, Henry, 68
Fielding, Sarah, 130–1
Fisher, John, 43–5, 156–7
Franklin, Benjamin, 79–80
Franks Casket, 14

gemination, 17
Germanic, 13–15, 24
Gil, Alexander, 142
GloWbE corpus, 78, 83, 159–60
graphemes, 2–5, 7–8
grapheme substitutions, 92
Great Vowel Shift, 54–5, 128
Greek, 7, 18, 24, 49, 61, 78, 111,
    125, 135, 138
greengrocer's apostrophe, 122

h-dropping, 9
Hanna, Ralph, 40
Hart, John, 113, 139–41
Hoccleve, Thomas, 38, 102
Hogg, Richard, 18, 21
homophones, 8, 50, 55
Hudson, Anne, 39–40

Indo-European, 15
informal spelling, 66–7
Initial Teaching Alphabet, 147–8
Instant Messaging, 88–9
insular minuscule, 15

Johnson, Samuel, 61–4, 66, 112,
    115–16, 131
Jones, Daniel, 115, 147

Latin, 5, 13, 15–16, 18, 24, 27, 45–6,
    50, 111, 114, 134, 138
Late West-Saxon, 20–2, 23, 29–31
A Linguistic Atlas of Late Mediaeval
    English, 34, 42–3, 155
Layamon, 23, 31
Lewis, C. S., 121
ligatures, 18, 148
Lindisfarne Gospels, 19, 97

literacy, 13, 22, 60, 79, 82, 87–8,
    106, 117, 123, 132, 140, 143,
    145–6, 148
logograms, 87–8
Lowth, Robert, 65, 114–15

Middle English Local Documents
    corpus, 153
Milton, John, 75, 142
minims, 28, 148
Mischsprachen, 33
Mugglestone, Lynda, 72, 118
Mulcaster, Richard, 141–2
Murray, James, 81, 143–4
Murray, Lindley, 131–2

Old Norse, 25, 99–100
Ormulum, The, 31, 32–3
Osselton, N., 66–7
Oxford English Corpus, 160

Paston Letters, 123, 124, 151–2,
    155–7
Peikola, Matti, 39
personal names, 9, 93
Philological Society, 72, 143
phonemes, 2, 4–8
printing, 21, 23, 51–4, 58, 67, 69,
    81, 144, 147, 154–5
Priscian, 4–5
Puttenham, George, 113–15

Received Pronunciation, 145
Richardson, Malcolm, 43–4
Richardson, Samuel, 130
Robertson, James, 132
Robertson, Joseph, 67
runes, 13–15

Samuels, M. L., 36–48, 53, 154,
    156
Scragg, Donald, 21, 51, 132
scribes, 15, 19, 20–3, 29, 31, 33, 38,
    40, 44, 48, 51, 53, 56, 63, 97, 123,
    125

Shakespeare, William, 50, 52, 56–7, 114, 144
Shavian alphabet, 147
Shaw, George Bernard, 147
Sheridan, Thomas, 68, 115
Simplified Spelling Board, 83
Simplified Spelling Society, 147, 148
Smith, Jeremy, 21, 43, 48, 105.
Smith, Thomas, 9, 138–9
Smollett, Tobias, 133
Solopova, Elizabeth, 40
SPAG test, 118
spelling bee, 118–20
spelling pronunciation, 50
Stanley, Eric, 21, 31

Sweet, Henry, 118
Swift, Jonathan, 65, 68, 112, 132–3

texting, 87–8
Tieken-Boon van Ostade, Ingrid, 65, 130, 131
Tolkien, J. R. R., 28–9, 33
trade names, 92
Trevisa, John, 39, 113
Twitter, 90–4, 158
typos, 87, 89

Upward, Christopher, 148

Webster, Noah, 79–80, 119–20